Science and Anthropology in a Post-Truth World

Science and Anthropology in a Post-Truth World

A Critique of Unreason and Academic Nonsense

H. Sidky

LEXINGTON BOOKS
Lanham • Boulder • New York • London

Published by Lexington Books
An imprint of The Rowman & Littlefield Publishing Group, Inc.
4501 Forbes Boulevard, Suite 200, Lanham, Maryland 20706
www.rowman.com

6 Tinworth Street, London SE11 5AL, United Kingdom

Copyright © 2021 The Rowman & Littlefield Publishing Group, Inc.

All rights reserved. No part of this book may be reproduced in any form or by any electronic or mechanical means, including information storage and retrieval systems, without written permission from the publisher, except by a reviewer who may quote passages in a review.

British Library Cataloguing in Publication Information Available

Library of Congress Cataloging-in-Publication Data Available

ISBN 978-1-7936-0651-8 (cloth)
ISBN 978-1-7936-0653-2 (pbk)
ISBN 978-1-7936-0652-5 (electronic)

*To the Memory of Dr. Perry L. Gnivecki,
Archaeologist, Scientist, and Dear Friend*

Contents

1	The War on Science and Reason and the Way to Post-Truth	1
2	Delegitimizing Science in the Academy: Ideological Underpinnings	19
3	Science Studies and the Anthropology of Science: How Postmodernists Sought to Demystify Truth	39
4	The Hermeneutics of Quantum Gravity, Incomprehensibility, and the Sokal Hoax	49
5	American Intellectual Contributions to Science Delegitimation: Kuhn and Feyerabend	57
6	Epistemic Relativism: Is the World Truly Unknowable?	69
7	Epistemology: How Do We Know What We Know?	81
8	The Problem of Pseudoscience in Post-Truth America	105
9	Postmodern Anthropology: Epistemic Relativism and Incoherence as an Experimental Moment?	125
10	Paranormal and Theistic Anthropology: From Postmodernism to Post-Truth Supernaturalism	141
11	From Postmodernism to Post-Truth United States	163
Bibliography		181
Index		211
About the Author		231

Chapter 1

The War on Science and Reason and the Way to Post-Truth

Post-truth first overtly appeared in public discourse in 2016. That year marked the apparent inauguration of a cultural and political environment characterized by obscurantism, sheer lying, demagoguery, incivility, misinformation, and authoritarianism. Post-truth means simply that all attempts to differentiate between fact and fiction, or efforts to distinguish between what true and false, are deemed obsolete. The idea of post-truth predates the presidency of Donald Trump. According to the *Oxford Dictionaries*, the expression post-truth was coined by the playwright Steve Tesich in a 1992 article in *The Nation* called "Government of Lies." He used it in reference to the deceptions associated with Watergate, the Iran-Contra Affair, and the first Gulf War. The term also appeared in Ralph Keyes' 2004 book *The Post-Truth Era: Dishonesty and Deception in Contemporary Life*.

Others trace the ancestry of post-truth to the nineteenth-century German philosopher Friedrich Nietzsche's (2003: 139) perspectivism, that is, that truth claims are relative to the perspective of the person or group making them (Higgins 2016; Papazoglou 2016; Wehner 2016). Nietzsche is significant in the context of this discussion because his ideas had a profound influence on postmodern academics who launched a systematic campaign to discredit science, rationality, and truth. Nietzsche is also one of the apostles of present-day anti-science populists, Alt-Right agitators, and white supremacists, although apologists past and present have tried to absolve him from such charges (e.g., Kaufmann 1968; Alloa 2017; Heit 2018). I shall say more about Nietzsche in a later chapter.

Whatever its pedigree, it was the 2016 U.S. presidential elections and Brexit that propelled the idea of post-truth into global collective consciousness. *The Oxford Dictionaries* declared it the word of the year of 2016 (Higgins 2016; Wang 2016). Other current euphemisms for such falsehoods, such as counter-knowledge, half-truths, alt-truth, conspiracy theories, and "fake news" came into vogue as well (Levitin 2016: xiv). The term "fake news," which plays a big part in Trump's rhetoric, was declared 2017's word of the year by the *Collins Dictionary*'s and denotes "false, often sensational, information disseminated under the guise of news reporting" (Hunt 2017).

What is important for this discussion is that truth is now irrelevant, and what passes for truth in this context depends on how one feels (McIntyre 2018: 10). As Tom Nichols (2017: xx) observes, there is now a new Declaration of Independence in the United States: "No longer do we hold *these* truths to be self-evident, we hold *all* truths to be self-evident, even the ones that are not true." If it feels true to you, it is true! In reference to scientific truths this means, as Stewart Lockie (2016) puts it, that what "matters is whether those listening to those [scientific] claims would like them to be true—truth being judged not by evidence but by consistency with listeners' existing beliefs and values." The witty author and social commentator, Charles Pierce had already recognized this as symptomatic of American culture in his humorous book *Idiot America* (2009):

> [America] decides, en masse, with a million keystrokes and clicks of the remote control, that because there are two sides to every question, they must both be right, or at least not wrong. And the words of an obscure biologist carry no more weight on the subject of biology than do the thunderations of some turkeyneck preachers out of the Church of Christ's Parking Structure in DeLand, Florida. Less weight, in fact, because our scientist is an "expert" and, therefore, an "elitist." Nobody puts him on cable. He's brilliant, surely, but no different from all the rest of us, poor fool.

With this new understanding of truth pretty much any view, no matter how nonsensical or irrational it is, can be offered as seemingly credible claims to knowledge. As psychologist Lewandowsky and his colleagues have succinctly put it:

> A hallmark of a post-truth world is that it empowers people to choose their own reality, where facts and objective evidence are trumped by existing beliefs and prejudices. This can be amplified by leaders who model deception and delusion as adequate means to garner support. In this world, lying is not only accepted, it is rewarded. Falsifying reality is no longer about changing people's beliefs, it is about asserting power (Lewandowsky et al. 2017: 361).

Post-truth politics is not about providing a coherent alternative model of reality, but rather entails operations to achieve political goals by generating uncertainty about whether anything is knowable thus undermining trust in facts and objective reality to the degree that these things become irrelevant or are even dismissed as nonexistent (Cook et al. 2017; Lewandowsky 2017: 361; Lewandowsky et al. 2016).

These topsy-turvy circumstances that seem to defy rational conventions are disconcertingly reminiscent of situations the philosopher and political theorist Hannah Arendt described in her book *The Origins of Totalitarianism* (1951), a study of the Nazi and Stalinist regimes published more than half a century ago. As she put it:

> Never has our future been more unpredictable, never have we depended so much on political forces that cannot be trusted to follow the rules of common sense and self-interest—forces that look like sheer insanity, if judged by the standards of other centuries (Arendt 1951: vii).

These are the same sorts of doubts many, including members of the Justice Department and jurists around the country have expressed regarding Trump erratic behavior and autocratic tendencies and the actions of his assemblage of henchmen in post-truth America. Such politics, Arendt (1951: 382) observed, depend upon a "curiously varying mixture of gullibility and cynicism" created by barrages of falsehoods, in which people come to a point where they concurrently "believe everything and nothing, think that everything was possible and nothing was true." What Arendt was describing was a version of a post-truth world in her time. She added:

> The totalitarian mass leaders based their propaganda on the correct psychological assumption that, under such conditions, one could make people believe the most fantastic statements one day, and trust that if the next day they were given irrefutable proof of their falsehood, they would take refuge in cynicism; instead of deserting the leaders who had lied to them, they would protest that they had known all along that the statement was a lie and would admire the leaders for their superior tactical cleverness (Arendt 1951: 382).

Reading this makes it challenging not to think about the indifference by Trump's followers to his fusillades of mendacity, moral and ethical failures, and vulgarity that in a previous era would have ended political careers. Such apathy and disbelief are explicable because the falsehoods are not intended to make people believe a particular lie, but instead to at once generate gullibility, skepticism, and incredulity, that is, that we cannot know anything, truth and falsehood are indistinguishable, experts are elitist, scientific knowledge is bogus, and so forth. Arendt (1968: 257) added:

> The result of a consistent and total substitution of lies for factual truth is not that the lie will now be accepted as truth, and the truth be defamed as lies, but that

the sense by which we take our bearings in the real world—and the category of truth vs. falsehood is among the mental means to this end—is being destroyed.

These circumstances produce the type of followers that dictators, autocrats, and totalitarian demagogues hopes for in their dreams (cf., Tesich 1992: 13). Here too Ardent's (1951: 474) observations are highly relevant:

> The ideal subject of totalitarian rule . . . [are] people for whom the distinction between fact and fiction (i.e., the reality of experience) and the distinction between true and false (i.e., the standards of thought) no longer exists.

When the distinction between truth and falsehood are blurred, and people lose their bearings in the real world, post-truth demagogues themselves become the sources and purveyors of knowledge/truth for their followers and are able to forward and spin whatever lies best suits their purposes but declared to be for the benefit of the people, to make the country great again, or something like that. Steven Levitsky and Daniel Ziblatt (2018) call attention to further signs of Americas' trajectory in this direction in their book *How Democracies Die* (2018):

> American politicians now treat their rivals as enemies, intimidate the free press, and threaten to reject the results of elections. They try to weaken the institutional buffers of our democracy, including the courts, intelligence services, and ethics offices (Levitsky and Daniel Ziblatt 2018: 2).

They specifically highlight the following political markers: (1) rejection of (or weak commitment to) democratic rules of the game; (2) denial of the legitimacy of political opponents; (3) toleration or encouragement of violence; and (4) readiness to curtail civil liberties of opponents, including the media (Levitsky and Ziblatt 2018: 23).

Many other aspects of post-truth politics also come straight from the playbook of fascist propagandists of a bygone period who were touting totalitarianism for the common good of "the people" (Snyder 2017: 12). Attacking and devaluing truth and expertise and undermining the credibility of educational institutions that harbor independent voices is an effective way of undermining public discourse and curtailing reasoned discussion and debate central to the democratic process (Stanley 2018: 36, 38, 53).

The reason contemporary observers have sought insights in Arendt's work, as the historian Jeffrey Isaac (2016) put it, is because it speaks "powerfully to our present moment." Post-truth has indeed come hand in hand with an alarming wave of authoritarianism, right-wing populism, xenophobia, racism, vulgarity, emboldened religious fundamentalism, and the subordination of democratic principles to the wisdom of the crowd (cf., Kakutani 2018: 14). Moreover, post-truth politics is the politics of debasement (Ott 2017). This is partly an effect of the spillover of lies and vulgarity by the paragons of the political system into public discourse which has granted Americans license to breach moral and ethical conventions (Murguía 2019: 7). These were all familiar terrain for Arendt.

Hence, at the close of the second decade of the twenty-first century, Americans find themselves living in a scary and confusing era of misinformation, "fake news," "counter knowledge," "weaponized lies," "alternative facts," conspiracy theories, magical thinking, fanaticism, and irrationalism (Jaffe 2017; Sidky 2018: 38–43). Alternative facts, according to the sociologist Salvador Murguía (2019a: 4), comprise a semantic strategy that contests substantiated knowledge by offering up alternative factoids. While such use of falsehoods in politics is not new, the scope and manner in which Trump and his followers use and defend such mendacities is entirely novel and is of growing concern among some observers (see Salvador 2019b).

Along the same lines, the professor of law, S. I. Strong (2017: 137) says that alternative facts, is "a term that quickly became synonymous with a willingness to persevere with a particular belief with complete ignorance of, or with a total disregard for, reality." This, she adds, has serious implications:

> The increasing incidence of alternative facts in the popular and political arena creates a critical conundrum for lawyers, judges, legislators, and anyone interested in deliberative democracy, since it is unclear how rational debate can proceed if empirical evidence holds no persuasive value.

It is well understood that a working democracy depends upon well-informed citizens (Kuklinski et al. 2000). Further, where people are misinformed the likelihood of poor personal and societal decisions are very high, such as not immunizing children or disregarding climate change (Lewandowsky et al. 2017: 354). Consider the fallout from Trump's efforts to mislead the American public about the dangers of the COVID-19 virus, which by mid-March 2020 had appeared in all fifty states, threatening millions of people and was poised to overwhelm the healthcare system (Smith et al. 2020). Trump systematically fabricated an alternate reality around the virus outbreak by dismissing scientific findings and the alarms issued by healthcare professionals as a hoax, "fake news," or a political conspiracy to undermine his presidency (Coppins 2020). This reprehensible tactic delayed testing as the pathogen was spreading among Americans. The reality of the situation, however, became evident as COVID-19 cases escalated, schools and universities shut down, public events canceled, and containment zones established by local authorities. By June 5, 2020, there were 1.9 million cases and 108,000 deaths in the

United States from the virus. By August 20, 2020 the total number of cases increased to 5.54 million with over 170,000 deaths. This is an unfortunate reminder that reality does not bend to our wishes and desires.

The sociologist of religion, Damian Thompson (2008: 1) characterizes these developments as a pandemic of credulous thinking. With truth now divorced from facts or evidence, there has indeed been an outpouring of purveyors of supernaturalism, anti-intellectual dogmas, medieval credulities, and bogus forms of knowledge. Social media is also profuse with various conspiracy theories and pseudoscientific nonsense. Conspiratorial thinking, which I shall discuss in a later chapter, is closely tied to post-truth rejection of science and scientific knowledge (cf., Lewandowsky et al. 2013a: 630).

Anti-intellectualism has a long history in the United States (Hofstadter 1963). Moreover, cranks and hacks have always lurked in the peripheries of mainstream American society (Sidky 2015: 105–122). This is not something new. As the scientist and author Isaac Asimov observed back in 1980:

> There is a cult of ignorance in the United States, and they're always has been. The strain of anti-intellectualism has been a constant thread winding its way through our political and cultural life, nurtured by the false notion that democracy means that "my ignorance is just as good as your knowledge."

Sociologists Colin Campbell (2002: 14) called this peripheral cultural space where such deviant or weird beliefs resided "the cultic milieu." What is new is that the purveyors of such ideas have now become mainstream actors invading previously inaccessible social and political spaces. This includes cyberspace, where the cultic milieu is thriving in virtual reality. What is also novel is the development of a politically driven post-truth alternative epistemology in which such beliefs thrive.

The internet where any nonsense can be creatively packaged and offered as reliable information is swarming with vendors of bogus knowledge, offering their own "truths" and "ways of knowing" with bluster as better substitutes for science and scientific knowledge (Thompson 2008: 10–11). In cyberspace, conspiracists and science deniers are able to reinforce each other's delusions and paranoia (Diethelm and McKee 2009; McKee and Diethelm 2010: 1310–1311). The irrational and nonsensical beliefs being disseminated range from creationism, Holocaust denial, NASA's moon landing hoax, to climate change denial, astrology, crystal healing, phony physics, anti-vaccine propaganda, 9/11 conspiracy theories, ancient aliens, reptilian overlords in the government, and much more (Lewandowsky et al. 2013). I discuss the problem of pseudoscience and alternative knowledge in post-truth United States in chapter 8 and conspiracy theories in chapter 11.

The dissemination of false facts has the execrable effect of not only undermining public trust in political institutions, it also corrupts intellectual standards and honest inquiry, and diverts attention from the actual issues by drawing lawmakers into protracted debates about already established science (Rabin-Havt 2016: 4). In this intellectual environment, pretentious and utterly unqualified post-truth politicians have found room where they can flagrantly and without accountability flaunt opinions on issues ranging from vaccines, human reproduction, stem cell research, the origins of the earth, human evolution, and the state of the biosphere, all of which are contrary to overwhelming historical and scientific evidence (Sidky 2018). As the Princeton philosopher Harry Frankfurt (2018: 17) observes, such ideologues "luxuriate in the production of bullshit, or lies, and of whatever other modes of fraudulence and fakery they are able to devise."

Trump and his supporters did not invent these circumstances, they simply co-opted it. As the commentator on American culture Kurt Andersen has put it in his book *Fantasyland: How America Went Haywire* (2017), Trump is "the apotheosis of post-truth," not its architect (Andersen 2017: 417). From the moment the Trump administration took office it began unleashing ongoing barrages of demonstrably false statements, ranging from bogus claims about the size of Trump's inauguration crowd, distortions regarding transgender persons in bathrooms, and claims about the rates of violent crime in the United States, among others without any culpability (Barerra et al. 2019: 1; Bridges 2017). Each of these lies, as already noted, creates uncertainty about established facts and enforces the perceptions that nothing can be known (Lewandowsky et al. 2017: 361). The essayist Adam Gopnik (2017) has made a relevant observation regarding such blatant prevarications:

> There is nothing subtle about Trump's behavior. He lies, he repeats the lie, and his listeners either cower in fear, stammer in disbelief, or try to see how they can turn the lie to their own benefit.

Consider Trump's bogus story about three million illegal votes to explain why he lost the popular vote (Phillip and DeBonis 2017; O'Reilly 2019; Quercia 2019). This is an account that no one familiar with the circumstances actually believed, including Republican congressmen or members of the administration. But that does not matter. Gopnik adds:

> The lie is not a claim about specific facts; the lunacy is a deliberate challenge to the whole larger idea of sanity. Once a lie that big is in circulation, trying to reel the conversation back into the territory of rational argument becomes impossible.

Such falsehoods, as Sean O'Reilly (2019: 139) points out, are what Adolf Hitler called the "big lies." This is yet another element in Trump's political discourse that has striking similarities with the tactics old-time fascist propagandists. Hitler explained that the bigger the falsehoods and the more often they are iterated the greater their effectiveness (Dreyfuss 2017). As he put it in his *Mein Kampf* (1939):

> in the big lie there is always a certain force of credulity; because the broad masses of a nation are always more easily corrupted in the deeper strata of their emotional nature than consciously or voluntarily; and thus in the primitive simplicity of their minds they more readily fall victims to the big lie than the small lie. since they themselves often tell small lies in little matters but would be ashamed to resort to large-scale falsehoods. It would never come into their heads to fabricate colossal untruths, and they would not believe that others could have the impudence to distort the truth so infamously.

Remarkably, post-truth falsehoods have been surprisingly resilient despite dedicated fact checking efforts to correct what is obviously false information (Nyhan and Reifler 2019; Nyhan et al. 2019). Research has shown that often such correction efforts not only fail to reduce misperceptions among the targeted ideological group, but due to the psychological phenomenon known as the backfire effect, in some cases such efforts actually increases misperceptions among the people in question (Bridges 2107; Nyhan, Brendan, and Jason Reifler 2010). These circumstances correspond with Alberto Barndolini's asymmetry principle that "the amount of energy needed to refute bullshit is an order of magnitude bigger than to produce it" (Williamson 2016).

Lewandowsky et al. (2017: 356) maintain that the post-truth malaise is better understood not as information deficits, or misinformation, that can be debunked, but through the lens of political drivers that have created an "alternative epistemology" that does not fit conventional standards of evidentiary validation. Statements from politicians and elements of the news media bolster this new epistemology. Consider James Inhofe (R-Oklahoma) who produced a snowball in the Senate Chamber in 2015 as proof that global warming is a hoax (Grim 2015). This boorish and scientifically illiterate politician, who does not know the difference between climate and weather (McIntyre 2018: 55), has written a book titled *The Greatest Hoax: How the Global Warming Conspiracy Threatens Your Future* (2012) in which he asserts that scientific institutions around the world have conspired in unison to perpetrate the global warming hoax to destroy the American way of life, bringing conspiracy ideation into mainstream American politics (Lewandowsky et al. 2017: 360). The new alternate epistemology in which there is space for such duplicities has resulted in a puissant amalgamation of "ignorance, anti-rationalism, anti-intellectualism" that Susan Jacoby described in her book *The Age of American Unreason* (2008) long before post-truth became a household word.

Opinion polls suggest that millions of Americans subscribe to the alternative post-truth epistemology (Lewandowsky et al. 2017: 360). In this alternate reality, climate change is a hoax devised by the Chinese, or scientists, the Bush administration and the Israeli intelligence masterminded the 9/11 attacks, the U.N. is bent on establishing a World Government, the Democratic Party runs a child prostitution enterprise from a pizzeria in Washington, D.C. (the 2016 "Pizzagate" conspiracy that has morphed into QAnon, see chapter 11), and NASA has established a child slave colony on Mars (see Kafka 2016; Lewandowsky, Gignac, and Oberauer 2013; Mathis-Lilley 2017).

Thus, in post-truth Americas, it is not the Enlightenment view based on rationality and science but supernaturalism, anti-intellectualism, and obscurantism that comprise the most potent forces in the private and national life of people in the land. These developments are astonishing in a country historically known for secularism, the separation of church and state, science-driven technological innovations, and the exulted ideal that public policy must look to scientific evidence instead of appealing to emotion, religious dogma, or authority. The latter was the view cherished and espoused by this nation's founding figures like Thomas Paine, Thomas Jefferson, and Benjamin Franklin (Sidky 2018: 42).

The flagrant assault on science and scientific knowledge is particularly worrisome. This is because, as the historian of religion Leonardo Ambasciano (2018: 172) points out, "science and democracy are intertwined." They both empower people and encourage critical thinking and rational debate. This is why, he adds, wherever they can right-wing reactionaries and conservative forces exert enormous amounts of effort and resources to "delegitimize science" and its significance in human life. It should not come as a surprise, therefore, that in comparison to multiple presidential administrations dating back to the 1950s, under Trump's regime the scope and scale of attacks on science, which began from the first day of the administration, has been unprecedented (Berman and Carter 2018; Carter et al., 2017, 2018).

In his book *Post Truth: The New War on Truth and How to Fight Back* (2017), Matthew D'Ancona summarizes these developments as

> a new phase of political and intellectual combat, in which democratic orthodoxies and institutions are being shaken to their very foundations by a wave of ugly populism. Rationality is threatened by emotion, diversity by nativism, liberty by a drift toward autocracy. More than ever, the practice of politics is perceived as a zero-sum game, rather than a contest between ideas. Science is treated with suspicion and, sometimes, with open contempt. At the heart of this global trend is a crash in the values of truth, comparable to the collapse of a currency or a stock. Honesty and accuracy are no longer assigned the highest priority (D'Ancona 2017: 7–8).

Explanations for the rise of anti-intellectualism and anti-science perspectives in this country would no doubt include many complex interconnected factors with lengthy histories. These comprise globalization, demographic shifts, changes in the socio-economic infrastructure, the powerful role social media, massive disparities in wealth and power, the disenchantment of the world by science and technology, and so forth (Sidky 2018: 39; Lewandowsky et al. 2017: 357–360). However, the genesis of post-truth, which is the culmination of a preexisting and decades long anti-science and anti-intellectualism campaign, can be clearly attributed to two separate and roughly concurrent enterprises.

The first involved corporate-funded science-denial efforts that began in the 1950s by the profit-hungry tobacco and fossil fuel and agrochemical industries seeking to dodge environmental and safety regulations. Their answer was to undermine the credibility of scientific research that was detrimental to profits (Oreskes and Conway 2010). The second was a methodical science de-legitimation campaign emanating from American universities and colleges during the 1980s and 1990s. As the philosopher and historian of science Lee McIntyre (2018: 24) points out, *science-denial* and *science de-legitimation* paved the way for post-truth.

Science denial means a refusal to believe in established scientific findings for ideological reasons (Diethelm and McKee 2009; McIntyre 2019). It relies on public relations to undermine the legitimacy of scientific conclusions (Specter 2009). Science de-legitimation refers to the efforts of American academics to undermine science as a valid or viable intellectual enterprise. In this study, I am primarily interested in the academic anti-science endeavor and its implications and far-reaching effects on various disciplines, including anthropology. However, to provide the necessary context, in this chapter, I shall cover corporate America's science-denial efforts.

The blueprint or roadmap for science denial was initially set into place by the tobacco industry and a cadre of turncoat scientists on its payroll working to mislead the American public about solidly established scientific evidence that smoking cigarettes causes cancer. The historians of science Naomi Oreskes and Erik Conway (2011: 9) described these events as follows:

> It is a story about a group of scientists who fought the scientific evidence and spread confusion on many of the most important issues of our time. It is a story about a pattern that continues today. A story about fighting facts, and merchandising doubt.

Their description of the scientists engaged in this untoward undertaking is instructive:

Over the course of more than twenty years, these men did almost no original scientific research on any of the issues they weighed in. Once they had been prominent researchers, but by [this time] they were mostly attacking the work and the reputation of others. In fact, on every issue, they were on the wrong side of the scientific consensus. Smoking does kill—both directly and indirectly. Pollution causes acid rain. Volcanoes are not the cause of the ozone hole. Our seas are rising and our glaciers are melting because of the mounting effects of greenhouse gases in the atmosphere, produced by burning fossil fuels. Yet, for years the press quoted these men as experts and politicians listened to them, using their claims as justification for inaction (Oreskes and Conway's 2011: 8).

This enterprise was not about supplying evidence or data but simply to manufacture uncertainty in the public mind. Ari Rabin-Havt (2016: 7) refers to this undertaking as "Lies Incorporated" comprising:

a highly organized industry built around the creation and dissemination of falsehoods supported by a media environment that aids and abets its works. Facts are conjured in purportedly academic studies that have the thinnest veneer of legitimacy.

The operational principle behind this is simple: if the facts do not support your argument discredit those facts at the source (Rabin-Havt 2016: 7). The shameful aspect of this undertaking is that tobacco firms were fully aware that their products were killing people. However, profits outweighed this bothersome fact. As Oreskes and Conway (2011: 33) observe, the tobacco manufacturers were fully aware of the dangers of smoking as early as 1953. Therefore, with no evidence on their side, their tactic was deception and distortion or fighting scientifically established facts by merchandising doubt (Oreskes and Conway 2011: 33). The long-term effects of this effort were remarkable. Americans went on thinking that smoking was harmless, and many still believe this. It was not until the 1990s, as the tobacco companies began losing court cases that the dangers became apparent. Yet the U.S. Congress did not authorize the FDA to regulate tobacco as a dangerous addictive substance until 2009.

The tobacco industry thus provided the roadmap for subsequent science denial operations (Rabin-Havt 2016: 27). In the ensuing years, several other groups and individuals would challenge scientific evidence that either endangered their commercial gains or undermined their religious beliefs and prejudices using strategies directly out of the tobacco industry's playbook (Oreskes and Conway 2011: 35). The issues included climate change, health care, gun control, and stem cell research, among others.

The strategy was to instill the impression that there is considerable disagreement among the experts on the issue, that "the jury is still out on the matter," and that there are two sides to the story that must have equal consideration. As Oreskes and Conway (2011: 242) point out, the media was instrumental in getting out the message that the scientific debate over tobacco was unsettled "long after scientists concluded otherwise."

The main ploy was to confuse the issue. The gist of this tactic is encapsulated in a leaked internal 1969 memo by a tobacco executive who said "doubt is our product . . . since it is the best means of competing with the 'body of fact' that exists in the minds of the general public" (in Oreskes and Conway 2011: 34). This deceptively leveled the playing field by placing bogus assertions on an equal plane with findings based on well-understood scientific evidence. By granting matching credence to both sides of an issue that do not have comparable evidentiary standing, the media thus set the precedent of creating a false equivalence (McIntyre 2018: 77; Stocking and Holstein 2009). Therefore, as Shawn Otto puts it in his book *The War on Science* (2016): "Major media outlets can thus give an equal platform to scientific outliers, celebrities, and political whack jobs on important issues ranging from climate disruption to vaccines" (Otto 2016: 199).

The now common media practice of covering "both sides" of an issue under the label of "fair and balanced" reporting, but without any consideration for evidentiary credence, thus routinely undermines truth by granting unwarranted credibility to lies (Rabin-Havt 2016: 194). This is a very corrosive trajectory with ominous implications. As the philosopher, Jason Stanley points out in his book *How Fascism Works* (2018):

> Allowing every opinion into the public sphere and giving it serious time and consideration, far from resulting in a process that is conducive to knowledge formation, destroys its very possibility (Stanley 2018: 70).

However, this is a very effective delaying tactic to impede policymaking while profits accrue. If the science behind a dispute is made to appear dubious or inconclusive, then it makes no sense to implement any changes that could needlessly affect the economic interests of the workers in the industry in question (Rabin-Havt 2016: 27). Add to this mix a scientifically illiterate American public lacking a basic understanding of cause and effect and rules of logic, and the desired outcome is almost guaranteed. Public relations, governmental lobbying, and the media became the medium of this science-repudiation message. The idea that there are two sides to the story is the foundation of alternative facts and counter-knowledge that paved the way to post-truth.

The next phase of the war on science was initiated by the fossil fuel industry, attempting to deflect environmental regulations seeking to limit the global emissions of greenhouse gases. The riposte was to hoodwink the public into believing that a significant scientific controversy exists regarding human-caused global climate change that is endangering the planet. Politicizing the issue in the minds of voters would lead to public pressure on policymakers.

Doubt once again became the scientific fact buster (Jacques et al. 2008; McCright and Dunlap 2003, 2010; Stocking and Holstein 2009). This was accomplished by once more driving home the message that the story has two sides and sway the media to grant equal coverage to both sides of the story as if they had equal weight. As Oreskes and Conway (2011: 33) put it:

> Until recently the mass media presented global warming as a raging debate—twelve years after President George H. W. Bush had signed the U.N. Framework Convention on Climate Change, and *twenty-five years* after the U.S. National Academy of Sciences first announced that there was no reason to doubt that global warming would occur from man's use of fossil fuels. "Balance" had become a form of bias, whereby the media coverage was in favor of minority—in some cases extreme minority—views. In principle, the media could act as gatekeepers, ignoring the charlatans and snake oil salesmen, but if they have tried, our story shows that at least where it comes to science they have failed. . . . it wasn't just obviously right-wing outlets that reported false claims about tobacco and. . . other subjects; it was the "prestige press"—indeed the allegedly liberal press—as well.

Under these conditions, facts and opinions become indistinguishable, and the concept of truth as something grounded on objective reality superfluous. Everyone can pick and choose the facts that best suites them. Remarkably, all of this is highly consonant with an idea that was being entertained by many in this nation's highest and most prestigious institutions of higher learning, that is the notion of "multiple truths," or epistemological egalitarianism, that I shall discuss in the chapters to follow.

The fossil fuel industry hired scientists tasked to create "industry-approved" facts or counter-science to combat real science. These functionaries were mostly elderly individuals near the end of their careers, still harboring anti-communist political beliefs from the Cold War days. In their political worldview, environmentalism was merely a disguised leftist or communist effort to assert control over this great nation. Motivated by a laissez-faire free-market ideology and an intense revulsion for governmental regulations made them the perfect collaborators (Lewandowsky et al. 2013a: 623; Rabin-Havt 2016: 35, 39). Such free-market worldviews have been found to be a significant predictor of the rejection of scientific findings that entail regulatory implications, such as climate science, but not necessarily of other scientific findings (Lewandowsky et al. 2013b: 1).

The efforts of the fossil fuel industry to cast doubt on established climate science has been all-encompassing, starting from grassroots organizations to the systematic creation and dissemination of false science, intimidation of scientists, and a comprehensive media blitz. Conservative think tanks are playing a central role in manufacturing doubt. Between 1972 and the present, the majority of books advocating climate science denial have been published by such entities (Jacques et al. 2008; Lewandowsky et al. 2013a: 622).

Climate-change deniers do not offer a sound alternative explanation of global climate, their claims are intrinsically incoherent, and their efforts constitute a political maneuver aimed at generating uncertainty in the public's mind (Lewandowsky et al. 2016: 360). Moreover, such deception is perpetrated by drawing upon a small number of highly flawed studies and the routine misinterpretation of the data (Abraham et al. 2014; Benestad et al. 2016; Doran and Zimmerman 2009; Lewandowsky et al. 2016). These efforts merely substitute an incoherent conspiracist body of pseudoscience to refute a coherent and well-established body of scientific facts (Lewandowsky et al. 2016: 190). Given that there is overwhelming scientific consensus on the issue, climate denialism like other forms of science denial is presented in non-scientific outlets such as websites, blogs, and conservative think tank publications (Anderegg et al. 2010; Lewandowsky et al. 2017: 360). This enterprise is not about evidence, but rather about public relations to advance a political objective.

As in the case with the tobacco firms, fossil fuel companies are fully aware of the impact of their product on the global climate and the risk it poses to billions of humans. Again profits, this time to the tune of trillions of dollars, have negated these annoying environmental issues (Rabin-Havt 2016: 41). For this reason, climate science has become more politicized than any other scientific field (Hamilton 2011; Lewandowsky 2013: 629; McCright and Dunlap 2011a, 2011b). In Rabin-Havt's (2016: 44) words, these combined tactics comprise "one of the largest attempts at mass deception in human history."

The ultimate outcome of these duplicities was to again set the stage, as McIntyre (2018: 33) says, where "facts" were irrelevant, and the media was conditioned to submissively present "both sides" of the story through a false equivalence on controversial scientific issues. In his book *Weaponized Lies* (2016), Daniel Levitin (2016: xiv) details the flaw with this approach:

> Two sides to a story exist when evidence exists on both sides of a position. Then reasonable people may disagree about how to weigh that evidence and what conclusion to form from it. Everyone, of course, is entitled to their own opinion.

But they are not entitled to their own facts. Lies are an absence of facts, and, in many cases, a direct contradiction of them.

The effects of these circumstances on the mass media have been startling. Gonzo journalism has become widespread, and few in the profession considered speaking truth to power or even objectivity in reporting as part of their responsibilities (Calcutt 2016; Otto 2016: 23,129, 200). In a way, this makes sense—if facts are no longer part of the equation in reporting, then why not invent stories? Fake news is, therefore, perfectly understandable. As Oreskes and Conway (2011: 236) observe:

> The network of right-wing foundations, the corporations that fund them, and the journalists who echo their claims have created a tremendous problem for American science.... Real science—done by scientists and published in scientific journals—is dismissed as "junk," while misrepresentations and inventions are offered in its place.

Consider Trump's embarrassing remarks on this topic: "Global warming has been proven to be a canard repeatedly over and over again," it is "mythical," "nonexistent," "bullshit," "based on faulty science," "a total, and very expensive hoax!" (in Andersen 2017: 424). Why are science and truth targets? Oreskes and Conway add:

> If science is about studying the world as it actually is—rather than as we wish it to be—then science will always have the potential to unsettle the status quo. As an independent source of authority and knowledge, science has always had the capacity to challenge the ruling powers' ability to control people by controlling their beliefs. Indeed, it has the power to challenge anyone who wishes to preserve, protect or defend the status quo (Oreskes and Conway 2011: 236–237).

All the details of this disconcerting tale about the birth and evolution of science denial in the United States are covered in Oreskes and Conway's book *Merchants of Doubt* (2011) and further details are unnecessary here. What is important to note is that the successful corporate-funded science-denial campaigns outlined here would have massive sociocultural and political ramifications in the years to come.

Daily life is now permeated with science-denying assertions that have morphed from uninformed skepticism about scientific knowledge into an overt hostility toward the very idea that objective knowledge is a possibility (Thompson and Smulewircz-Zuker 2018: 7). Once outrageous lies and conspiracy theories are reiterated through radio, television, and print, they become entrenched in the public mind and are extraordinarily difficult to undo (cf., Goertzel 2010: 493). The disseminators of false information are abetted in their untoward efforts by the fact that many prevarications strike emotional chords and are "sticky" and easily take hold (Heath and Heath 2007: 3–51).

Bogus ideas continue to have believers even after they have been refuted, rising from the dead over and over, impacting political discourse and public opinion (Rabin-Havt's 2016: 190). Augmenting this process is that once lies are set into motion by interested parties, they are perpetuated by ordinary citizens unwittingly ensnared in the misinformation campaign (McIntyre 2018: 21). The sociologist Tristan Bridges (2107) explains this phenomenon as follows:

> As a rule, misinformed people do not change their minds once they have been presented with facts that challenge their beliefs. But beyond simply not changing their minds when they should, research shows that they are likely to become *more* attached to their mistaken beliefs. The factual information "backfires" [known as the backfire effect] When people don't agree with you, research suggests that bringing in facts to support your case might actually make them believe you *less*. In other words, fighting the ill-informed with facts is like fighting a grease fire with water. It seems like it should work, but it's actually going to make things worse.

If it is so easy to blatantly obfuscated well-established scientific conclusions about the hazards of smoking and the human causes of global climate change through systematic misinformation and public relations, why not extend the prescription to other issues to be politicized? How about immigration, gun control, stem cell research, voter reform, vaccines, gay marriage, abortion, and COVID-19: the possibilities are endless. What about evolutionary theory? In a *New York Times* piece (October 29, 2000), George W. Bush used the lexicon of post-truth science-denial when he asserted the "the jury is still out" on evolution." What about the invasion of Iraq? That disastrous decision that caused close to a hundred thousand Iraqi casualties and contributed to the rise of ISIS was based on hubris, gut feelings, and bluster of some conceited politicians, not rational policy decision-making, the weighting of evidence, and assessment of intelligence data. Iraq did not attack the United States on 9/11and it did not possess chemical and nuclear weapons of mass destruction (cf. Kakutani 2018: 31). In fact, there was overwhelming evidence to the contrary. Yet, the American public fell for these deceptions. Bush and his fear-mongering cronies contemptuously sold a disastrous and pointless war to the American people based on false pretensions. None but a few raised any objections.

The Iraq war was a foretaste of the full-blown post-truth to come. It demonstrated that facts were becoming increasingly irrelevant in American political discourse and that cynical, self-serving politicians could audaciously and without accountability promote just about any spurious claims based solely on political fiat or personal interest. It now seems that falsehoods are not a matter of public concern anymore. Years ago, the astronomer and astrophysicist Carl Sagan (1995: 241) made a near oracular observation for our time:

> One of the saddest lessons of history is this: If we've been bamboozled long enough, we tend to reject any evidence of the bamboozle. We're no longer interested in finding out the truth. The bamboozle has captured us. It's simply too painful to acknowledge, even to ourselves, that we've been taken. Once you give a charlatan power over you, you almost never get it back. So the old bamboozles tend to persist and the new ones rise.

So, as Rabin-Havt (2016: 197) says: "We have become a society and a political class that has become desensitized to the impact of falsehood." "However," he adds, "lies have consequences." What are these consequences? Trump's post-truth America characterized by emboldened right-wing populism, xenophobia, racism, vulgarity, religious extremism, and concerted efforts to undermine deliberative democracy.

Chapter 2

Delegitimizing Science in the Academy

Ideological Underpinnings

Regrettably, a significant contribution to science-denial and a post-truth mentality was imparted by a cadre of American academics, the so-called New Left. Paradoxically, the very people who were supposed to be the guardians of truth, rational discourse, and science—esteemed professors in institutions of higher learning—undertook a comprehensive effort to delegitimize science and propagate and encourage irrationalism and anti-intellectualism (Andersen 2017: 309; Sidky 2018: 39). These developments are especially problematic for me because anthropology, the discipline to which I belong, had a pivotal role in the assault on truth, scientific knowledge, and rationality in institutions of higher learning.

These circumstances involved a remarkably weird twist. As Richard Wolin observes in his book *The Seduction of Unreason* (2004), deep-seated skepticism about reason and democracy, that was at one time the trademark of right-wing reactionary thought, now became the forte of the Left in American universities and colleges (Wolin 2004: 4). In unanticipated ways, the academic Left's intense skepticism about knowledge and its persistent decades-long derision of science paved the way to today's post-truth cultural landscape, with its counter-knowledge, alternative facts, fake news, and all the rest. Their diatribes were propagated from departments of "science studies," sociology, anthropology, political science, literary criticism, cultural studies, English, journalism, education, gender studies, and the other humanities on campuses around the country during the 1980s and early 1990s. As Shawn Otto (2011: 112) observes, the impact of academic science delegitimation on American society and culture was as momentous as the efforts of the religious right with the same objective. Moreover, he adds, its thinking bolstered those on the other fronts against science—namely, religious fundamentalists and incumbent industry—justifying their case in public discourse by offering them powerful tools, thereby magnifying their effectiveness (Otto 2016: 173).

Why the contempt for science became the preoccupation of radical thinkers in the United States during the 1980s and early 1990s has a great deal to do with the particular and rather abysmal circumstances in which these intellectuals found themselves. By the 1980s, they comprised a "residual intelligentsia" of 1960s radicalism still hanging on long after their popular base had withered away (Gross and Levitt 1994: 34). Their ideologies were faltering along with their hopes of achieving real social change. By the late 1970s, they had already to come to grips with the bitter fact that they had turned out to be less relevant than expected (see Rorty 1992: 17). Social justice and economic equality appeared more evasive than ever. The global capitalist system emanating from the United States was continuing to expand unabated. Racism appeared more obstinate than ever before. New demographic patterns were not leading to benevolent coexistence but a widening of socioeconomic differences. Feminists who made up the ranks of the radical Left felt they were getting nowhere. Also dashed were their expectations of truly socialist orders in the Soviet Union and Eastern Europe, free of their horrifying totalitarian regimes and the long-awaited development of an alternative to capitalism (Benson and Stangroom 2006: 44; Gross and Levitt 1994: 26).

Under these conditions, American radicals sought different ways through which they could once again regain their relevance. The alternative was found in some theories espoused by an odd assemblage of unconventional French philosophers: Michel Foucault, Jacques Derrida, Jean-François Lyotard, Bruno Latour, Jean Baudrillard, Jacques Lacan, and others. The intellectual movement they started was known variously as *social constructivism, deconstructionism, post-structuralism, post-positivism,* and *postmodernism* (see Aylesworth 2015). However, many of the paragons associated with these perspectives did not necessarily self-identify as such and were unclear about what these labels represented. Rather than becoming engrossed with the nuances of terminology necessary to differentiate postmodernism from say poststructuralism, or deconstructionism, and so forth, I shall use the designation postmodernism. Following Sokal and Bricmont (1998: 183), this term refers to the brainchild of a segment of Parisian intelligentsia, a perspective characterized by the following features:

> A fascination with obscure discourses; an epistemic relativism linked to a generalized skepticism toward modern science; an excessive interest in subjective beliefs independently of their truth or falsity; and an emphasis on discourse and language as opposed to facts to which those discourses refer (or worse, the rejection of the very idea that facts exist or one may refer to them).

Wolin describes the circumstances under which American academics became disciples and proxies of the French savants espousing such views. In his words:

> During the 1970s and 1980s, a panoply of texts by Derrida, Foucault, Deleuze, and Lyotard were translated into English, provoking a far-reaching shift in American intellectual life. Many of these texts were inspired by Nietzsche's anticivilization animus: the conviction that our highest ideals of beauty, morality, and truth were intrinsically nihilistic. Such views found favor among a generation of academics disillusioned by the political failures of the 1960s (Wolin 2004: 8).

The link between postmodern philosophy and Nietzsche, whose work also directly inspired Mussolini's fascist politics and Hitler's Nazis ideology of genocide, is particularly problematic and requires discussion. There have been generations of apologists, as Ronald Beiner (2018: 18) points out, who have tried and some continue to try and "sanitize" Nietzsche by arguing that such an association is based on misunderstandings or misinterpretations (e.g., Kaufmann 1968; Alloa 2017; Berel 2002; Golomb 2002; Helmut 2018; Nehamas 2002; Sznajder 2002). Such arguments are wholly unpersuasive. Beiner (2018: 18) correctly points out that Nietzsche was complicit in "the Hitlerite appropriation of his legacy because there were things in his oeuvre that invited that appropriation and that made it attractive for Hitler to lay claim to him."

Consider the following passages in which Nietzsche advocates the extermination of inferior races, extolls violence and autocratic rule, disparages truth, calls for the subordination and subjugation of the masses, rationalizes the abuse of women, and talks about the master race or the supermen (*übermensch,* plural *übermenschen*) who are above morality, transcend good and evil, and exert a will to power to heroically triumph.

> The great majority of men have no right to life, and serve only to disconcert the elect among our race; I do not yet grant the unfit that right. There are even unfit peoples (*The Will to Power*, in Beiner 2018: 4).

> A declaration of war on the masses by *higher men* is needed. . . . A doctrine is needed powerful enough to work as a breeding agent: strengthening the strong, paralyzing and destructive for the world-weary. The annihilation of the decaying races. . . . Dominion over the earth as a means of producing a higher type (Nietzsche, *Will to Power*, in Wolin 2004: 53).

> The possibility has been established for the production of international racial unions whose task will be to rear a *master race*, the future "masters of earth"—a

new, tremendous aristocracy, based on the severest self-legislation, in which the will of philosophical men of power and artist tyrants will be made to endure for millennia (Nietzsche, *Will to Power*, in Wolin 2004: 56).

No act of violence, rape, exploitation, destruction is intrinsically "unjust," since life itself is violent, rapacious, exploitative, and destructive (Nietzsche, *Genealogy of Morals*, in Wolin 2004: 56).

"All truth is simple"—Is that not a compound lie? (Nietzsche, *Twilight of the Idols* 1990 [1888]: 33).

No amount of laundering can obscure or put a non-malevolent spin on the meaning of these assertions. A great deal of Nietzsche's philosophy directly lends support to fascist and Nazi ideologies and projects without the need to twist, distort, or manipulate his statements (Stellino 2017: 474–475). It is no surprise that totalitarians, fascists, Nazis, racists, relativists, and present-day post-truth white power activists in America and Europe find the rantings of this genocidal, sexist, racist, and nihilistic madman highly appealing. Nietzsche's ideas were also embraced by Martin Heidegger, a philosopher near and dear to the postmodernists. He was politically committed to and publicly endorsed National Socialism (Nazism) between 1930 and 1945 (see Bambach 2003: 31–38; Faye 2009: 30–31).

Postmodernists also found Nietzsche a friend and ally because he disparaged modernity, democracy, and the Enlightenment ideals, espoused moral relativism, relentlessly attacked truth and rationality, and argued that truth (scientific or otherwise) is linked to and is in the service of power (Baghramian 2010: 45–46). In this regard Beiner (2018: 6–7) observes:

> One notable case in point is the Nietzschean doctrine claiming that appeals to truth are largely ideological, designed to obfuscate the deeper realities of power and resentment. This doctrine was enthusiastically taken up by Michel Foucault with his attempt to see truth as a normative aspiration exposed as a mask for what are in reality cynical "regimes of truth." And what do we have today? "Post-truth"! Nietzschean notions, mediated by supposedly emancipatory appropriations of Nietzsche, seem to have left us vulnerable to harsh new ideologies that appear to regard respect for truth as a snare for the strong set by the weak, as Nietzsche largely presents it.

Wolin (2004: 53) makes a very relevant observation regarding the postmodernists' reception of Nietzschean ideas:

> Ironically, whereas an earlier generation of critics took Nietzsche's philosophy to task for its repugnant political message, the postmodern approach is fond of celebrating his apoliticism. But no special interpretive talent is needed to see

that [his ideas] . . . far from being "apolitical," are fraught with political directives and implications.

For this reason, Beiner (2018: 5) admonishes the postmodern savants for the imprudent and uncritical manner they received Nietzsche's problematic aphorisms, observing that:

> great thinkers can be dangerous thinkers. And to the extent that their ideas contribute to bad ideological currents in the present, we have to be alert to their noninnocence and do our utmost not to become their apologists.

Aside from their abhorrent political implications, Nietzsche's ideas also contributed to hostility toward science. The passage most often cited in support of this assertion comes from Nietzsche's notebook written in the spring of 1887:

> Against positivism which halts at the phenomenon "There are only facts" I would say: no, precisely facts do not exist, only interpretations. We cannot determine any fact "in itself": perhaps it is a nonsense to want such a thing. "Everything is subjective," you say: but that itself is an interpretation, the "subject" is not a given, but an added-on-fiction, tucked-behind—Is it at last necessary to posit the interpreter behind the interpretation? Even that is poetry, hypothesis. Inasmuch as the word "knowledge" has any meaning at all, the world is knowable: but it is variously interpretable; it has no meaning behind it, but countless meanings "Perspectivism" (Nietzsche 2003: 139).

As Pinker (2018: 446) correctly observes, Nietzsche may be seen as the godfather of the twentieth-century anti-science movements, including critical theory, deconstructionism, and postmodernism. Post-truth can be added to this list.

The question to address here is: Why did the aphorisms of Nietzsche's unorthodox and eccentric French acolytes have such great appeal to leftist academics in the United States? Well, the French savants were saying exactly what disillusioned American professors in humanities and social sciences departments wanted to hear, namely that rationality and reason are the instruments of oppression and "truth" is a mirage or hoax (Andersen 2017: 307). These ideas provided a convenient explanation for their failure to bring about social change. Indeed, the powerful seductive appeal of these ideas among members of the Academic Left was the basis of the celebrity of the French philosophers (Andersen 2017: 308; Benson and Stangroom 2006: 40).

As the historian John Diggins (1992: 356–357) puts it, the new philosophy provided the American academics "ready-made answers to their defeat and disillusionment." They thought that they had discovered a new theory of social emancipation. Also, there was consolation in the idea that they had hitherto been fooling themselves and that the world is after all unknowable because everything is about power, language, perspective, subjective interests, and so forth. The key to emancipation, therefore, resided not in protests and shedding blood in the streets, but rather, as the French savants were saying, in language and texts, the careful scrutiny of which become a principal preoccupation of these radicals, as discussed below.

Foucault stressed, for example, that human life is organized around language. However, language is not neutral but is structured and distorted by prevailing relations of power and domination. What is considered to be knowledge or truth, he added, is the product of power. "Truth," Foucault (1980: 133) said, "is linked in a circular relation with systems of power which produce and sustain it, and to the effects of power which it induces and which extends it." Furthermore:

> It is not a matter of emancipating truth from every system of power (which would be a chimera, for truth is already power), but detaching the power of truth from the forms of hegemony, social, economic, and cultural, within which it operates at the present time (Foucault 1980: 133).

Therefore, truth/knowledge cannot grasp power because what is defined as such is itself the result of power (Diggins 1992: 351). Truth is an ideological construct of the power-wielding elite and, therefore, truth is the real adversary of the people. To state it differently, "truth" is what *passes* for truth, and what passes for truth is established by hegemonic power (Lynch 2005: 38). The reception of such sublime insights planted the seeds that today have bloomed into the standpoint that there is no such thing as truth, and the very concept is ridiculed and spurned by many.

The view of power being advocated was ultra-idealist because power was construed to be a disembodied force that permeates everything, yet is unconnected to social structures, human social relations, or earthly conditions (Foucault 1978: 92). Clearly, there is a great deal of Hegelian mystification here that Karl Marx so desperately tried to avoid (Rosdolsky 1977). Power, according to Foucault (1978: 92):

> [is not simply] a group of institutions and mechanisms that ensure the subservience of the citizens of a given state . . . or a mode of subjugation . . . or a general system of domination exerted by one group over another . . . these are only the terminal forms power takes. . . . Power is the multiplicity of force relations immanent in the sphere in which they operate and which constitute their own organization.

Foucault thus eliminated human agency and intellectual aspirations from the equation. What remains, therefore, is the mysterious, terrifying, and impenetrable force of power that dominates and oppresses, but which manifests itself as an effect without a cause—there is control without a controller and domination without a dominator (Diggins 1992: 352). Power becomes akin to a supernatural force that by definition cannot be specified or proven to exist by any empirical criteria. This was remarkable and scary stuff. But, what it left out was the good old-fashioned kind of power that emanates from institutional structures, the power that comes from the barrel of guns, and the control over what I call the "material means of destruction" that has devastated countless societies and suppressed hundreds of thousands of humans around the planet. I am talking about the kind of tangible, earthly power that actually subjugates and dominates the wretched of the earth who are oppressed and ruled (D'Andrade 1999: 98; Sidky 2007a: 861).

Language was a central concern of many of the postmodern philosophers, such as Jacques Derrida (1930–2004). He was the founder of Deconstructionism or the deconstructionist approach to textual analysis. In his view, everything begins and ends in the realm of language, and language is disconnected from any objective reality. Language, moreover, is an arbitrary and artificial creation—it is a "construct" in the same way as meaningful cultural behavior, which is like a language with its own narrative structure. We know the world through existing linguistic categories and knowledge itself is a product of language. Linguistic categories, moreover, refer to themselves—they are "self-referential"—and not to objects existing outside language. According to this view, if language has no referents or constraints outside itself, then linguistic meanings can change randomly, as do its truth postulates (Layton 1997: 200–201). Truth is, therefore, relative and knowledge, which is an artifact of language, is as arbitrary as language itself rather than being linked to some objective reality (cf., Layton 1997: 195). Along the same lines, postmodernists in anthropology averred that it is impossible to demonstrate the independence of reason, logic, or mathematics, from "the discourses that constitute them" (Tyler 1986: 37). I shall discuss the anthropological incarnation of postmodernism in chapter 9. For now, all we need to know is that such clever and sublime notions were resonating among certain American cultural anthropologists.

So what was the answer to the enigma of power? Well, to expose its exact nature, one had to look at the linguistic context of truth claims. Science, the French philosophers asserted, is merely a social discourse, or "myth," and they treated it as a textual or rhetorical construct, "a kind of writing" minus the slightest possibility that it can get anything right" (Norris 1997: 7). Teasing apart texts, as I have already said, thus became a central preoccupation across the humanities and social sciences, including cultural anthropology, which was already toying with the ideas of culture as text, ethnography as fiction, and so forth.

What I found baffling is why so many took these assertions about the prison of language as novel philosophical insights. As the cognitive psychologist and linguist Steven Pinker (2007: 134, 149) points out in his book *The Stuff of Thought* (2007), various literati have advanced something comparable, that is, that language is "a prison house of thought," including Nietzsche, Wittgenstein, Heidegger, and others. Another source for the assertion that experience and representations are texts and it is impossible to go outside of the text is the debatable thesis of the Swiss linguist Ferdinand de Saussure (1857–1913). He said that language does not refer to an objective reality or meaning outside itself, namely that it is self-referential. Hence, "black gets its meaning exclusively from its opposite white," and so forth with no connection to the real world (Franklin 2009: 43). This is not an innovative insight but is a version of the sophist rhetorician Gorgias's (ca. 483–375 BCE) position that knowledge is impossible and that even if anything could be known, it could not be communicated. As the philosopher C. Francis Higgins (2006) points out, postmodernists found Gorgias's ideas on truth and language a highly useful addition to their philosophical repertoire.

The postmodernists were not merely unoriginal in their assertions about language, they had succumbed to a long-standing difficulty in Western philosophy. "Delusions about the power of words," as the ever-perceptive Australian philosopher David Stove (1991: 32) pointed out:

> are an occupational hazard with philosophers. In fact that is putting it mildly. The truth is that a difficulty of distinguishing words from the world . . . is a weakness to which philosophers as a class are peculiarly and painfully prone.

He added that the premise that we are prisoners of language, the delusion about the power of words, or the notion that the world comprises, embodies, or is ruled by "a *sentence-like* entity, a 'logos' is an idea almost as old as Western philosophy itself." In the Bible the word is the beginning and, Stove pointed out, this "sums up pretty accurately one of the most perennial, as well as most lunatic, strands in philosophy."

Pinker (2007: 124) adds that this idea had become a staple of courses on language through the early 1970s, and by then it had also entered popular consciousness (for an overview, see Baghramian and Carter 2019a). Also, this is all the stuff of anthropology 101. In anthropology, a similar relativistic idea was encapsulated in the strong version of The Sapir-Whorf Hypothesis proposed by the anthropologists Edward Sapir and Benjamin Whorf. The critical paper that was the basis of this premise was Whorf's article "The Relation of Habitual Thought and Behavior to Language" (written in 1939 and published in 1941), in which he compared the way English speakers and speakers of the Hopi language referred to time (see Leavitt 2006; Webster and Peterson 2011: 3). Here is Sapir's (1929: 209, 214) explanation:

> [Language] powerfully conditions all our thinking about social problems and processes. Human beings do not live in the objective world alone, nor alone in the world of social activity as ordinarily understood but are very much at the mercy of the particular language which has become the medium of expression for their society. It is quite an illusion to imagine that one adjusts to reality essentially without the use of language and that language is merely an incidental means of solving specific problems of communication or reflection. The fact of the matter is that the "real world" is to a large extent unconsciously built up on the language habits of the group. No two languages are ever sufficiently similar to be considered as representing the same social reality. The worlds in which different societies live are distinct worlds, not merely the same world with different labels attached. . . . We see and hear and otherwise experience very largely as we do because the language habits of our community predispose certain choices of interpretation.

Most anthropologists and cognitive scientists, however, reject the strong version of the linguistic relativity thesis (Kay and Kempton 1984; Wolff and Holmes 2011; for an overview, see Lucy 1997).

Sokal and Bricmont (1998: 100) point out a seldom recognized issue that the radical relativism inherent in the Sapir-Whorf hypothesis (a.k.a. linguistic relativity) lends itself to the atomization of all humans into disparate cultures with their own conceptual universes—even their own "reality"—and hence virtually incapable of communication with each other, that is, that cultures are incommensurable. This thesis certainly impacted the relativistic views of the philosopher Paul Feyerabend (1975: 241–242), one of the apostles of postmodernism whose work is discussed in chapter 5. The idea that cultures are incommensurable, a correlate of the radical relativity thesis, is problematic because if this were the case cultural anthropologists whose task it is to fathom unfamiliar conceptual worlds would be out of business.

Assertions regarding the all-encompassing power of language upon perception and knowledge are facile and not very convincing. As Pinker (2007: 437) adds:

> People sense that their words are about things in the world, and are not just definitions trapped in a self-referential circle of terms (as we see in intuitions about the semantics of names). In a similar way, people can think of propositions as being objectively true or false, not just as things they suppose to be true or false (as we see in intuitions about the semantics of factive verbs like learn and

know). The intuition that ideas can point to real things in the world or can miss them, and that beliefs about the world can be true or just believed, can drive people to test their analogies for fidelity to the causal structure of the world, and to prune away irrelevant features and zero in on the explanatory ones.

Derrida's (1976: 46–48) construal of language went further, however, claiming that writing rather than speaking is the significant feature of language, and he defined writing as any aspect of communication that leaves a vestige or imprint. Speech is a form of writing even though it is incomparably ephemeral in comparison with words inscribed on paper: "And thus we say 'writing' for all that gives rise to an inscription in general, whether it is literal or not" (Derrida 1976: 9). All experiences and representations are texts and it is impossible to go outside of the text. Reality is thus reduced to discourse, and the need to worry about tangible, earthly power relations and circumstances is lifted from the postmodern philosopher's shoulders. Given the definition of reality and experience as text or discourse, Derrida claimed that the only form of cultural analysis and critique is literary analysis (Kuznar 2008: 12).

So what did Derrida mean by deconstruction? For him, this involved the uncloaking of hidden rhetorical devices, metaphors, metaphysical assumptions, and contradictions that exist within texts (Diggins 1992: 354). The meaning in a text, it was argued further, is unrecognized by its author because he or she employs culturally entrenched tropes (a dreadful jargon term for metaphors). Through deconstruction, the argument went, the meanings or intentions inside a text were revealed, as were the writer's culturally defined assumptions, motivations, and agendas. The philosopher Christopher Norris (2002: 18–19) provided a concise précis of deconstruction as follows:

> Derrida refuses to grant philosophy the kind of privileged status it has always claimed as the sovereign dispenser of reason. Derrida confronts this claim to power on its own chosen ground. He argues that philosophers have been able to impose their various systems of thought only by ignoring, or suppressing, the disruptive effects of language. His aim is always to draw out these effects by a critical reading which fastens on, and skillfully unpicks, the elements of metaphor and other figurative devices at work in texts of philosophy. Deconstruction in this, its most rigorous form acts as a constant reminder of the ways in which language deflects or complicates the philosopher's project. Above all, deconstruction works to undo the idea—according to Derrida, the ruling illusion of Western metaphysics—that reason can somehow dispense with language and achieve knowledge ideally unaffected by such mere foibles.

Zeroing in on language, "blind-spots of metaphor," "rhetorical strategies," and "figurative devices," Derrida aimed at nothing less than the deconstruction· of Western logocentrism and its truths as encapsulated in science. For Derrida, scientific texts were just like any other texts and had to be deconstructed and the falsely exalted position of scientific discourse demonstrated as merely a delusion stemming the presumptuousness and misplaced arrogance of Western metaphysics (Gross and Levitt 1994: 78). This is how he thought one could achieve emancipation.

It is crucial to bear in mind, however, that deconstruction of texts was a rather "slippery business" (Carneiro 1995: 11). There were no rules, handbooks, no incorrect interpretations, and no wrong answers. The presumed shrouded and unstated meanings and hidden "codes of power" that were said to exist in all texts do not yield themselves readily. Careful reading does not suffice. Such encrypted significations came to light only after the ingenuity and prodigious insights of the postmodern savants were brought to bear upon the matter, and what they revealed depended mostly on who was deconstructing the text and their political and ideological orientations. Slippery business indeed.

This became embarrassingly evident during a crisis that arose for these thinkers when it was revealed posthumously that one of their own, the much celebrated luminary, Paul de Man (1919–1983), a professor of French and comparative literature at Yale University, was a fascist in his earlier years. The revelation was based on the discovery of articles he had written during the war for two Nazi-controlled Belgian newspapers. This disclosure raised pressing questions and generated considerable criticism of deconstruction, and the moral relativism upon which it was grounded. Some followers of de Man, fearful of their own reputations, took a vow of silence on the matter. Others, employing their sharpest hermeneutical tactics or interpretive skills, sought to differentiate between de Man's early years as a fascist and his later years as a literary critic. Still, others opted for full disclosure by releasing two books, *Wartime Journalism* (1988) and *Responses: On Paul de Man's Wartime Journalism* (1989) (De Man et al. 1988; Hamacher et al. 1989). But as Harvard professor Louis Menand (2014) points out, all of these were bad ideas because: "As it turned out, full disclosure did not make the case any less unpalatable. The record showed that, for all intents and purposes, the young de Man was a fascist."

Derrida (1988) took up the defense. He argued that when carefully deconstructed, the articles were not saying what they appeared to be saying, "or they were saying it and unsaying it at the same time" (Menand 2014). Critics were not kind. They pointed out that using Derrida's approach and logic, one could deconstruct Hitler's *Mein Kampf* into a Zionist tract (Lehman 1991: 238; Harris 1995: 70). Menand (2014) comes to the following conclusion:

> Deconstruction started to run into the sands when it got used to interpret texts in conformance with the political views of the interpreter (a type of self-fulfilling

prophecy that afflicts many schools of criticism). Deconstruction is not a train you can get off of at the most convenient station.

The postmodernists' moral relativism, subjective truths—that is, truth claims provided by the authors—thus preceded to awkward conclusions.

What is remarkable is that nowhere did any of these sages provide any evidence for their claims about the nature of power and the all-encompassing enveloping force of language. Nor did they offer any compelling reasons why only they were exempt from the shackles of language that imprisoned all other philosophers from Plato to Hegel. Their perspective was entirely an ideological one based upon a priori thinking (cf., Otto 2016: 199–200). Using specious arguments, or more correctly dogma, the French philosophers sought to undercut the view that humans can grasp any knowledge about some external reality. We could justifiably say that this project was a thoroughly anti-intellectual perspective in orientation and goals. Their target was knowledge in general, but specifically, science became their singular preoccupation. It was as if they were somehow afraid of knowing or the possibility of knowledge. I called this epistemophobia (Sidky 2007b: 69).

As will become apparent, this epistemic stance regarding the power of language hinged upon undermining the separation of thought from reality and the premise that belief may be based on objective evidence or facts (Franklin 2009: 50). As the philosopher James Franklin (2009: 43) puts it:

> As applied to "poststructuralist" and postmodern "discourse," it acts as a universal solvent of claims to truth, scientific or other. As with the move from logic to sociology, the purpose of this ploy is to undercut any talk about people believing something because there is good reason to, thus opening up the way to endless "deconstruction" and speculation on the political and psychopathological causes of their beliefs.

Why is this assertion specious? Simply because it is implausible. If there were nothing to be known, then the problem of knowledge itself would not exist in the first place (Lett 1987: 24). It is also important to note, as the philosopher of science Larry Laudan (1990: vii) pointed out, that at the time no one outside the social sciences and humanities departments took postmodern postulates regarding knowledge and knowing seriously. This was especially true among those engaged in the philosophy of science proper who attributed such beliefs to an episode of "cultural silliness" that would wither away and die. But social scientists, historians, and the rest were awe-stricken and completely sold on the sublime truths they had discovered in the apothegms of a few eccentric Continental thinkers.

David Stove (1995: 66–67) nominated the postmodernist construal of language—which can be condensed to "we can only speak through our conceptual schemes; therefore we cannot speak about things in and of themselves"—as the Worst Argument in the World (Franklin 2009: 46–47). Stove's assessments involved the degree of badness of the argument (50 percent) and degree of endorsement by philosophers (50 percent). In other words, he was seeking a case that was both very bad and very prevalent (Franklin 2002). The versions of this thesis offered by Gorgias, Saussure, Derrida, and other European literati all qualify as winners of the worst argument contest. This is what the philosopher Reuben Abel (1976: 27) said about this type of epistemological cynicism long before postmodernism was formulated:

> It seems to me safe to deny the thorough-going skepticism of Gorgias, who argued that nothing existed; and if it did, it could not be communicated; and if it could be apprehended, that apprehension could not be communicated. If he could tell us that, how can knowledge not be communicated?

Others have reached a similar conclusion. Thus, as the philosopher of science, Lee McIntyre (2015: 105) says:

> The relativist and postmodernist criticisms of science are based on terrible arguments and . . . anyone who doesn't already buy into their politics will not buy their criticisms either.

The absence of evidentiary corroboration for their argument necessitated that the purveyors of postmodern epistemic relativism resort to politicking to make converts accept "a universal truth" that there is no such thing as "a universal truth." McIntyre (2015: 105) adds that it is "the mark of a weak theory that one must be an advocate in order to understand it." Based on my experiences as a Ph.D. student in anthropology and in the department where I work, the more appropriate term is proselytizing rather than advocacy. For this reason, postmodern acolytes were immune to criticisms. This is because they were indoctrinated instead of adopting their beliefs through logic, argumentation, evidence, and comparison. Such true believers are not open to rational debate or challenge. Hence the many critics pointing out the absurdities of their epistemic position did not stem this rising tide of irrationality in universities and college campuses.

Such problems, notwithstanding, the academic Left was wholly committed. What they obtained from the French theorists was a method—deconstruction and textual analysis—a rationale for using it, and a target, Western logocentrism, at which to direct it. As Diggins (1992: 356) adds:

Having lost the confrontation on the streets in the sixties, they could later, as English professors in the eighties, continue it in the classroom. A new nemesis haunted the Left. Everything wrong with modern society would be explained no longer by the mode of production but by the mode of discourse.

Upon adopting the received wisdom from Paris, members of the academic Left shifted their focus from mundane earthly political affairs to the task of investigating and uncovering the mysterious almost supernatural forces of domination and power which, as they saw it, made freedom impossible (Diggins 1992: 349). Thanks to French postmodern sagacity, failed American critical thinkers now saw a path forward (cf., Chomsky 1994: 163).

More remarkably, the direct effect of this was to transform radicalism into an entirely academic and purely intellectual enterprise (Diggins 1992: 16, 373). As Wolin (2004: 12) notes, the postmodernists preferred to operate in the confined realm of theory where the dangers of radical opposition become conceptual and "concrete politics were reduced to the 'ethereal.'" He adds: "It seems that the seduction of "theory" helped redirect formerly robust political energies along the lines of acceptable academic careers" (Wolin 2004: 9). This was something new, a kind of radicalism that posed no risks, did not endangered careers, but instead furthered them (Gross and Levitt 1994: 74). These academics now felt entitled to explore the most esoteric topics as bold political initiatives against the forces of oppression. Also, university administrators and boards of trustees were perfectly comfortable with such an enterprise because in those days the "call to arms" amounted to nothing more than ominous adages in obscure journals (Gross and Levitt 1994: 74).

As Gross and Levitt (1994: 74) pointed out, the assumption was that somehow paying careful attention to the words, tropes, and rhetorical postures in texts bestowed upon the analyst some world-changing capacities. The problem is that the postmodern radicals attributed too much significance to words and texts. In this regard, the sociologists Ruth Wallace and Alison Wolf (1991: 328) made the following insightful observation:

> Those who write and tell tales, and whose words survive, are only a fraction of society. They are unquestionably its products in the sense of being the people they are because of when and where they live. However, especially in the written word, there is much that is individual to the writer and much more that is specific to the outlook of the "writing" classes alone. It is dangerous to believe that one can somehow deduce · social institutions directly from ideas, just as it is dangerous to see ideas as simply a "superstructure" minoring the economic institutions below.

To put it differently, what the savants did, as anthropologist Steven Sangren (1988: 411) noted, was to "conflate authority in texts with authority in society." While authority in texts may have a part in the creation and perpetuation of power in society, Sangren sarcastically added, textual authority is not as forceful as they wish, "otherwise writers would be kings."

This new intellectual enterprise was not about creating genuine social change in the world, as the radical thinkers of previous generations had attempted by taking to the streets, but to undermine the validity of all the values and ideals cherished by Western culture since the Enlightenment. Science and reason, which they equated with the "episteme" of the modern world, were indicted as the instruments of totalitarian regimes for oppression and domination (Harris 1999: 155). Science became the embodiment of authority, expertise, and hierarchy of power. There was a lot of post-truth sounding stuff here, skepticism toward science, denigration of expertise, and an overt anti-intellectualism. The key to social emancipation was to demystify this endeavor called science and divest it of the claim to universality and ageless un-contextual validity. It had to be exposed for what it truly is, merely a product of a particular historical epoch and its truths applicable only to one specific configuration of power relationships (Benson and Stangroom 2006: 49; Gross and Levitt 1994: 38, 50). A key point that is often overlooked is that while pontification about science became the specialty of the postmodernists in American universities and colleges, none of them or their French apostles whose ideas they mimicked were trained as scientists. It is accurate to say that they were almost entirely scientifically illiterate academics trained in the humanities who did not understand what they were studying (see Sokal and Bricmont 1998).

How would denigrating science lead to emancipation? Simple. By undermining science, alternative anti-establishment perspectives and belief systems regarded as superstition or irrationalism by science could be made to appear more valid (Gross and Levitt 1994: 48). In anthropology, this was articulated as making "space" in texts for the voices of "the other" to be heard. Fostering and promoting such ideas were thus seen as acts of emancipation. In retrospect, this all sounds very silly and absurd. However, at the time, the proponents of such views were fanatically committed to these ideas with the zeal and dedication of the most devoted religionists and cult members.

There is more. There was little consolation in merely adopting the tenets of the French icons. Instead, like the many recipients of new religious revelations, these intellectuals found additional solace by spreading the word. This gave these votaries a pious fervor and missionary zeal to carry the word to anyone who would listen. Ironically, given that their enterprise was about social justice, egalitarianism, and human dignity, those who did not accept their premises—usually colleagues down the hall—were labeled racists, sexists, right-wing oppressors, colonialists, neocolonialists, and the instruments of a defunct materialist worldview. The terms of opprobrium were endless. In the case of my department, the career trajectory of these ideologues toward tenure, promotion, and preferential treatment was zealous self-righteous moral one-upmanship, tenacious denigration of opposing perspectives, and politicking with administers and board members rather than offering coherent arguments or sound scholarship.

In the halls of American academia, postmodern cults acquired scary authoritarianism similar to religion. It was complete with self-styled saviors, infatuated acolytes, sacred tomes, dress codes, secret mantras, taboo words, moral injunctions, and the intense certitude common to all true-believers. The anthropologist Robin Fox (1997: 339) made the following observation:

> What was a shift in emphasis in the social sciences has become a revolutionary, relativistic, antiscientific political ideology, with a frightening tendency, in the United States, at least, to harness the worst forces of puritanical fanaticism, forces that seem so eager to burst out and have their day, in a new wave of campus totalitarianism that threatens with academic gulags and thought reform those who do not accept the moral absolute of the cultural relativists (Logic has been the most obvious loser in the whole sorry history).

Retrospectively, Christopher Norris (2002: 178) pointed out the irony in all of this:

> It is a pity that the old, still simmering dispute between traditionalists and theorists in departments of literature so quickly gave way to the kinds of intra-theoretical skirmishing that have flared up at regular intervals over the past two decades. Thus the celebrants of difference, heterogeneity, and openness to "the other" as the high-point of postmodern ethical doctrine seem oddly disinclined to tolerate any criticism of their views or any suggestion . . . that such thinking might be philosophically and ethically questionable.

That the postmodernists acquired a cult-like or religious orientation is not surprising. Their enterprise was always an ideology disguised as scholarship. By rejecting rational argumentation and the "leveling evidence from science," to borrow Otto's phrase, their philosophy did not provide a method for establishing knowledge apart from depending on the authority of its leading figures (Otto 2016: 199–120, 2011: 137). Thus, as Otto (2011: 133) points out, postmodern thinking led to a dependence on authority, the very thing its proponents wanted to avoid. The same thing happened to postmodernism's spiritual counterpart or dubious shadow outside college campuses, namely the New Age movement, and an array of other mystical views all with their own authorities in the form of gurus, wizards, sages, vatics, and, of course, flying shamans.

There were other problems as well. While Euro-American academicians were advancing radicalism as textual analysis, the inherent problems of exorcising truth from the equation and spurning the "leveling evidence from science" did not escape critics. As the noted British political scientist Alan Ryan (1992: 21) observed:

> It is. . . pretty suicidal for embattled minorities to embrace Michel Foucault, let alone Jacques Derrida. The minority view was always that power could be undermined by truth: that it was unjustly distributed, that its holders wanted this overlooked and purchased all sorts of intellectual disguises for the purpose, that it would be an uphill struggle getting the truth in front of the public, but that that was what had to be done. Once you read Foucault as saying that truth is simply an effect of power, you've had it. Those with power have "truth" on their side, and the old radical hope that we can undermine power with truth is incoherent. But American departments of literature, history, and sociology contain large numbers of self-described leftists who have confused radical doubts about objectivity with political radicalism, and are in a mess.

These issues notwithstanding, the American radicals vigorously unleashed their ideas on campuses, through the media, and upon cultural life. Their intense skepticism toward objective knowledge and science, their hyper-relativism, and systematic assault on truth would pave the way further on to the development of post-truth to come, as discussed below.

The paragons of this movement, Foucault, Derrida, Lyotard, Baudrillard, Latour, may have had their differences, but they all shared a disdain for the rationalist tradition of the Enlightenment and a disregard for empirical data and logic or rationality. These became the primary targets for demystification or delegitimization (McIntyre 2018: 126–129). Steven Pinker (2018: 406) with justification describes postmodern philosophy as "defiant obscurantism, self-refuting relativism, and suffocating political correctness" and its proponents as:

> moros cultural pessimists who declared that modernity is odious, all statements are paradoxical, works of art are tools of oppression, liberal democracy is the same as fascism, and Western civilization is circling the drain.

There is nothing new or innovative about this purported critical insight regarding the nature of culture and society on offer by the postmodernists. This premise was central to and was coopted from Nietzsche, which Beiner

(2018: 23) encapsulates as: "Western civilization is going down the toilet because of too much emphasis on truth and rationality and too much emphasis on equal human dignity."

Beyond the definition provided earlier, it is challenging to characterize the intellectual enterprise adopted by the America Left more precisely by reading the original major texts by the iconic French literati. Also, postmodernism has different meanings in art, architecture, philosophy, and social thought, which does not help matters (Bereiter 1994: 4). Hence, as the philosopher Michael Lynch (2005: 35–36) points out, it is impossible to define postmodernism, the popularity of which was primarily due to its obscurity. Perhaps the most explicit statement of sorts was made by Lyotard in his book *The Postmodern Condition: A Report on Knowledge* (1979). He said: "I define postmodern as incredulity toward metanarratives" (Lyotard 1984: xxiv). This was the holy book of the movement that the historian Michael Gordin (2012: 205) refers to it as the "ur-text of academic postmodernism."

Such imprecision is why it is often challenging to pin down what exactly someone like Foucault, Lyotard, or Latour actually meant (cf., Benson and Stangroom 2006: 56–57; Lynch 2005: 36, 38). As the philosopher James Franklin (2009: 42) points out:

> There are obvious difficulties with presenting the arguments in the original works of Derrida, or Lacan, or Baudrillard. They do not write in any natural language, they do not put the premises before the conclusion, the conclusion is distributed over the text rather than appearing in any one sentence, positions are assumed to have been established outside the texts one is actually reading, in previous texts, or perhaps future ones, and so on.

The impenetrable prose, obtuse rhetoric, and "gnomic murkiness" through which the French savants dispensed their wisdom gave their ideas an undeserved air of erudition (Anderson 2017: 307). The anthropologist Robert Carneiro (1995: 14) was puzzled by this:

> If literature is their forte and the discovery of meaning their aim, why do post-modernist couch their discourse in language so elusive and obscure? I have a private theory about this . . . that post-modernists . . . don't *want* to be understood. In the guise of bringing enlightenment, they enjoy sowing the seeds of confusion. Deep down in their hearts, they relish being arcane and unfathomable. Why? Because they hold to the secret premise that *to appear abstruse is to be thought profound.*

Why did those reading the works of the French sages take them seriously and failed to recognize the absurdity of what was on offer? The philosopher Peter Slezak (1994b: 335) suggests the following:

Presumably, their incomprehension was attributed to the impenetrable profundity of the work and their own limitations. Still, the willingness to overlook what surely could not have been understood is a remarkable insight into the sociology of the sociology of science.

The cognitive scientist Dan Sperber (2010) refers to this phenomenon as "the guru effect." As he puts it:

> Obscurity of expression is considered a flaw. Not so, however, in the speech or writing of intellectual gurus. All too often, what readers do is judge profound what they have failed to grasp. Obscurity inspires awe, a fact I have been only too aware of, living as I have been in the Paris of Sartre, Lacan, Derrida and other famously hard to interpret *maîtres à penser* [masters for thinking].

Three decades ago, the philosopher of science Larry Laudan (1990: ix) noted the astonishment of his colleagues over why epistemic relativism had caught on and persisted. He had no answers. Along the same lines, Paul Boghossian (1996: 14–15) asked:

> Given what the basic tenets of postmodernism are, how did they ever come to be identified with a progressive political outlook? And given how transparently refutable they are, how did they ever come to gain such widespread acceptance?

One could speculate that the reply to such questions was not that the postmodern literati had good arguments, they did not, but because of particular human cognitive biases. These include the proclivity for soaking up specific types of fantasies, and the tendency to trust what authority figures say that rendered the recipients of such sublime truths susceptible to certain cognitive irrationalities. Among these is the confirmation bias, the phenomenon of group-think, the backfire effect, and the Dunning-Kruger Effect (see chapter 6). There was also a heavy dose of intellectual dishonesty to be discussed later.

Chapter 3

Science Studies and the Anthropology of Science

How Postmodernists Sought to Demystify Truth

Postmodern cultural critics went on to establish an array of disciplines or perhaps more accurately pseudo-disciplines almost as diverse as Protestant denominations that cropped up in Europe following the Reformation (Andersen 2017: 308). A specific area of inquiry called "science studies" was devoted solely to demystifying science and rationality. There was already a sociological study of science established by the Columbia University sociologist Thomas K. Merton (1979). However, the earlier effort was aimed at offering sociological explanations for the origins and institutional organization of science and not its methods or content (Gorham 2017: 117). By contrast, the field of science studies was entirely about the content of science, or the generation of scientific knowledge (Boghossian 2006: 113).

For the academic critics, debunking the authority of science, objective knowledge, and truth was the road to social emancipation. This marked the start of the so-called "Science Wars," which refers to the concerted effort by American academics to delegitimize science as the ideological tool of the powerful devised to exploit and oppress minorities, women, and the impoverished and the weak (McIntyre 2015: 104). The two opposing factions in this conflict were scientists on one side and the postmodern relativists on the other.

At issue was whether scientific theories deliver an objective understanding of reality, that is, tangible knowledge about the structure of reality, or whether it produces agenda-driven and self-serving ideological constructs no different from astrology, magic, or pseudoscience. The evolutionary biologist Stephen J. Gould (2000: 253) described this squabble as follows:

At the close of this millennium, the favored dichotomy features a supposed battle called "the science wars." The two sides in this hypothetical struggle have been dubbed "realists" (including nearly all working scientists), who uphold the objectivity and progressive nature of scientific knowledge, and "relativists" (nearly all housed in faculties of the humanities and social sciences within our universities), who recognize the culturally embedded status of all claims for universal factuality and who regard science as just one system of belief among many alternatives, all worthy of equal weight because the very concept of "scientific truth" can only represent a social construction invented by scientists (whether consciously or not) as a device to justify their hegemony over the study of nature.

What is remarkable is that this courageous enterprise to address the content of scientific theories was not undertaken by scientists or anyone trained in scientific methodology, mathematics, logic, and so forth. No, it was taken up by a coterie of anthropologists, sociologists, political scientists, historians, and those working in departments of literary criticism, English, gender studies, education, and other humanities, and hence by individuals who did not understand what they were studying and were, therefore, among the least suited to undertake such an assignment (cf., Windschuttle 1998: 1).

Consider Bruno Latour, a self-styled "anthropologist of science" and the postmodern luminary who inaugurated "science studies" (for an overview, see Sokal and Bricmont 1998: 124–133). Latour devoted his whole career to disclose how science is really done, as opposed to how scientists say it is done. He and those who emulated his work believed that they could reveal a hitherto unknown mystery that had escaped all other philosophers and intellects. The mystery was that knowledge and facts are a social construction, and that they found the answer in a domain of inquiry where no one had hitherto suspected, namely science and the process of how scientific knowledge is generated (Boghossian 2006: 18). For these valiant seekers, science thus became a subset of the humanities.

In the book *Laboratory Life: The Social Construction of Scientific Facts* (1979), written in collaboration with the sociologist Steve Woolgar, Latour proclaimed that his objective was to "penetrate the mystique" of science (Latour and Woolgar 1979: 18). What were Latour's qualifications to glean such insights and penetrate the heart of the mystery of the scientific process? None. Latour and his coauthor state in the second edition of *Laboratory Life* (1986): "Professor Latour's knowledge of science was non-existent; his mastery of English was very poor; and he was completely unaware of the existence of the social studies of science" (Latour and Woolgar 1986: 273). As the philosopher Peter Slezak (1994b: 336) pointed out, these science studies anthropologists did not see such deficiencies as handicaps, but rather indispensable assets for gaining unique insights.

Here is their explanation: "[Latour] was thus in the classic position of the ethnographer sent to a completely foreign environment" (Latour and Woolgar 1986: 273). This only illustrates that these writers knew as little about science as they did about ethnographic fieldwork, which requires a command of the local language, learning anthropological field techniques, and considerable research regarding the society in question prior to entering the field. If *Laboratory Life* planted anthropologists in the scientific laboratory to make informative observations, as one sympathetic commentator says (Zimring 2019: 290–292), these were highly incompetent and embarrassingly methodologically inept anthropologists. It is astonishing that such ideologues were actually taken seriously by so many academics and public intellectuals.

So, what deep insights did these luminaries obtain? First, they claimed that scientific facts are not discovered, they are "constructed" or made up. Second, the scientific enterprise is merely a process for the "construction of fictions" (Latour and Woolgar 1979: 17, 28, 284). In this view, scientific findings arise from non-epistemic factors, such as self-interest and ideology that impinge upon the scientists, and not from empirical evidence or objective facts (Boghossian 2006: 8). This became one of the core concepts of social constructivism, which is occasionally used as a descriptor for the movement under discussion. Here is how Latour (1983: 141,160) described the earth-shattering insights offered by the new discipline of science studies:

> Now that field studies of laboratory practice are starting to pour in, we are beginning to have a better picture of what scientists do inside the walls of these strange places called "laboratories." . . . The result, to summarize it in one sentence, was that nothing extraordinary and nothing "scientific" was happening inside the sacred walls of these temples. . . . Nothing special, nothing extraordinary, in fact, nothing of any cognitive quality was occurring there.

In another book *Science in Action: How to Follow Scientists and Engineers Through Society* (1985), Latour unveiled yet another mystery, namely that scientific truths are established as a result of "dialogic" agreement among members of the scientific community and have no bearing upon or relationship to any objective evidence (Latour1985: 99, 186, 258). He perceived science as nothing but a language game and a game of power, anchored solely upon appeal to received authority. In his book *Pandora's Hope: Essays on the Reality of Science Studies* (1999), Latour brazenly challenged the possibility that the scientist can maintain a critical distance from the object of study or the validity of the subject-object dichotomy (Latour 1999: 149).

Slezak (1994b: 330) made the following pertinent observation regarding such acuity:

> Sociologists of science, belatedly discovering that scientific knowledge is less than absolutely certain, have concluded that all knowledge must be entirely delusory. Feeling a little twinge in their epistemology, they have found solace in absolute skepticism; noticing that the inference from evidence to theory is not apodictically certain, they have concluded that science is a fiction.

Contra assertions by admirers that Latour revealed "all of the problems with human observations [with] which science struggles" (Zimring 2019: 290), philosopher of science have known this since at least the time of Francis Bacon (1902 [1620]: 23–24; for a discussion, see Sidky 2020: 147–160). Here is what the philosopher Reuben Abel (1976: 39) stated long before Latour:

> The influence of belief, or hypothesis, on perception is so striking that one might almost say, not that seeing is believing, but that believing is seeing. There is abundant experimental evidence that what people report about their own after images depends on what they are told to expect.

It is important to clarify a few issues at this stage. Yes, it is without question that science is conducted by humans with endless arrays of prejudices, biases, and perversions. After all, science is a human enterprise—it is not done by or for the benefit of insects, birds, polar bears, or chimpanzees. It serves human purposes, and its findings are rendered in human terms. In other words, science provides approximate understands in *human terms* of "something" (call it "reality, "the empirical world," of whatever) that seems to exist apart from out perceptual and cognitive apparatus rather than being generated by it (Lett 1987, 1997). There is nothing novel or earth-shattering about these observations, although Latour, his colleagues, and like-minded irrationalist philosophers, such as Thomas Kuhn and Paul Feyerabend (see chapter 5) made careers out of such bogus pseudo-profound acumens. The real question is not that human biases or ideology are factors in the process of scientific research—that is well known—but whether the methodology of science is capable of dampening such biases to a degree as to render approximate reliable understandings of that "something," call it objective reality, the empirical world, or whatever. The scientific method was developed because science is a human enterprise and humans are biased and prejudiced. By ignoring the latter question, the postmodern savants and the irrationalist philosophers, *misrepresented* science as solely the product of human biases and prejudices without the possibility of getting anything right.

To put it in other words, beginning with a reasonable assertion that cultural and linguistic factors intrude upon knowledge, which is something many philosophers have known for a very long time (Lynch 2015: 36), Latour transformed it into a universal statement that no knowledge of the empirical world is possible. Everything, including facts, is culturally or socially assembled. Maintaining that all knowledge is relative to particular cultural and historical contexts, social background, class, gender, and the like, Latour inferred that the idea that science can comprehend reality was a world-wide deception.

Many philosophers would agree that particular descriptions are accepted in relation to practical interests (i.e., some facts are socially constructed) rather than because of any correspondence they may have in and of themselves with an external objective reality. In other words, beliefs and social interests impinge upon certain types of knowledge. But this is not what Latour and other constructivists were asserting. Their claim was that there are no such things as facts or an objective reality that exist in and of themselves independent of our descriptions (Boghossian 2006: 31). These ideologues devoted considerable time and effort to establish the mind-dependent nature of facts or the dependence of thought and reality, that is, that "thought and reality are one and the same" (Williams 2001: 138). Hence, their axiomatic rejection of the separation of the observer and observed.

Unsurprisingly, such views found many receptive audiences in the prevailing dreary climate of irrationalism, anti-intellectualism, pseudoscience, and supernaturalism already on the rise in the United States at the time, of which they were a manifestation. The overall accomplishment of this intellectual enterprise was that it delivered ideological weapons for others to deploy, which is a factor that cannot be overemphasized. The recipients of these anti-science armaments include present day right-wing populists, Christian fundamentalists, industry front groups, New Age mystics, teachers, and journalists who now had the intellectual tools to use in their efforts to confuse the public about the role and function of science (Cailin and Weatherall 2019: 32; Otto 2016: 7, 172).

Omitted from the equation of the science critics was the possibility of "foundational truths," or mind independent objects, or the notion that somethings are valid irrespective of our thoughts and feelings about them (Benson and Stangroom 2006: 43; Lynch 2005: 43; McIntyre 2018: 11). There was, of course, a considerable degree of intellectual dishonesty behind such denials. Why? If true, then we would have to believe that the earth did not start revolving around the sun until Nicolaus Copernicus (1473–1543) decided that it did and convinced others to accept his views. Also, we would have to believe that there was no gravity until Isaac Newton (1642–1727) stated the law of universal gravitation and convinced others of it. And we must consider that the principles of aerodynamics work and heavier than air machines fly because of an agreement by a group of scientists and engineers. I will return to the idea of the social or cultural construction of reality later on.

These examples might seem absurd, but postmodern philosophers made even more ludicrous claims. Consider Latour's reply to the assertion that the Pharaoh Ramses II may have died of tuberculosis; a hypothesis developed after an examination of his mummified corpse by French scientists. Here is what he said:

> The attribution of tuberculosis and Koch's bacillus to Ramses II should strike us as an anachronism of the same caliber as if we had diagnosed his death as having been caused by a Marxist upheaval, or a machine gun, or a Wall Street crash. Is it not an extreme case of "whiggish" history, transplanting into the past the hidden or potential existence of the future? (Latour 1996: 248).

By whiggish, Latour meant that one could not judge the past in light of the present. Ramses could not have died in the manner suggested, he reasoned, because the bacillus that causes the disease was unknown in ancient Egypt. Latour added that before 1882, when Robert Koch discovered the bacterium, the pathogen did not exist.

Or take another postmodern luminary, Jean Baudrillard, whose textualism led him to view history itself, in this case the Gulf War (August 1990–February 1991), as a "simulacrum," imitation, or fictive construct (on Baudrillard, see Sokal and Bricmont 1998: 147–153). The relationship of the Gulf War to actual war, he asserted, was similar to the relationship between computer pornography and actual sex (Baudrillard 1995: 62). These ideas were expounded in three articles published in the newspaper *Libération* between January and March of 1991 and republished in the book *The Gulf War Did Not Take Place* (1995).

Baudrillard proclaimed that the Gulf War did not happen because the ideas of truth, falsehood, and reality are obsolete Enlightenment dogmas associated with positivist philosophies (Norris 1992; Slezak 1994a: 290). Nothing is real, he added, outside texts, discourses, and free-floating language games (Norris 1992: 13–19). It is all a "simulacrum," simulated, or fake. This is an early iteration of the idea of "fake news" that characterizes present-day politics in the United States. One wonders if the families of the tens of thousands of Iraqi conscripts and civilians killed in the desert trenches of Kuwait, in Baghdad, or on "the Highway of Death" during that pointless war ever thought that it was all a "simulacrum."

Such absurd statements make one wonder if these savants sincerely believe what they were saying? A more puzzling question is: Why did so many people take someone like Baudrillard seriously? Many of my anthropology colleagues did so, profusely citing Baudrillard's sublime axioms in their lectures and there were plenty of admirers in other disciplines (e.g., Merrin 1994; Pfohl 1997; Strehle 2014). As Norris (1992: 17) says, his arguments were indeed taken seriously "to the point where Baudrillard [could] deliver his ludicrous theses on the Gulf War without fear of subsequent exposure as a charlatan or of finding those theses resoundingly disconfirmed by the course of real-world events." However, others not seduced by or inducted into the inner mysteries of postmodern wisdom saw the absurdity of Baudrillard thesis. The Middle East expert Daniel Pipes (1996) aptly described *The Gulf War Did Not Take Place* as "a book of profound error and transcendent stupidity, the most inane ever reviewed in these pages."

Perhaps David Stove was justified in his unrelenting and contemptuous characterization of such cavalier and intellectually irresponsible ideologues and their nonsensical declarations. He described postmodern doctrines as "philosophical folly," and an example of "a stupid and discreditable business" whose originators are "beneath philosophical notice and unlikely to benefit from it." He also alluded to their intellectual dishonesty, adding that these ideas are exemplars of the "fatal affliction and corruption of thought" in which people utter bizarre things that they know to be false (Stove 1991: 68). "Questions like these, beyond doubt," he added, "can only be asked either insincerely, or by someone seriously disordered in mind" (Stove 1991: 68).

Such intellectual dishonesty, bizarre utterances, and callous contempt for the importance of intellectual life are evident, as Slezak (1994b: 333) pointed out, in the "nihilistic indifference" these savants adopted regarding "the ultimate cogency of their own thesis." Consider what Latour and Woolgar said about their book:

[It] recognizes itself as the construction of fictions about fiction constructions, and that all texts are stories. This applies as much to the facts of our scientists as to the fictions "through which" we display their work (Latour and Woolgar 1986: 284).

They go on to admit that their own efforts do not possess a determinate meaning because "it is the reader who writes the text" (Latour and Woolgar 1986: 273). Reveling in the mischievous obscurity and perverse incomprehensibility of their text, Latour and Woolgar (1986: 273) contemptuously referred to the continued foolish attempts of their readers who "years after the initial publication" of their book continue to argue over "what was actually intended by its authors."

There was an interplay here between a great deal of vanity, pomposity, audacity, and intellectual dishonesty on the part of these literati who were basking in their superstardom and relishing the credulity and incapability of their audiences to penetrate their deliberately obtuse texts. Years ago, the noted sociologist Stanislav Andreski published a book with the clever title *Social Sciences as Sorcery* (1972) in which he criticized the reigning paradigms of postwar American sociology that had also developed an obscure and intimidating jargon with no connection to reality. What is surprising is that Andreski's observations fit the epistemic skeptics during the late 1980s and early 1990s as they did the theorists of his day. Andreski (1972: 9) asked, for example, whether academic superstars who tout fashionable nonsense really believe what they espouse:

> A renowned author would have to have a most extraordinary character . . . to be able to write prolifically in full knowledge that his works are worthless and that he is a charlatan whose fame is entirely undeserved and based solely on the stupidity and gullibility of his, admirers. Even if he had some doubts about the correctness of his approach at some stage of his career, success and adulation would soon persuade him of his own genius and the epoch-making values of his concoctions. When, in consequence of acquiring a controlling position in the distribution of funds, appointments, and promotions, he becomes surrounded by sycophants courting his favors, he is unlikely to see through their motivation; and, like wealthy and powerful people in other walks of life, will tend to take flattery at its face value, accepting it as a sincere appreciation (and therefore confirmation).

Another factor probably at work was the socio-psychological phenomenon of group-think I have already mentioned. This becomes operational when enthusiastic people with similar beliefs and attitudes interact. In such settings, individuals may express an even stronger version of the ideas that brought them together to obtain in-group approval, popularity, and dominance (French and Stone 2014: 119–120). In such circumstances in classrooms, faculty lounges, and conference halls, contrary views are not sought out and, if expressed, are ignored or ostracized. The cognitive scientist Dan Sperber (2010: 591) describes this, without using the term "group-think." As he says:

> Participating in such a collective process involves not just an intellectual but also—and more surely—a social benefit, that of belonging, of getting recognition as a person in the know, capable of appreciating the importance of a difficult great thinker. Not participating, on the other hand, may involve the cost of being marginalised and of appearing intellectually stale and flat. . . . Here emerges a collective dynamic typical of intellectual schools and sects, where the obscurity of respected masters is not just a sign of the depth of their thinking, but a proof of their genius . . . sharing their interpretations and impressions with other admirers, readers find in the admiration, in the trust that other have for the master, reasons to consider their own interpretations as failing to do justice to the genius

of the interpreted text. In turn these readers become disciples and proselytes. ... competition [now develops] among disciples for an interpretation that best displays the genius of the master, an interpretation that, for this purpose, may be just as obscure as the thought it is meant to interpret. Thus a thinker is made into a guru and her best disciples in gurus-apprentices (Sperber 2010: 592).

Sadly, while the postmodern literati may have found their intellectual deceit and the ease with which they hoodwinked others about the profundity of their narrative exhilarating, what they accomplished, as Slezak (1994a: 289) pointed out, was "to corrupt the standards of critical thought and honest inquiry." The fruits of these literati's fools' errand are all around us today in Trump's Fantasyland post-truth America, where critical thought and scrupulous inquiry have become terms of opprobrium.

Similarly, the philosopher of science Larry Laudan (1990: x) called attention to what many others should have recognized at that time, namely the inappropriate and deceptive use of conclusions from the philosophy of science in support of various "social cum political causes." In his words:

> Feminists, religious apologists (including "creation scientists"), counterculturalists, neoconservatives, and a host of other curious fellow-travelers have claimed to find grist for their mills in, for instance, the avowed incommensurability and underdetermination of scientific theories. The displacement of the idea that facts and evidence matter with the idea that everything boils down to subjective interest and perspective is—second only to American political campaigns—the most prominent and pernicious manifestation of anti-intellectualism in our time (Laudan 1990: x).

Laudan perceptively recognized what was happening three decades ago, circumstances that many of those concerned about post-truth, anti-intellectualism and a culture of falsehoods today are just now apprehending.

Remarkably, armed with the sorts of insights described, the agenda the academic radicals set for themselves was to promote epistemological egalitarianism open to diverse viewpoints and to create a more tolerant, multicultural society free of all the evils of modernity. In retrospect, some writers are partially sympathetic to the postmodernist cause because it brought to attention the need to consider multiple voices in an increasingly pluralistic society (D'Ancona 2017: 91). However, it is difficult to be sympathetic. These ideologues share responsibility for the present cultural climate that has transfigured Idiot America into a post-truth nation characterized by emboldened religious extremism, right-wing populism, xenophobia, scapegoating of ethnic minorities, and where outright racism, bigotry, incivility, and religious superstitions have replaced political correctness, cultural sensitivity, and multiculturalism (Ott 2017; Sidky 2018: 42).

Chapter 4

The Hermeneutics of Quantum Gravity, Incomprehensibility, and the Sokal Hoax

One critic who braved grappling with the intimidating impenetrable prose and pseudo-profundity that characterized postmodern philosophical discourse realized that the savants were incapable of differentiating between what they were writing and deliberate nonsense (Franklin 2009: 44; Sokal and Bricmont 1998: 3). This person was the New York University physicist Alan Sokal who brought the problem to light by submitting a parody article full of absurdities and blatant *non-sequiturs* to *Social Text*, then one of the prestigious postmodern journals. The paper, with the delightful but preposterous title "Transgressing the Boundaries: Towards a Transformative Hermeneutics of Quantum Gravity," was accepted and published in a special issue called "Science Wars," ironically devoted to refuting the critics of postmodernism. Here is an excerpt from Sokal's essay:

> There are many natural scientists, and especially physicists, who continue to reject the notion that the disciplines concerned with social and cultural criticism can have anything to contribute, except perhaps peripherally, to their research. Still less are they receptive to the idea that the very foundations of their worldview must be revised or rebuilt in the light of such criticism. Rather, they cling to the dogma imposed by the long post-Enlightenment hegemony over the Western intellectual outlook, which can be summarized briefly as follows: that there exists an external world, whose properties are independent of any individual human being and indeed of humanity as a whole; that these properties are encoded in "eternal" physical laws; and that human beings can obtain reliable, albeit imperfect and tentative, knowledge of these laws by hewing to the "objective" procedures and epistemological strictures prescribed by the (so-called) scientific method. . . . But deep conceptual shifts within twentieth-century science

have undermined this Cartesian-Newtonian metaphysics; revisionist studies in the history and philosophy of science have cast further doubt on its credibility; and, most recently, feminist and poststructuralist critiques have demystified the substantive content of mainstream Western scientific practice, revealing the ideology of domination concealed behind the façade of "objectivity." It has thus become increasingly apparent that physical "reality," no less than social "reality," is at bottom a social and linguistic construct; that scientific "knowledge," far from being objective, reflects and encodes the dominant ideologies and power relations of the culture that produced it; that the truth claims of science are inherently theory-laden and self-referential; and consequently, that the discourse of the scientific community, for all its undeniable value, cannot assert a privileged epistemological status with respect to counter-hegemonic narratives emanating from dissident or marginalized communities.

Several commentators have pointed out that anyone with even a high school level science background would have realized that this was a prank because it was so nonsensical as to be self-evidently untrue (Franklin 2009: 45; Weinberg 1996; Windschuttle 1998). The title of the article alone should have been a dead giveaway.

Sokal (1996b) revealed his hoax in an article in the journal *Lingua Franca*. Here is how he explained his motivations for undertaking this task:

> For some years I've been troubled by an apparent decline in the standards of rigor in certain precincts of the academic humanities. But I'm a mere physicist: if I find myself unable to make heads or tails of *jouissance* and *différance* [jargon term associated respectively with Jacques Lacan and Jacques Derrida], perhaps that just reflects my own inadequacy.... So, to test the prevailing intellectual standards, I decided to try a modest (though admittedly uncontrolled) experiment: Would a leading North American journal of cultural studies . . . publish an article liberally salted with nonsense if (a) it sounded good and (b) it flattered the editor's ideological preconceptions? (Sokal 1996b).

The revelation caused an uproar, received substantial press coverage, and more than twenty scholarly public forums were organized to discuss its fallout, including meetings at Princeton, Duke, The University of Michigan, and New York University (Boghossian 1996: 14). There are several books dealing with the subject, including *The Sokal Hoax: The Sham that Shook the Academy* (2000) compiled by the editors of *Lingua Franca*, Alan Sokal and Jean Bricmont's *Fashionable Nonsense: Postmodern Intellectuals' Abuse of Science* (1998), and Sokal's *Beyond the Hoax: Science, Philosophy and Culture* (2008), among others. Here, I shall provide only a few of the highlights of the scandal.

Overall, the parody was a clear demonstration of the abstruse metaphysics, incautious relativism, and scientific illiteracy of postmodern writers involved in the study of science (Gorham 2017: 123). The texts produced by the savants are incomprehensible, as Sokal and Bricmont (1998: 6) later observed, "for the excellent reason that they mean precisely nothing." For the philosopher Paul Boghossian (1996: 15):

> Alan Sokal's hoax has served as a flashpoint for what has been a gathering storm of protest against the collapse in standards of scholarship and intellectual responsibility that vast sectors of the humanities and social sciences are currently afflicted with.

Sokal's reaction to what his hoax revealed was a decisive admonition of the entire postmodern philosophical project:

> My concern over the spread of subjectivist thinking is both intellectual and political. Intellectually, the problem with such doctrines is that they are false (when not simply meaningless). There *is* a real world; its properties are *not* merely social constructions; facts and evidence *do* matter. What sane person would contend otherwise? And yet, much contemporary academic theorizing consists precisely of attempts to blur these obvious truths—the utter absurdity of it all being concealed through obscure and pretentious language.
>
> *Social Text*'s acceptance of my article exemplifies the intellectual arrogance of Theory—meaning postmodernist *literary* theory—carried to its logical extreme. No wonder they didn't bother to consult a physicist. If all is discourse and "text," then knowledge of the real world is superfluous; even physics becomes just another branch of Cultural Studies. If, moreover, all is rhetoric and "language games," then internal logical consistency is superfluous too: a patina of theoretical sophistication serves equally well. Incomprehensibility becomes a virtue; allusions, metaphors and puns substitute for evidence and logic. My own article is, if anything, an extremely *modest* example of this well-established genre (Sokal 1996b).

Many embarrassed literati simply went into a state of denial and refused to address the issues brought to the fore by Sokal (Franklin 2009: 49). Others reacted with anger, hostility, and by using the only weapons they had: special pleading, specious rationalizations, and *ad hominin* attacks. Two true-believers asserted that Sokal lacked the intelligence or an understanding of the profundity of the sources he quoted and was "himself the victim of an obsolete positivist ideology of science" (Best and Kellner 1997: 247). In an article in the French newspaper *Le Monde,* Latour glibly attributed the scandal to the work of "a very small number of theoretical physicists, deprived of their fat Cold War budgets, [who] are searching for a new threat" and are targeting postmodern intellectuals (in Sokal 1997). The coeditors of *Social Text*, Bruce Robbins and Andrew Ross (2000: 54) even deceptively suggested that "Sokal's parody was nothing of the sort, and that his admission represented a change of heart, or a folding of his intellectual resolve." It seems that intellectual dishonesty was not restricted to just a few advocates of postmodernism at the apex of the intellectual movement, but was rampant across the entire cohort of converts and believers.

The sardonic reaction of those outside the academia is captured in the following commentary in the June 10 issue of *The Nation* (1996):

> You've got to hand it to Alan Sokal, the New York University physicist who tricked *Social Text*, the cultural studies journal, into publishing in its special "Science Wars" issue—as a straight academic article—his over-the-top parody of postmodern science critique. "Transgressing the Boundaries: Toward a Transformative Hermeneutics of Quantum Gravity" is a hilarious compilation of pomo gibberish, studded with worshipful quotations from all the trendy thinkers—Derrida, Lacan, Lyotard, Irigaray, *Social Text* board member Stanley Aronowitz (cited thirteen times) and issue editor Andrew Ross (four times). Its thesis, barely discernible through the smoke and fog of jargon, is that the theory of quantum gravity has important affinities with assorted New Age and postmodern ideas; it concludes with a call for "emancipatory mathematics." The whole production was rigged so that anyone who knew physics would realize how preposterous it was. I tried it out on the Last Marxist and had to leave the room, he was laughing so hard. To judge by the gleeful e-mail that's been zipping around academia since Sokal revealed his prank in the current issue of Lingua Franca, the L.M. is far from alone (Pollitt 2007: 113, 9).

On a more somber note, the theoretical physicist and Nobel laureate Steven Weinberg (1996) observed that Sokal did not invent the profusion of nonsensical aphorisms quoted in the paper, he simply found such passages in the writings of the postmodern savants themselves (see Holquist et al. 1996 for responses to Weinberg's analysis from perturbed academics in various humanities departments, such as comparative literature, critical theory, and so forth). Take the following passage by Jacques Derrida (1970: 267), the principal expositor of deconstructionism:

> The Einsteinian constant is not a constant, is not a center. It is the very concept of variability—it is, finally, the concept of the game. In other words, it is not the concept of some*thing*—of a center starting from which an observer could master the field—but the very concept of the game.

Perhaps someone trained in the humanities might think there is something profound or meaningful here, but, as Weinberg correctly says, it is nonsensical for anyone who understands physics.

Weinberg goes on to point out the equally ludicrous assertions by the other major postmodern sages who Sokal cleverly cited with "mock approval." Consider Bruno Latour's bogus statement about special relativity:

> How can one decide whether an observation made in a train about the behavior of a falling stone can be made to coincide with the observation of the same falling stone from the embankment? If there are only *one*, or even *two*, frames of reference, no solution can be found.... Einstein's solution is to consider *three* actors: one in the train, one on the embankment and a third one, the author [enunciator] or one of its representatives, who tries to superimpose the coded observations sent back by the two others.... [W]ithout the enunciator's position (hidden in Einstein's account), and without the notion of centres of calculation, Einstein's own technical argument is understandable.

This is a deceptive assertion, as Weinberg points out, because there is no difficulty in comparing the results of two, three, or any number of observers in relativity theory. He concludes that "such errors suggest a problem not just in the editing practices of *Social Text*, but in the standards of a larger intellectual community."

Finally and significantly, as if divining the future, Weinberg warned of the broader dangers of the irresponsible and deceptive anti-science discourse on offer:

> If we think that scientific laws are flexible enough to be affected by the social setting of their discovery, then some may be tempted to press scientists to discover laws that are more proletarian or feminine or American or religious or Aryan or whatever else it is they want. This is a dangerous path, and more is at stake in the controversy over it than just the health of science. As I mentioned earlier, our civilization has been powerfully affected by the discovery that nature is strictly governed by impersonal laws. ... We will need to confirm and strengthen the vision of a rationally understandable world if we are to protect ourselves from the irrational tendencies that still beset humanity.

While Sokal convincingly demonstrated the obscurantist nature of postmodern thought, he did not emphasize the fact that the mind numbing and inscrutable soliloquies were a central and indispensable aspect of what was being dispensed. The attack on science depended entirely upon rhetorical force, equivocation, appeal to emotion, and strawman arguments. Thus, as the philosophers, Ophelia Benson and Jeremy Stangroom (2006: 48) observe: "The counter-intuitiveness, the perversity, nonsensicality of many of the claims were in fact the point." Once evidence and reasoned debate are rejected, all that remained with which the savants could wow their adulating fans was proselytizing, advocacy, emotive aphorisms, opinions, and impenetrable rhetoric. The postmodern savants were compelling propagandists and their audiences were generally scientifically illiterate.

In the ensuing epistemological free-for-all these philosophers encouraged, any sort of assertion no matter how nonsensical seemed credible. In the context of this ideological trajectory, feminists went on their own warpath. They asserted that science is and has always been an exclusionary male chauvinist enterprise and should be condemned. One prodigy, Sandra Harding, looked at the works of early scientists and philosophers, such as Isaac Newton, Francis Bacon, and David Hume and described their efforts to understand nature in terms of rape metaphors with the lecherous male scientists forcing a reluctant Mother Nature to submit her secrets (O'Connor and Weatherall 2019: 34). In her words: "Why is it not as illuminating and honest to refer to Newton's laws as 'Newton's rape manual' as it is to call them 'Newton's mechanics'?" (Harding 1987: 113). What an astonishing remark! The seduction of unreason and sermonizing nonsense seems to have been corollaries of each other among many of these academic stars.

Yes, science was a male-dominated enterprise, but so was religion and an array of other activities. And yes, that was mistaken, but not much can be done about that. As philosophers Benson and Stangroom (2006: 54) observe, just as we cannot travel back in time to give Shakespeare's sister a grammar school education and start her on a career as a novelist, we cannot change the history of science. Harding assumed that with women running the show somehow, the epistemology of science would be reconfigured. Not so, Benson and Stangroom say, the topics of investigation would perhaps be different, but not the process of evaluating the evidence. Unless they add that with a large assembly of women running the show, they would be more open to accepting mistakes, faked evidence, and adulation in place of peer review (Benson Stangroom 2006: 54).

It is clear from Harding's comments that, like the other postmodern professors, as I shall discuss, the feminist cultural critics did not understand science. They mistakenly honed in on the scientists themselves as a specific group with a distinct background—in this case, a group comprised of misogynistic, racist, rich white men—rather than focusing on science as a method. All of this illustrates these radicals' skewed understanding not only of science but also of emancipation and egalitarianism. The initiates privy to the inner secrets and brilliant precepts of postmodern philosophy perhaps extolled Harding's comment that Isaac Newton's classic *Principia Mathematica* was a "rape manual" as a daring and awe-inspiring insight (cf., McIntyre 2015: 104). I doubt that non-initiates did.

Yes, gender inequalities and misogyny exist here and elsewhere and should not be tolerated under any circumstances. But is Harding's approach, which casts doubt on the credibility and rationality of its expositor, really the right path to emancipating the sisters? Looking at Harding's overall ill-founded and badly justified claims, Benson and Stangroom (2006: 55) sarcastically ask whether her case itself is "an object lesson in how epistemology is 'improved' by the addition of feminism." They also marvel at the fact that a prestigious university press published her work.

Overall, the new vision was epistemic relativism (for an overview, see Baghramian 2004: 138–162). From such a relativistic point of view, truth refers to consensual reality or agreed-upon ideas. In other words, a belief is true if and only if one's intellectual community agrees that it is true. Thus, if we all agree that climate change is a hoax, then that is the case. Indeed, isn't that what Trump and his supports are doing? What the relativists left out of the picture is that this kind of truth does not mean "true of the world" (cf., Hospers 1988: 117; Williams 2001: 117–137). For example, no matter how many Republican politicians and their voters mutually agree that climate change is not real, or join denialist James Inhofe (R-OK) in group prayer for the Lord to make it so, sea levels will continue to rise. Or consider how Trump, with the concurrence of his Senate Republican cronies, sought to bluff his way out of the reality of the COVID-19 pandemic on U.S. soil that by August 20, 2020 reached 5.54 million cases with over 170,000 deaths (Levitz 2020).

Relativism has a long history in Western thought, the origins of which go back to the Greek philosopher Protagoras (Baghramian and Carter 2019b; Lynch 2005: 31; Nagel 2014: 15). However, the type cynicism about knowledge dispensed by the postmodern literati is closer to that associated with Pyrrho of Elis (fourth century BCE). The leading advocate of Pyhrronian skepticism was Sextus Empiricus (second or third centuries BCE), who argued that we must refrain from making judgments about the truth because there are always numerous equally compelling arguments for and against a belief (Thorsrud 2014: 17–35).

The French luminaries repackaged relativism and made it fashionable once more. In their lectures and public addresses, they stressed in unison that all knowledge is culturally constructed and some even said that reality itself was so configured, articulating a thoroughgoing skepticism about the impossibility of knowing and knowledge. Baudrillard offered this insight in the typical postmodernist grandiloquent pseudo profound fashion:

> The secret of theory is, indeed, that truth doesn't exist. You can't confront truth in any way, only play with some kind of provocative logic. Truth constitutes a space that can no longer be occupied. The whole strategy is not to occupy it but to work around it so that others get caught in it (Lotringer and Baudrillard 1986: 142).

Objective truth was declared a grand hoax and the embodiment of power relations. In its place, these ideologues offered the ideas of "multiple truths," "multiple ways of knowing," or alternative epistemic systems. If there are multiple truths, it followed, then who is to say what is false. All types of "theories" or understandings could now be entertained on a level playing field. Liberation was at hand.

These writers also facilitated another condition relevant to this discussion. It was no longer politically correct to criticize magical thinking, fortunetelling, New Age mysticism, alternative healing, astrology, crystal power, and an array of other archaic credulities that today are prominent features in the post-truth cultural landscape of Idiot America or Fantasyland, United States. Sokal (2008: 263–370) dubbed these the non-academic counterparts of postmodernism. It is essential to point out, however, that pseudoscientific irrationalism and paranormalism did not merely develop autonomously in parallel to the irrationalism inside the academy. No, the postmodern philosophers encouraged and celebrated the public expression of such irrational and nonsensical views, as I shall discuss in later chapters. These were the "voices" of the marginalized, ridiculed, and repressed "other" that had to be heard (cf., Andersen 2017: 311). Hearing their voices would mean setting them free from the shackles of modernity.

Chapter 5

American Intellectual Contributions to Science Delegitimation

Kuhn and Feyerabend

In the United States, a uniquely American contribution to postmodern thought was derived from the work of Thomas Kuhn (1922–1996). Kuhn is considered by some to be among the influential philosophers of science, and he still has many defenders who object to any associations between his ideas and postmodern epistemic skepticism. Nevertheless, his work had a significant influence on the American version of postmodern anti-science discourse, impacting not only the philosophy of science but also a range of other disciplines, such as sociology, anthropology, as well as intellectual culture at large (Okasha 2016: 71).

In his highly acclaimed book, *The Structure of Scientific Revolutions* (1970 [1962]), Kuhn presented ideas that echoed those espoused by the paragons and gurus of postmodern philosophy. He argued, for example, that scientific truths depend upon consensus, dialogue, negotiation, and agreement among groups of scientists rather than "the nature of nature," that is, empirical data (Kuhn 1970: 43). These, he maintained, are the defining conditions of scientific knowledge (Kuhn 1970: 168–169). In other words, such notions as knowledge, discovery, and progress are merely the language used by the partisans of any paradigms (research/methodological frameworks), meaning that all of these are "paradigm relative" (Stove 1991: 10). Moreover, Kuhn implied that knowledge is embedded in social, linguistic, and discursive practices and what exists outside these practices, if we even grant such a possibility, can never be known.

Before Kuhn, many viewed the scientific enterprise as a dispassionate investigation of the natural world (Cailin and Weatherall 2019: 32). However, the influence of belief on theory was well known by philosophers of science for a very long time, as discussed in chapter 3. So Kuhn's ideas were not really new, although admirers make such claims (e.g., Barker and Kitcher

2014: 78–105; Staley 2014: 70). It was the equivocal way Kuhn presented his case that made it appear that sometime thing more was the case, namely, that evidence does not substantiate theories, and furthermore, that there is no distinction between science and pseudoscience (cf., Franklin 2000). The idea that facts do not justify theories is known as underdetermination, which holds that:

> no matter how extensive our acquaintance with the natural world, there will remain an indefinitely many—arguable infinitely many—compatible theories all of which are equally compatible with the available evidence. Indeed, even if we had a God's eye perspective and could ascertain that all of a theory's potential observational consequences were correct, we still could not tell if the theory were true since it would have indefinitely many rivals with the same observational consequences (Laudan 1990: 49).

These tenets became indispensable to the postmodern savants in their science de-legitimation endeavors. As the historian Keith Windschuttle says, Kuhn's book became one of the canonical texts of science studies. Similarly, the philosopher of science Christopher Norris (1997: 82) says that Kuhn's book established the idea that knowledge is relative to some "linguistic" or "cultural framework of belief" that define what counts as knowledge. Indeed, Kuhn's attack on the extant rational models of how scientific knowledge develops and grows inspired numerous social science and humanities professors to take up the task of uncovering the hidden social determinants of scientific knowledge by bringing to bear historical, anthropological, literary, postcolonial, and feminist perspectives (Gorham 2017: 118, 121; Windschuttle 1998: 4).

KUHN'S ATTACK ON THE RATIONALITY OF SCIENCE

In Kuhn's view, an established scientific endeavor, what he called paradigms (models of how research should be done), persist for a time, and guide research. This is a period of "normal science," when the enterprise becomes entrenched, and begins to solve scientific problems. However, in the course of normal science, new facts/phenomena, or anomalies, are encountered that cannot be addressed. Eventually, such glitches can no longer be ignored and this leads to the adoption of an alternative set of assumptions. This is a period of "extraordinary science," or a "scientific revolution," which leads ultimately to the founding of an entirely new paradigm (Kuhn 1970: 68). The examples he used was the shift from the Ptolemaic to the Copernican astronomy and the change from Newtonian to Einsteinian physics.

The new paradigm, according to the argument, is "incommensurable" with the previous one, being constructed upon dissimilar conventions linked to a separate set of sociopolitical factors and there are no neutral-vantage points or a God's eye perspective from where one can assess the claims of different paradigms (cf., Okasha 2016: 81). In other words, the old and the new orientations are incompatible and share no common ground. According to Laudan (1990: 121):

> Incommensurability between rival perspectives refers to the fact that the advocates of those perspectives subscribe to different evaluative standards. Two bodies of discourse—whether theories, worldviews, paradigms or what have you—are incommensurable if the assertions made in one body of discourse are unintelligible to those utilizing the other.

Kuhn contended that conceptual schemes that comprise theories, methods, and other criteria employed to develop theories, or scientific "truths," that is, paradigms, determine the construal of reality as well as research questions and the manner of their investigation (Schick and Vaughn 2014: 307). In Kuhn's (1970: 125) words:

> When paradigms change, the world changes with them. . . . Even more important, during revolutions scientists see new and different things when looking with familiar instruments in places they have looked before. It is rather that the professional community had been suddenly transported to another planet where familiar objects are seen in different light and are joined by unfamiliar ones as well . . . paradigm changes do cause scientists to see the world of their research differently . . . we may want to say that after a revolution, scientists are responding to a different world.

Kuhn appeared to be saying that prior theoretical assumptions impinge upon observations, which is well understood. But he meant something more, namely that the meaning of concepts and facts themselves derive from the paradigm of which they are a part, not some objective reality (Okasha 2016: 82). In this view, the acceptance of a fact that denotes a dinosaur is not because it corresponds with the world/nature, but is entirely due to our contingent needs and practical interests. In other words, there are no facts that correspond to the way the world is "in and of themselves" apart from our denotations (Boghossian 2006: 31). This is known as the theory-ladenness argument. Laudan (1990: 35) provides a concise description:

> All observations are theory-laden . . . there is nothing we can say about the world which does not go well beyond what we are "given" by our senses. Every

act of cognizing involves applying language or concepts. Our language, like our conceptual structures, pigeonholes experience in various ways. The categories in terms of which we carve up the world and make it intelligible to ourselves are not given by the external world but arise from . . . earlier linguistic practices, our technical and practical interests as cognizers, and our built-in neurogenetic equipment.

If correct—if facts are defined solely relative to one's paradigm—then researchers operating under the auspices of different paradigms live in entirely different thought worlds. This is exactly what Kuhn (1970: 149) says: "[The] most fundamental aspect of the incommensurability of competing paradigms . . . [is that] the proponents of competing paradigms practice their trades in different worlds." Here, as Okasha (2016: 78) points out, Kuhn was explicitly espousing "a radical form of anti-realism about science."

From this perspective, a Copernican and Ptolemaic astronomer would be unable to enter into a debate because they would not be able to agree on the astronomical data (Okasha 2016: 82–83). But this is an exaggerated perspective because the astronomers are empirical beings situated in a common empirical reality. They could certainly agree that the earth exists, it has a moon, that the sun rises at certain times regardless of whether they are adhering to a geocentric or heliocentric paradigm. "Such statements," as Okasha (2016: 82–83) points out, "are sufficiently theory-neutral to be acceptable to proponents of both paradigms."

There is another implication to all of this. From Kuhn's (1970: 206) perspective, there can be no growth, accumulation, or progress in scientific knowledge, but merely one paradigm displacing another, with each orientation representing a new start, built upon a new set of conventions linked to a new world view. While a new paradigm is adopted in part because it solves the anomalies that stumped and toppled the earlier framework, for Kuhn it is the irrational sociopolitical and ideological factors that account for the shift, not because the new research scheme is better able to explain the facts (Kuhn 1970: 167–169).

This is an irrationalist view of how scientific knowledge grows because it dispenses with objectivity and empirical facts as sources for beliefs. There is more. Given that sociopolitical factors determine a paradigm's ascendancy over another, there are no compelling reasons or body of facts to convince the recalcitrant old-timers laboring under the former approach of the validity of the new perspective. The core of the new paradigm merely comprises a set of ideological beliefs that prevailed over the core ideology of the previous model for political reasons. The expositors of the defunct approach eventually retire, die-off, and disappear and the new generation of scientists, the victor in the paradigm war, then shifts to a "normal science" phase (Kuhn

1970: 121). This portrays scientific communities as political congregations each seeking to outmaneuver the other, with the winner getting to install their approach and deciding what constitutes knowledge and truth (Franklin 2000).

If correct, this would mean that our knowledge of the world/universe today has not increased beyond the state of knowledge since the Scientific Revolution circa 1580, which verges on the ludicrous and is a misrepresentation of the history of science. Yet, oddly enough, Kuhn (1970: 149) also acknowledges that displaced paradigms are not abandoned altogether, and therefore implies that there is building upon what was established before. For example, he notes that Newtonian dynamics are "a special case of" and is "derivable from Einsteinian theory" (Kuhn 1970: 99). However, the thrust of his work is that paradigms are incommensurable, and each one is a new beginning.

In his devastating critique, the Australian philosopher David Stove explained how philosophers such as Kuhn have been able to get away espousing irrational views of science:

> Much more is known now than was known fifty years ago, and much more was known then in 1580. So there has been a great accumulation or growth of knowledge in the last four hundred years. This is an extremely-well known fact, which I will refer to as (A). A philosopher, in particular, who did not know it, would be uncommonly ignorant. So a writer whose position inclined him to deny (A), or even made him at all reluctant to admit it, would almost inevitably seem, to the philosophers who read him, to be maintaining something extremely implausible. Such a writer must make that impression, in fact, unless the way he writes effectively disguises the implausibility of his suggestions that (A) is false (Stove 1998: 21).

For this reason, *The Structure of Scientific Revolutions* is an odd mixture of rationalist and irrationalist views of the development of scientific knowledge. Stove (1998: 21–50) points out that throughout his book Kuhn relies on evocation, ambiguity, false equivalencies, and clever inconsistencies (cf., Bell 1994: 206–208; Boghossian 2006: 119; Franklin 2000; Masterman 1970: 59–90). Hence, his vision of science is amenable both to a rationalist and to an irrationalist reading. The cumulative nature of scientific knowledge is undeniable, and Kuhn is wise not to contest the issue overtly. Yet, as Stove points out, Kuhn, through his strategy of equivocation also says that such is not the case and that "the world is somehow plastic to our paradigms" (Franklin 2000; Stove 1998: 25). Stove (1998: 24) describes this as "an extreme form of mixed strategy . . . [based on] simple inconsistency: that is, assert an irrationalist thesis, but also assert others which are inconsistent with it."

Like the postmodern savants, Kuhn took a reasonable assertion that sociocultural factors impinge upon scientific research/knowledge and converted it into the unreasonable proposition that *the only things* that impinge upon scientific knowledge are sociocultural factors. This is simply untrue. The philosophers Schick and Vaughn (2014: 309) point out one of the principal flaws in Kuhn's understanding of the history of science:

> If our paradigms determine everything that we observe, then it would be impossible to observe anything that did not fit our paradigm. But if we never observe anything that didn't fit our paradigm—if we never perceived any anomalies—there would never be any need to undergo a paradigm shift. So Kuhn's theory undermines itself—if we accept his theory of observation, we must reject his history of science.

In other words, if theoretical frames shape all observations, then no one would ever observe anything new (Schick and Vaughn 2014: 310). In this regard, the philosopher Paul Boghossian (2006: 124) calls attention to the fact that Einstein comprehended Newtonian mechanics as well as the theory of relativity, which would not be the case if scientific paradigms are truly incomprehensible. The concept of incommensurability does not hold true for scientific paradigms, the culture of scientists, or even human cultures in general. For example, there have been no instances in which an anthropological fieldworker has returned from a research site and reported that the particular culture being investigated was so alien that it was utterly incomprehensible (see Brown 1991). The issue of incommensurably of paradigms or cultures—an idea at the center of anthropology's version of postmodernism—is nonsensical.

Contra to defenders (e.g., Levine 1999), it is irrelevant whether Kuhn himself was unhappy that his ideas were used to support radical anti-science relativism, which he expresses in the postscript of the second edition of his book (Benson and Stangroom 2006: 39–40), as well as in his article "The Road Since Structure" (1990). However, as Windschuttle (1998: 6) observes, while Kuhn may have rebuked the charge of relativism, his writings undermined this rejection. The point is that his ideas became the underpinning of anti-science radicalism and its premise that "science is no different from other types of knowledge," and that "truth is irrelevant to explaining scientific conclusions" (Franklin 2000).

The influence of Kuhn's ideas on the social sciences, especially anthropology, and related fields, has been massive (Okasha 2016: 87). As Stove (1991: 9) observed: "In the intellectual slums, where resistance of any kind is weak—among sociologists, educationists, anthropologists, and the like—the execution done by this book has been simply terrific." I can recall dozens of times at anthropological conferences, where exponents of postmodernism mentioned Thomas Kuhn in support of their arguments. Kuhn's ideas also became central for sociologists of science, especially by members of a movement called "the strong program" in Britain in the 1970s and 1980s, associated with David Bloor (1976) and his Edinburgh School Strong Programme. Starting with Kuhn's ideas, these sociologists went further and openly repudiated truth and rationality (Bloor 1976, 1981). Their ideas, in turn, had a direct impact on Latour's science studies enterprise as well as postmodern thinking in general. The take away from Kuhn for the postmodernists, as the true-believer Michael Bérubé (2011) recalls, was that he revealed that scientific knowledge is not cumulative and that science was subject to the same historical contingencies and irrational factors as other perspectives.

Finally, Kuhn's views also offered industry seeking to dodge environmental and safety regulations and undermine policymaking based on scientific evidence an expedient and concise argument that scientific research is biased by the interests, morals, private perversions, and ideological allegiances of the scientists themselves (Cailin and Weatherall 2019: 32). Hence, these opponents of science could argue that the entire endeavor is untrustworthy, and it is necessary to be very cautious before accepting their research findings. This became a powerful delaying tactic used by incumbent industry in environmental policymaking.

The Kuhnian perspective is not an accurate depiction of how scientific knowledge develops and grows. His discussion of Newtonian dynamics, although intended to illustrate the irrational nature of the growth of scientific knowledge, is, in fact, a demonstration that paradigms are indeed commensurable and knowledge grows (Kuznar 2008: 57). In other words, solutions under previous standards do not become "un-solutions" after paradigm shifts despite the equivocations (Stove 1998: 25). Hence, scientists still use Newton's law of gravity to calculate the orbit of rockets and spacecraft (Stenger 2008: 114–115). Indeed, there are only a few instances of Kuhnian-type revolutions in the history of science. For this reason, Weinberg (1998) refers to Kuhn's ideas as "the revolution that didn't happen."

I have already mentioned how postmodern thought encouraged the proliferation of a variety of irrational and pseudoscientific perspectives. Kuhn's ideas also emboldened paranormalists to challenge science. For instance, the Harvard University psychiatrist John Mack, who in his book *Abduction: Human Encounters with Aliens* (1994) averred that alien abductions were real occurrences rather than imaginary or hallucinatory phenomena, acknowledged his intellectual debt to Kuhn. As he put it, Kuhn made him realize that:

> [the scientific view of the world] had come to assume the rigidity of a theology, and that this belief system was held in place by the structures, categories, and polarities of language, such as real/unreal, exists/does not exist, objective/subjective, intrapsychic world/external world, and happened/did not happen (Mack 1994: 20).

Chapter 5

PAUL FEYERABEND AND THE PROLIFERATION OF THEORIES

Kuhn was not the only font of wisdom for American academics resolved to delegitimize science. Another source of inspiration was the Austrian-born American philosopher Paul Feyerabend (1924–1994). He argued that the idea of the incommensurability of rival scientific theories—a notion he contrived together with Kuhn during intense conversations (Hacking 2010: xi)—applied not merely to theories and paradigms, but to science entirely vis-à-vis other perspectives that purportedly also make truth claims about the world (Hoyningen 2000b; Windschuttle 1998: 5). In his major work *Against Method: Outline of an Anarchic Theory of Knowledge* (1975), he forwarded an even more intransigent view of the history of science or an anarchistic philosophy of science where he refers to science as a particular superstition. It is for this reason that some annoyed physicists dubbed him the "the worst enemy of science" (Horgan 1993: 36; Preston et al. 2000).

Ruling out any general criterion that provides science special priority over other perspectives or ways of knowing, in this philosopher's work science became merely one belief system, among many others. In his words:

> Science is much closer to myth than a scientific philosophy is prepared to admit. It is one of the many forms of thought that have been developed by man, and not necessarily the best. It is conspicuous, noisy, and impudent, but it is inherently superior only for those who have already decided in favour of a certain ideology, or who have accepted it without ever having examined its advantages and its limits (Feyerabend 1975: 295).

Feyerabend (1975: 308), therefore, advocated that science should be approached "together with other fairy tales such as the myths of 'primitive societies.'" He went on to say that "leading intellectuals with their zeal for objectivity . . . are criminals, not the liberators of mankind" (in Horgan 1993: 36). He further observed that the privileged status of science in determining the truth about the world and universe had to be retracted in the same way that those espousing a secular approach in education broke the nexus between church and state (Feyerabend 1975: 5–6). In his words:

> Thus, while an American can now choose the religion he likes, he is still not permitted to demand that his children learn magic rather than science in school. There is a separation between the state and Church, there is no separation between state and science (Feyerabend 1975: 299).

Stated differently, for this anarchistic philosopher, there was no difference between science, sorcery, voodoo, witchcraft, or religion. He added further that in the modern world, science is simply in the position that theology occupied in earlier times. Thus, that people in early modern Europe believed that witches were real and could fly through the air, and so forth, is no less reasonable or valid than present-day Americans believing that the Apollo astronauts walked on the moon. I think Feyerabend would have been pleased to know that today some 16 million people in this country think that the Apollo moon landings were a hoax staged in a Hollywood film studio (Lewandowsky et al. 2013).

His solution for achieving real emancipation was to combine an extreme skepticism toward scientific truths with the acceptance of all modes of knowledge and an anything-is-admissible approach in the pursuit of knowledge. This was related to his "principle of proliferation," which called for the development of many incommensurable alternatives to orthodox theories to fight it out in the market place of ideas as the only way toward genuine knowledge, which was the basis of his epistemic anarchism. We are back to the "underdetermination of theory" argument already discussed. What Feyerabend and others who used this contention overlooked is the fact, however, as the philosopher Paul Achinstein (2000) observes, that yes, there are many logically possible alternative positions, but these will lead nowhere unless they are bolstered by evidence.

Relevant for our discussion is that Feyerabend's call for an egalitarian and anarchic approach to knowledge provided intellectual space for all sorts of pseudoscientific views, such as magic, astrology, New Age mysticism, and creationism. In other words, he was prescribing "methodological opportunism," as captured in such statements as "anything goes" and "let a hundred flowers bloom" (Gorham 2017: 84). What he meant was that scientific laws should be decided by democratic vote. For this reason, Stove (1991: 11) remarked that "it is impossible to convey briefly the unique absurdity of [Feyerabend's] book."

Feyerabend's stance on these issues led him to support the efforts of Christian fundamentalists, whom he compared to Galileo, to have biblical creationism taught in American schools alongside Darwinian evolutionary theory (Horgan 1993: 36). However, Feyerabend (1975) recommendations that such arcane subjects be taught in schools had an entirely different aim than the postmodern project. As Slezak (1994b: 352) pointed out:

> [For him] this was a heuristic device to maintain the novelty and creative vigor of scientific inquiry whereas [postmodern] doctrines [aimed to] simply undermine the very conception of such inquiry which has been developed and refined since the presocratics.

FEYERABEND: SCIENCE AS A RELIGION

Feyerabend's assertion that science and religion have epistemic parity is a colossal misrepresentation and requires a comment. Picking up Feyerabend's idea, contemporary science-deniers frequently assert that science has no exclusive authority and is merely a faith-based belief system, or religion (e.g., Roy 2005; Smith 2015). Joan Roughgarden (2006a, 2006b), a Christian biologist, adds that because science is a religious belief system, its postulates are no more authoritative than the precepts of the Bible. Here is yet another example of how academic epistemic relativism has in our time, emboldened purveyors of supernaturalism to forward their superstitions as comparable to science.

But the assertion is untrue for several reasons. First, science is not a system of inviolate or sacrosanct beliefs like religion, but a method of discovering how the world and universe operate (Schick and Vaughn 2014: 160). It is erroneous, therefore, to link science to any particular worldview, equate science with its applications, or link it with its results (Schick and Vaughn 2014: 160). Second, of all the ways of knowing, science alone turns critical judgment and skepticism upon itself. No religious belief systems have ever allowed or can afford to permit this option. Religious premises lack evidential foundations, and such belief systems provide no non-arbitrary means of differentiating between various and often conflicting theological assumptions. For this reason, because an appeal to objective evidence is impossible, disputes over matters of theology, invariably deteriorate into charges of heresy, apostasy, and atheism, along with intimidation, physical force, and, of course, religious violence (Sidky 2020: 89–91). Third, in contrast to religious premises whose validity is based on appeals to higher powers and postulated paranormal or supernatural beings outside the spatiotemporal confines of the universe, the evidentiary foundations of science are of this world, are open for assessment by others, and scientific claims are subject to testing and falsification by independent and impartial parties. Unlike religion, it is a requirement that all scientific propositions be publicly verifiable and testable, that is, tested in relation to publicly ascertainable evidence.

It is astonishing that an ideologue such as Feyerabend was taken seriously by so many people. Remarkably, toward the end of his life, he shifted his views on relativism and incommensurability of theories, stating that "if on almost every university toilet door there are relativistic theses, then it's time to distance oneself from relativism" (in Hoyningen 2000: 14). His change of heart is also reflected in one of his later papers:

> How can [science] depend on culture in so many ways, and yet produce such solid results? Most answers to this question are either incomplete or incoherent. Physicists take the fact for granted. Movements that view quantum mechanics as a turning-point in thought—and that include fly-by-night mystics, prophets of a New Age, and relativists of all sorts—get aroused by the cultural component and forget predictions and technology (Feyerabend 1992).

Here we have equivocation on the part of a committed irrationalist thinker (see also Feyerabend 1995: 151–152). Several such luminaries have subsequently renounced aspects of their anti-science relativistic stance.

Given this discussion, it is understandable why science studies drew its rational from the works of writers such as Kuhn and Feyerabend, along with French postmodernist literary theory (Windschuttle 1998: 11). Today, the viewpoints of these two philosophers are extensively cited by science-deniers on all fronts, as well as empowering an array of irrational counter-culturalists and religious extremists whose beliefs are refuted by scientific findings, including the proponents of Intelligent Design Creationism (Pennock 2010) to be discussed in chapter 8 (cf., Otto 2016: 187).

Chapter 6

Epistemic Relativism
Is the World Truly Unknowable?

David Stove (1991: 61–62) dubbed perspectives claiming that reality is unknowable as "veil-doctrines," which he described as:

> doctrines to the effect that a certain impenetrable veil cuts us off from knowledge of the actual universe; or that we are prevented by some insuperable obstacles from climbing the one vantage-point from which the cosmos can be seen rightly.

Advocates of such ideas maintain that reality is a social construct because humans are the helpless prisoners of language, and the key to unmasking this truth lies in paying careful attention to the nuances of writing and texts. This was the premise on which the paragons of postmodern philosophy grounded their foremost conclusion upon, namely that reality and hence knowledge are culturally constituted with no correlation to anything called an empirical reality or an objective world. The same reasoning was at the basis of the notion of the incommensurability of cultures, whether that of scientists or different human populations. Remarkably, however, nowhere did any of those advocating such ideas provide any proof in support of their assertions. Also, remarkably, no one at the time in these circles was asking for any. It was all an a priori assumption, pure and simple. Yet, this premise was at the core of the false portrayal of science by these epistemic critics and today is still considered a plausible idea in various quarters of our post-truth world, including among many cultural anthropologists. Here I will examine the plausibility of this science delegitimizing avowal.

First, let us ponder what other philosophers have said. Yes, humans everywhere hold some fuzzy beliefs that stem from sociological factors rather than evidentiary foundations, such as why many people in the American South are

Christians, and many in Iran are not (Boghossian 2006: 112). There are also agreed-upon things like money. However, this does not justify extending this proposition to all beliefs. The critical point is, as Gorham (2017: 128–129) observes, that whether a fact is socially constructed or is mind independent cannot be decided a priori or "legislated by philosophical fiat," but is a matter of historical and empirical analysis. Postmodern philosophers assumed this to be a universal condition beforehand, without any such inquiry.

Benson and Stangroom (2006: 40–43) point out, that while at first glance, the claim that reality is unknowable and everyone has their own truths appears to be alluring, every person knows that this is untrue viscerally and physically. Similarly, the philosopher Harry Frankfurt (2018: 10) talks about our "innocent commonsense understanding" of what is real and true and what is not. And Dew and Foreman (2014: 50) observe that everyone has an overwhelming intuitive sense that the world in which they live is real. They add:

> We may debate what propositions are actually true and at times have difficulty identifying them, but the vast majority of human beings throughout history have had an overwhelming conviction that there is such a thing as truth and that we can know it, at least in part.

The philosopher John Searle refers to such an understanding of truth as a default position that is central to thinking, speaking, and theorizing about the world and universe that makes knowledge possible. In his words:

> Default positions are the views we hold pre-reflectively so that any departure from them requires a conscious effort and a convincing argument (Searle 1998: 9).

Pre-reflective positions include the following:

> There is a real world that exists independently of us, independently of our experiences, our thoughts, our language.
>
> We have direct perceptual access to that world through our senses, especially touch and vision.
>
> Words in our language, words like rabbit or tree, typically have reasonably clear meanings. Because of their meanings, they can be used to refer to and talk about real objects in the world.
>
> Our statements are typically true or false depending on whether they correspond to how things are, that is, to the facts in the world.
>
> Causation is a real relation among objects and events in the world, a relation whereby one phenomenon, the cause, causes another, the effect (Searle 1998: 10).

Searle adds that in day-to-day life, these propositions are taken for granted to such a degree that it would be incorrect to describe them as merely opinions or points of view. People do not hold the opinion that the world exists in the same way that they would hold the opinion that George Lukas is or is not a great director. He adds that "These taken-for-granted presuppositions are part of what I call the Background of our thought and language" (Searle 1998: 10).

Along the same lines, the mathematician and philosopher of science Martin Gardner (1983: 15) made the following observation:

> The hypothesis that there is an external world, not dependent on human minds, made of something, is so obviously useful and so strongly confirmed by experience down through the ages that we can say without exaggerating that it is better confirmed than any other empirical hypothesis. So useful is the posit that it is almost impossible for anyone except a madman or a professional metaphysician to comprehend a reason for doubting it.

Pragmatic grounds and everyday epistemology, or the crucible of experience, are alone sufficient to cast doubt on the type of epistemic relativity advocated by the academic cultural critics (Lett 1997a: 67; Sidky 2018: 40). Everyday epistemology reveals that walls are solid, fire burns, knives cut, rain is wet, there are mountains, and airplanes fly because of their aerodynamic design. Then there is our fear of falling and why we do not walk off cliffs, our inclination not to step in front of moving traffic, and the reason we do not willingly put our hands in blazing fires. These things confirm that there are "foundational truths" about the world and demonstrate that epistemological relativism is false (Benson and Stangroom 2006: 43). In other words, our perceptions do not systematically deceive us all the time and this is a compelling indicator that there are external objects that accord with those perceptions (Sokal and Bricmont 1998: 53). In this regard, as Lett points out, no postmodernist ever genuinely doubted these things in their personal life, despite whatever epistemological nonsense they might have uttered in their scholarly life. This is yet another example of the intellectual dishonesty of the adherents of this ideology (Lett 2020, personal communication).

To put it differently, we are not hopeless prisoners caught inside the webs of our languages and linguistic categories. This issue was already addressed in chapter 2. It is also important to note that philosophers addressed this problem long before postmodernism or post-truth were conceived. Reuben Abel (1976: 33) noted, for example, that:

> the road that leads from my sense perceptions to my knowledge of a world outside myself is full of gaps, brambles, and obscurities. But it is the only road I have. . . . It is true that inference to the independent existences of external

objects cannot be demonstrated. . . . But our justification of such a belief is pragmatic: we survive and act successfully in the world by assuming it.

Then there is the agreement between theory and experiment in thousands of cases, sometimes with great precision, that suggests that there is an external world/reality and that science has acquired vast amounts of reliable knowledge about that world (Bernard 1995: 17). There is also the undeniable and astonishing success of science. As Stove (1991: 24) stated in this regard, "the history of Western science has been, since about 1600, almost entirely a *success* story. This is hard luck for . . . the bohemian enemies of success, but that is how it is. But not only have we learnt much. We have learnt something even more important: *how to learn*." These successes include antibiotics, organ transplants, telecommunications, computers, airplanes, GPS, space-flights, and landing humans on the moon several times that demonstrate that truth is knowable (Dew and Foreman 2014: 51; McIntyre 2015: 105). To put it differently, the idea that there is a world out there, an external reality independent of the thoughts we have about them, and the words we use in reference to them constitute "the best explanation for our experiences" (Schick and Vaughn 2014: 300).

We navigate the world using the same principles encapsulated in the scientific method, by continuously making decisions about our perceptions according to the rules of inductive/deductive hypothesis testing and refutation (Fox 1997: 341). Sokal and Bricmont (1998: 56) explain this as follows:

> The scientific method is not radically different from the rational attitude in everyday life or in other domains of human knowledge. Historians, detectives, and plumbers—indeed all human beings—use the same basic methods of induction, deduction, and assessment of evidence as do physicists or chemists. Modern science tries to carry these operations in a more careful and systematic way, by using controls and statistical tests, insisting on replication, and so forth. Moreover, scientific measurements are often much more precise than everyday observations; they allow us to discover hitherto unknown phenomena; and they often conflict with "common sense." But the conflict is at the level of conclusion, not the basic approach.

Similarly, the noted philosopher of science Karl Popper (1972: 31) said: "All science, and all philosophy, are enlightened common sense." What is puzzling to me is how the postmodern philosophers were able to convince so many to accept their bogus claims about the structure of reality and the impossibility of knowledge and truth.

Finally, in addition to these arguments, a strong reason to reject epistemic relativism comes from evolutionary biology. We apprehend the world and universe in human terms through the sensory apparatus and mental faculties that are part of our evolutionary heritage. Creatures that possess sensory organs that fail to reflect the outside world more or less accurately are unlikely to survive for very long. As Carl Sagan (1993: 19) observed in this regard:

> The universe forces those who live in it to understand it. Those creatures who find everyday experience a muddled jumble of events with no predictability, no regularity, are in grave peril. The universe belongs to those who, at least to some degree, have figured it out.

Given these factors that prevent anyone from genuinely believing in the truth of epistemic relativism, we must ask why the postmodern savants made such claims? Was it merely a matter of intellectual dishonesty? Was it due to a disordered mind? One could certainly make such claims. But there is something else going on. The Princeton University philosopher Harry Frankfurt's discussion of bullshit offered in his amusing but cogent book *On Bullshit* (2005), is relevant to the present study. Frankfurt makes a distinction between someone who is lying and one who is "bullshitting." A liar assumes that there are facts that are knowable and discernible and presupposes that we can get things right or wrong (Frankfurt 2005: 56, 61). The bullshitter, in contrast, does not oppose himself to the truth he simply pays no attention to it. He is unconcerned whether his assertions correctly represent reality, he simply makes them up to suit his purpose. In Frankfurt's words:

> Someone who lies and someone who tells the truth are playing on opposite sides, so to speak, of the same game. Each responds to the facts as he understands them, although the response of one is guided by the authority of truth, while the response of the other defies that authority and refuses to meet its demands. The bullshitter ignores these demands altogether. He does not reject the authority of the truth, as the liar does, and oppose himself to it at all. He pays no attention to it at all. By virtue of this. Bullshit is a greater enemy of the truth than lies are (Frankfurt 2005: 60–61).

Frankfurt's assertions fit the concepts offered by the French literati and their disciples. Lies that fit this qualification are also a hallmark of post-truth politics. In such cases, the narrative is more important than whether or not it is true or false (Ball 2017: 6). A slight emendation in reference to postmodern assertions might be to label them "pseudo-profound bullshit," as suggested by psychologist Gordon Pennycook and his colleagues (2015), by which they mean statements that "consists of seemingly impressive assertions that are presented as true and meaningful but are actually vacuous."

Frankfurt goes on to say that the prevalence of bullshit in contemporary public discourse emanates from the "antirealist doctrines" in academic circles (i.e., postmodern epistemic relativism) that repudiate the idea that reliable access to an objective reality is possible or that such a reality even exists (Frankfurt 2005: 66). We have now come across the crux of post-truth Fantasyland America where the crowd's reaction to various narratives has become the criteria for what passes as truth and knowledge (cf., Lewandowsky et al. 2017; McIntyre 2018: 9–10).

MISREPRESENTATIONS OF SCIENCE

The Left's assault on science was as disingenuous as those of corporate America and the efforts by fundamentalist Christians. Excluding the empirical dimension of the scientific enterprise, the postmodern luminaries misrepresented science as merely a "story" or narrative like any other that relies on rhetorical ornamentation and "language games"—Wittgenstein's metaphor—to persuade people of its legitimacy and authority. Or, as Boghossian (2006: 123) puts it, they conflated "a difference in representation with a difference in the things represented." The self-styled "anthropologists of science" who were engaged in science studies also confused the authority of science with that of the persons conveying scientific knowledge. I have already mentioned this error in connection with Harding's feminist critique of science in chapter 4.

As Otto (2016: 189) notes: "Postmodern thinking mistakenly focused on scientists as a group with a distinct ideological background rather than on science as a process of ideas, as something anyone can do regardless of their group." He adds that the savants did not really understand science and mistook the "authority and theatrics of the white lab coats and the way science was being used by the military-industrial complex" (Otto 2016: 172). Kuhn made the same blunder in thinking that scientific knowledge had more to do with the scientists themselves than with the structure of reality (Cailin and Weatherall 2019: 32–33).

As we shall see, science is not an authority system, but the opposite—its authority comes from the non-authoritarian investigation of nature—this is not anchored in the scientists, but in objective reality (Otto 2016: 172). In other words, in science, the ultimate arbiter is the evidence; it is gravity, not the scientist asserting that an apple will plummet to the ground that is the defining condition of knowledge in the end. Sadly, relativist anti-science writers remain befuddled about this issue (e.g., the anthropologist Herzfeld 2017). It is an epistemological blunder to confuse the assertions of facts (e.g., the words used to describe gravity) with the facts themselves (that apples fall from trees) as aspects of the external world that exist irrespective of how we know or which words we use to write about them. By taking this stance, postmodernists transformed a reasonable position that "facts do not speak for themselves" into the absurd conclusion that "there are no facts," and that no knowledge of the empirical world is possible, which is a gross *non-sequitur* (Spaulding 1988: 264).

RHETORIC AS EVIDENCE

Epistemic relativism dictates that no representations of reality or story can be privileged because there are multiple and equally valid realities and truths. Moreover, to reiterate, because all truths are relative, as the argument went, whose truth prevails is a coefficient of power and coercion (Foucault 1984: 75). The West is dominant and hegemonic, and hence its "truths"—meaning science and scientific knowledge—are privileged and not because science has gotten anything correct about the world and universe. Their solution to this problem was to denigrate science and extoll, encourage, and underwrite any kind of fiction, falsehood, or bunkum as long as they emanated from among the powerless and the marginal elements of society (Andersen 2017: 311).

In other words, trained academics in American universities were encouraging science illiteracy and irrational thinking! If nothing else, this factor alone is sufficient indication of the impact of postmodern academics on the present-day political and cultural climate where science and reason are denigrated and pseudoscientific preposterousness is flourishing. The list of such absurdities includes Trump advocating bogus and dangerous remedies for COVID-19, such as injecting disinfectants, inserting UV lights in human bodies, and taking *hydroxychloroquine*. Another snake oil concoction Trump is touting is a deadly plant poison called oleandrin because a sycophant grifter attested to its efficacy.

The problem that postmodern philosophy ran into is this: How does one make claims to knowledge if reason, truth, and objective facts are discredited? Well, all the epistemic relativist is left with are opinions, ideology, faith, appeal to authority, and rhetoric, as I have said already. We have now verged upon the realm of post-truth because rhetorical force often wins arguments despite the soundness of the opposing position. As Benson and Stangroom (2006: 172, 178) point out: "All rhetoric has to do to win is convince people, it doesn't have to do it legitimately or reasonably or honestly." Rhetoric without evidence, they add, cannot be emancipatory because it is not a communication aid, an addition of reliable evidence, or sound inference. It is a substitute for the absence of sound evidence and reasoned argumentation. Epistemological relativism enables bad arguments devoid of any evidentiary foundations to prevail in public debates over justified arguments based on sound evidence. Think about how this is playing out today in the public and political arenas in Fantasyland, United States. In their words:

> It is not emancipatory because it helps emotive rhetoric to prevail over reason and evidence, which means it helps falsehood to prevail over truth. Being trapped in a world where lies can't be countered seems a strange idea of emancipation (Benson and Stangroom 2006: 172).

As pointed out earlier, postmodernism was ideology disguised as scholarship. It was a duplicitous enterprise by imprudent professors. This is not an unfair assertion because their premises were incoherent and absurd.

There were other problems with the perspective under discussion. Having transformed scientific discourse into texts by means of dubious rhetorical argumentation, and forwarding the claim that one text is no more privileged than another, the relativists avowed a privileged status for their own approach. Remarkably, none of the postmodernist luminaries addressed this "reflexivity thesis," or did so in a sardonic and disingenuous fashion, as in the case of Latour (cf., Gorham 2017: 127). In other words, why don't the postmodernists' assertions about knowledge apply as well to their own claims to knowledge? Why isn't postmodern philosophy itself merely another social construction? If it does apply, then the postmodern theory is defeated. If it does not, then its proponents have to demonstrate why only their perspective is free from the contingencies impinging on all other knowledge claims?

Perhaps one reason why they refused to address this issue is that it would be playing the enemy's rationality game involving the abhorred logic and reason (cf., Franklin 2009: 42). I also suspect that the Dunning-Kruger Effect was powerfully at play here as well throughout the ranks and files of these thinkers. This refers to "being ignorant of one's own ignorance" or to the cognitive bias that leads ignorant and unqualified people to inflated self-assessment of how smart and competent they are (Dunning 2011; Kruger and Dunning 1999). How else does one explain why individuals without requisite training in science, and hence least qualified to pontificate about the subject, felt entitled to undertake the deconstruction of scientific knowledge?

The savants operated as if through some unique insight, empathic power, or subjective capacity and intuition, with which they alone were endowed, they could penetrate into the mysterious forces and occult codes of power that shackled and oppressed everyone else. As Stove (1991: 62) pointed out in this regard, the proponents of such veil-doctrines comprise:

> people who have so far succeeded in transcending the cognitive limitations of their own "class-situation" as to be in a position to inform the rest of us that no one can ever transcend the cognitive limitations of his class-situation. They will tell you for a fact that there is no such thing as a fact.

Postmodernists claimed that they could decipher the mystery of power by looking at seemingly inconsequential aspects of language that are invisible to conventional analysts and even the authors of those texts. That other people did not possess such sublime insights was because they lacked the requisite imagination or intelligence. Thus, while these academics relegated everyone, including the unenlightened anthropologists, historians, economists, chemists, biologists, mathematicians, and physicists to the prison of language, they allotted themselves the dispensation of alone being able to break free from the mysterious fetters of linguistic templates (Gross and Levitt 1994: 56). This is claiming privileged status for one's self, a sin for which postmodernists constantly admonished their rivals (Kuznar 2008: 156).

But there are more defects and inconsistencies in this philosophy that both ensured its ultimate failure and sadly rendered its proponents entirely irrelevant as a political force today—in post-truth America, the cultural Left is in shambles politically and is utterly marginalized (cf., Woolin 2004: 13). First, as I have already alluded, the postmodern perspective of comprehensive relativism (as opposed to domain-specific relativism, such as systems of supernatural beliefs) was fundamentally incoherent and self-contradictory. The reason for this, as already noted, is because it claimed that all truths were relative to social class, gender, ethnicity, and cultural background, but excluded itself from the constraints of culture, history, and context (Boghossian 2006: 53; Sidky 2004: 399). Schick and Vaughn (2014: 311–312) have this to add:

> To say that everything is relative is to say that no unrestricted universal generalizations are true (an unrestricted universal generalization is a statement to the effect that something holds for all individuals, societies, or conceptual schemes). But the statement that "No unrestricted universal generalizations are true" is itself an unrestricted universal generalization. So if relativism in any of its forms is true, it's false.

Thus, like other hardcore skeptics, by claiming that they have proved that nothing can be proven, they contradicted their own perspective (cf., Musgrave 1993: 19).

Second, there were no specified rules for extracting the purported occult codes of power and encrypted significations from texts. As noted before, careful reading does not accomplish this task. Recall Derrida's embarrassing conundrum defending Paul de Man. So how does one proceed? Remarkably, the answer was through subjective means, using the postmodern scholar's personal and often oversimplified moral categories of exploitation versus resistance, with truth conflated with "good" provided by and suited to the analyst's moralistic sensibilities. This enterprise was not about the discovery of new knowledge or truth because the analyst herself or himself provided the "truth" (Salzman 2001: 136). These writers professed a self-righteous desire to "speak truth to evil" (Scheper-Hughes 1995), however, it was their own "truth" arrived at using extraordinary capacities and hermeneutic ingenuities with which they credited themselves and denied everyone else (Sidky 2007: 68).

Third, the relativists were awful writers. Their books and articles were full of strategic ambiguities upheld by means of glaring *non-sequiturs,* a pompous contempt for facts and reason, mystification, impenetrable language, and heavy doses of rhetoric and pseudo-profound technical jargon. The success of their ideas was not due to their intellectual merits but because as masters of language the savants sought to impress their audience with the "clever abuse of sophisticated terminology" (Sokal and Bricmon 1998: 8). To borrow sociologist Stanislav Andreski's (1972) phrase, these works involved a "smokescreen of jargon." The passages are full of obscure literary allusions, neologisms, baroque rhetorical forms, and contrived scientific-sounding jargon, such as "non-Euclidian space," "chaos theory" "reversal of cause and effect," and my favorite one from anthropology, the "endorphin of culture" (Tyler 1987: 102). All of this sounded erudite but were in actuality barrages of "pseudo-profound bullshit" that made for incomprehensible texts (cf., Carniero 1995: 14; Sokal and Bricmont 1998: x–xi).

Embarrassingly, as I have already mentioned, many cultural anthropologists soaked up and recapitulated these ideas by becoming disciples of the French literati or commentators upon their works. They were thus an instrumental party in the assault on truth and knowledge in the United States (see Otto 2016: 175–176). I cannot admonish my colleges harshly enough because they were on the scene and well situated to study the incursion of irrationalism in American universities and colleges and address the important anthropological question: Why do people believe in premises for which there is either no evidence or are demonstrably false? Instead of analyzing this perplexing phenomenon in terms of scientifically meaningful categories following the tradition of systematic skepticism, cultural anthropologists became converts, endorsers, proxies, and proselytizers of bogus irrational ideas and nonsensical philosophical precepts. They were thus complicit in the contamination of intellectual life and honest inquiry. Sokal (1996b) was fully justified in his condemnation of such intellects:

> Politically, I'm angered because most (though not all) of this silliness is emanating from the self-proclaimed Left. We're witnessing here a profound historical *volte-face*. For most of the past two centuries, the Left has been identified with science and against obscurantism; we have believed that rational thought and the fearless analysis of objective reality (both natural and social) are incisive tools for combating the mystifications promoted by the powerful—not to mention being desirable human ends in their own right. The recent turn of many "progressive" or "leftist" academic humanists and social scientists toward one or another form of epistemic relativism betrays this worthy heritage and undermines the already fragile prospects for progressive social critique. Theorizing about "the social construction of reality" won't help us find an effective treatment for AIDS or devise strategies for preventing global warming. Nor can we combat false ideas in history, sociology, economics, and politics if we reject the notions of truth and falsity.

To sum it up, the critical theorists in question were engaged in nothing less than a concerted but disingenuous misinformation campaign against science and rationality. If postmodern philosophy was anything other than a colossal pretext, it would still be a viable intellectual enterprise. Where are the promised grandiose theoretical breakthroughs? Where are the remarkable insights into sociocultural processes that would lead to a kinder and more just society? There are none because postmodernism was an intellectual sham, which, as I have said, was an ideology disguised as scholarship. Its shameful legacy is post-truth and anti-democratic right-wing populism. What the savants offered were "pseudo-profound bullshit," propaganda, and an intellectually dishonest enterprise. They accomplished nothing aside from bewildering an already scientifically illiterate American public about the role and function of science (Sidky 2018: 42).

Chapter 7

Epistemology
How Do We Know What We Know?

The lasting contribution of the academic Left's disinformation about truth and objectivity was to corrupt standards of critical thought and honest inquiry. They also promoted a reckless form of anti-intellectualism. Thanks to their ideas, there is now a prevalent post-truth conjecture that science is dubious because scientific inferences from evidence to theory are not clearly established and scientific truths are provisional rather than proven in an absolute sense.

In this chapter, I shall examine the nature of scientific knowledge and some of the principles underlying the scientific approach. I wish to clarify two questions: first, why of all the ways of knowing, science alone holds our best hope of garnering reliable knowledge of humankind, the world, and the universe; and second, to show why scientific knowledge is different from all other modes of understandings, including pseudoscientific, mystical, poetic, intuitive, and allegorical approaches. This discussion is necessary because alternative ways of knowing and pseudoscientific absurdities have not only become mainstream, but they have intruded into fields such as anthropology. Hence, I want to know if such views are warranted.

All claims to knowledge whether they are about rocks, cultures, human nature, genes, the COVID-19 virus, the existence of ghosts, ancient aliens, miracles, UFOs, the evolution of life, and so forth, are epistemological issues. Epistemology comes from the Greek word episteme (ἐπιστήμη) or knowledge. It is concerned with the investigation of the nature and sources of knowledge and whether claims to knowledge are justified (Audi 2011; Creel 2001; Goldman and McGrath 2015; Greco and Sosa 1999; Hales 2002; Williams 2001).

Epistemology forces us to ask: How we know what we know? How do we know whom to believe? How do we discern what is justified, and what is not justified? Thus, epistemology challenges us to stipulate precisely how we know what we know by revealing the nature and sources of our knowledge (Brook and Stainton 2000: 1–3; Dew and Foreman 2014: 9; Lett 1987: 15, 20).

The drive to understand the world and universe, as the philosopher of science Geoffrey Gorham (2017: vii) expresses, is a profound and unique aspect of our kind. Aristotle was well aware of this when he said in the opening passage of his *Metaphysics* (350 BCE) that "All men by nature desire to know." Similarly, the philosopher of science Samir Okasha (2016: 36) says, an important aim of science, aside from explanations for practical ends, is to satisfy our intellectual curiosity about the world. Thus, those who espouse epistemic skepticism and related bogus assertions block us from the principal human goal of understanding the operation of the world and the universe. For this reason, the inimitable Carl Sagan (1993: 55) said:

> Those who make uncritical observations or fraudulent claims lead us into error and deflect us from the major human goal of understanding how the world works. It is for this reason that playing fast and loose with the truth is a serious matter.

The problem of knowledge occurs because the world abounds with many different types and often contradictory claims to knowledge or ways of knowing. However, not all of these are equally useful if our goal is to obtain reliable understanding of the world and universe (Sidky 2004: 32). Thus, if that is our objective, then we must make distinctions between different ways of knowing (Gellner 1992: 38). Compare, for instance, the warnings issued by scientists and healthcare professionals about the imminence of the COVID-19 epidemic on U.S. soil in the early months of 2020 and Trump's disastrous assertion that the entire thing was a hoax and a conspiracy to undermine his presidency. Thus, if our objective is to understand the world and act responsibly and reasonably in it, then we must make distinctions between different ways of knowing (Gellner 1992: 38).

Of concern here are the particular set of epistemological premises upon which science is based. This is not a simple task because, as Okasha (2016: 15) correctly points out, science is a heterogenous enterprise involving a range of disciplines and theories. It is, therefore, challenging to offer a single all-encompassing rendering of what distinguishes science from other perspectives. In philosophy, this is referred to as the demarcation problem. However, while this is true, it is also the case that science in general "is based on a systematic and finely honed set of tools that humans have developed over the centuries to compensate for our species' 'biases'" (Lilienfeld 2018: xiii).

Moreover, all of the diverse scientific endeavors operate upon the key premise that there is an objective reality that exists independently of the imperfect perceptions, interpretations, motivations, feelings, wishes, and desires of human beings. Reality, in other words, exists apart from our perceptual and cognitive apparatus rather than being generated by it. Hence, as the philosopher Paul Boghossian (2006: 22) points out, the world would have all of its attributes even if humans never evolved. Many facts are, therefore, independent of the thoughts, social interests, and values people have about them. Boghossian (2006: 20) adds, for example, that the belief that at one time dinosaurs lived on earth is not dependents on us, but is a natural fact that obtains without input from us:

> What is independent of our social make-up is the fact that the fossil records we have discovered constitutes *evidence* for the existence of dinosaurs—contribute to making it rational, in other words, to believe in their existence. That we should have discovered the evidence for dinosaurs may not be independent of our social context; *but that it is evidence* for that hypothesis is (Boghossian 2006: 21).

It is, therefore, possible that evidence alone can dictate and justify why we believe in what we believe (Boghossian 2006: 21, 39). If we aim to arrive at the correct understandings of the world, our beliefs must accord with those mind-independent facts (Boghossian 2006: 13, 59). This is why it is unwise to exclude the leveling effect of objective scientific evidence through political fiat or because of wishful thinking, which has become a routine in Trump's Idiot America.

For the epistemic relativists, in contrast, what constitutes a fact that denotes a dinosaur is determined not because it corresponds with the world or nature but is entirely due to our contingent needs and practical interests. The assertion here is that there are no facts that correspond to the way the world is "in and of themselves" apart from our denotations (Boghossian 2006: 31). To make this assertion leads to an epistemological quandary. The reason, as already mentioned, is that the claim is fundamentally incoherent and self-undermining because it holds that the only absolute fact is that all facts are mind-dependent facts because of our needs and interests (Boghossian 2006: 54–55).

Returning to our discussion, related to the stated assumptions of science is the premise that reality is amenable to rational inquiry, meaning that it is comprehensible through direct sensory experience (Lett 1997a: 42). Moreover, reality is intelligible without recourse to supernatural forces and powers (Bernard 1994: 168). Science begins by acknowledging the problems of knowledge, but unlike epistemological skeptics, it does not consider knowledge to be unattainable. As Albert Einstein (1936) stated: "The eternal mystery of the world is its comprehensibility." These features together give science consilience, or a unified view of the world where conclusions from various fields tend to converge (Mahner 2013: 38).

As discussed in chapter 6, the idea that there is a world out there, an external reality independent of the thoughts, constitutes "the best explanation for our experiences" (Schick and Vaughn 2014: 300). Moreover, this external reality cannot be altered and made subject to our wishes and desires no matter how much "faith" we have, how diligently we try, how many votes we take, how much we flex our political muscles, and how many other people we convert to our views (Sidky 2004: 398).

Observation of the provision that our understanding of the world must accord with the reality of the world is why science has been so successful. However, we ignore this reality at our peril. A tragic example of this was the Challenger disaster in 1986. That misfortune occurred on January 28, 1986, when the craft exploded and broke apart seventy-three seconds from Cape Canaveral, Florida, killing all crew members on board, including a school teacher Christa McAuliffe. This was Challenger's tenth mission. The engineering was sound. However, there were worries that the circular rubber gaskets or O-rings that sealed the rocket boosters would fail in the unseasonably cold temperatures that day. For this reason, the engineers advised postponing the launch until favorable weather conditions. NASA administrators, however, relied on their "gut instincts" or intuition, believing that they could somehow override the facts. The launch proceeded as scheduled.

Why did NASA officials disregard the protest by the engineers? Nobel-prize winning physicist Richard Feynman (1986), who was part of the committee investigating the Challenger disaster, suggested that their decision may have been "an attempt to assure the government of NASA perfection and success to ensure the supply of funds." Alternatively, he said that they might have sincerely believed that the launch conditions were safe, demonstrating an "incredible lack of communication between themselves and their working engineers." Feynman admonished the officials for not dealing with "the world or reality," adding that "For a successful technology, reality must take precedence over public relations, for nature cannot be fooled." As McIntyre (2018: 172) sums it up: "Facts were the facts. No amount of spin, lies, bullshit, or happy talk could contradict them."

Of all the ways of knowing, only science strives to ground its conclusions in reality and empirical facts. Or, as McIntyre (2015: 120) adds: "Science is perhaps the best way of respecting truth because it has a built-in mechanism for elimination bias and providing for the correction of error." Long ago, the philosopher Bertrand Russell (1961: 782) called attention to the leveling effect of evidence, stating,

> The concept of "truth" as something dependent upon facts largely outside human control has been one of the ways in which philosophy hitherto has inculcated

the necessary element of humility. When this check upon pride is removed, a further step is taken on the road towards a certain kind of madness—the intoxication of power which invaded philosophy with Fichte, and to which modern men, whether philosophers or not, are prone. I am persuaded that this intoxication is the greatest danger of our time, and that any philosophy which, however unintentionally, contributes to it is increasing the danger of vast social disaster.

And as Einstein put it, "Science is one of the most precious things we have" (Hoffmann 1972: 261). It is valuable not because it guarantees absolute truths, free of bias, error, and deception, but because it is a unique self-correcting method for reducing bias, mistakes, and fraud to advance our understanding of the social and natural worlds (Sidky 2018: 42).

SCIENCE AND THE MEANING OF TRUTH

In philosophy, there are different understandings of truth. We may talk about (1) truth by coherence, (2) truth by consensus, (3) truth by pragmatism, and (4) truth by correspondence (see Capps 2019; David 2016; Young 2018). It is significant to stress that these different understandings of truth do not have epistemic parity contra to what epistemic skeptics aver.

Truth by coherence refers to a set of ideas and assemblages of propositions that are consistent with and support one another but may have no external points of reference (Williams 2001: 117–137). Or to put it another way, a proposition is true if and only if it coheres with a system of propositions (Crumley 1999: 40). The social constructivist notion about many ways of knowing—or many self-referential epistemic systems—is based on this idea. The postmodernist epistemic plurality clause holds that there are multiple internally coherent alternative epistemic systems, each one as valid as the next. Moreover, in each one of these systems, beliefs are justified relative to their accepted epistemic parameters rather than objective facts. Finally, the belief is that there are no independent facts or a God's eye perspective to enable the determination of which, if any, of these systems is or is not correct. All of these systems, therefore, have epistemic parity.

Hence, the anthropological view that the first inhabitants of the Americas came from Asia by way of the land bridge connecting Siberia and Alaska and the view of some contemporary Native Americans that their ancestors originated in an underground spirit world have equal epistemic status. Paul Boghossian (1996) referred to such a case in his commentary on the Sokal hoax:

> A front-page article in the *New York Times* of October 22, 1996 provided a recent illustration. The article concerned the conflict between two views of

where Native American populations originated—the scientific archeological account, and the account offered by some Native American creation myths. According to the former extensively confirmed view, humans first entered the Americas from Asia, crossing the Bering Strait over 10,000 years ago. By contrast, some Native American creation accounts hold that native peoples have lived in the Americas ever since their ancestors first emerged onto the surface of the earth from a subterranean world of spirits. The *Times* noted that many archeologists, torn between their commitment to scientific method and their appreciation for native culture, "have been driven close to a postmodern relativism in which science is just one more belief system." Roger Anyon, a British archeologist who has worked for the Zuni people, was quoted as saying: "Science is just one of many ways of knowing the world. [The Zunis's world view is] just as valid as the archeological viewpoint of what prehistory is about."

Epistemic relativists may find such a view fully acceptable. However, it violates the law of noncontradiction because, in these terms, something can be true while its precise opposite is concurrently true as well. Epistemic plurality is, therefore, incoherent and self-contradicting, and a declaration against its own reliability. A self-contradictory position is epistemologically meaningless. As Dawes (2001: 3) has put it, "The conclusions it generates are always false because conclusions about the world that are self-contradictory cannot be accurate ones." Or, as Dew and Foreman (2014: 59) say, for propositions to be valid, they must be logically consistent by not contradicting each other.

Another issue overlooked was that if we apply the epistemic plurality clause consistently to all systems, that is, the origins of the people of the Americas in relation to Native American creation myths, then science should not be excluded. If other perspectives are justified in this manner, then it is contradictory to stipulated that science, which is based upon on the premise that beliefs are justified by correspondence to objective facts, is false.

Science recognizes that some truths are constituted in terms of coherence. For example, different systems of geometry consist of coherent and internally consistent propositions. The witchcraft beliefs among the Azande or in early Modern Europe are other examples (see Evans-Pritchard 1937; Sidky 1997: 101–116). Coherence thus offers justification for such beliefs. However, while such systems are true by coherence, they are not necessarily "true of the world" (Hospers 1988: 117). As Boghossian (2006: 16) has put it, "If a belief is to count as knowledge, it must not only be justified; it must also be true."

Truth by consensus holds that a belief is true if and only if one's intellectual community agrees that it is true. Such beliefs, in other words, are a matter of convention, things that groups of people agree to be "true," that is, they are intersubjective (Bailey 1991: xviii). Cultural constructivists have this in mind when they talk about science, the culture of scientists, and the development of scientific knowledge as a dialogic enterprise among scientists.

Pragmatic truth claims relate to particular groups of people, that is, it's true for us, or because of its specific useful outcomes in accomplishing certain tasks. In other words, a proposition is true if it works, meaning that acting on or believing the proposition produces desired consequences (Crumley 1999: 40) Philosophers such as Richard Rorty (1998) subscribed to this type of truth concept. As an example, consider the theories for the peopling of the Americas again. In these terms, the account of the Asiatic origin of the inhabitants of the Americas based on the archaeological record and scientific anthropological and genetic data may count as evidence for us in relation to our epistemic system suited to our purposes. However, this is not the case for the Native Americans. For them, their ancestors originated in an underground spirit world, which counts as evidence in relation to their epistemic system that is better suited to their purposes (Boghossian 2006: 24). Pragmatic truths of this kind can also violate the law of noncontradiction, which stipulates that something can't be true while its opposite is concurrently true as well. For example, this understanding of truth leads to the assertion that the first Americans came from Asia and that they originated in a subterranean supernatural realm (Boghossian 2006: 40).

Of the types of truths discussed, coherence and pragmatism, while not adequate justifications of truth on their own, comprise necessary conditions for truth. This means that the criteria associated with each have to be present, but on their own are not sufficient to establish the truth of a proposition. Or as Dew and Foreman (2014: 59) have put it, coherence and pragmatism may be used as a test for truth.

Science is based on truth by correspondence This premise holds that the truth of propositions depends upon "the way the world is," or whether they correspond to empirical facts (Williams 2001: 139). Norris (1997: vii) provides the following description:

> Realist philosophers of science . . . insist that what makes our theories and beliefs true or false is the way things stand in reality and not just the way reality is "constructed" in accordance with this or that type of cultural world-view, descriptive scheme, communal belief-system or whatever.

Or to put it another way, we live in an external world/universe that exists independently of our perceptual apparatus rather than being generated by them, and these external conditions comprise the conditions of knowledge (Williams 2001: 32, 138). True propositions must accord with reality. Science aims to supply accurate descriptions of this external reality (Okasha 2016: 54).

Its goals are explanations and the validation of those explanations (Reyna 1994: 556). An explanation is a proposition made up of sets of related concepts that explain "how and why reality is constituted as it is" (Reyna 1994: 556). Highly abstract propositions are called theories; while less abstract ones are referred to as empirical generalizations or hypotheses.

This understanding of truth is not a fiction invented by power-hungry madmen in white lab coats, as epistemic skeptics alleged. It is a notion of truth that has been a predominant assumption among virtually all people across space and time and is foundational to human thinking, as was discussed in chapter 6. Stated differently, it is pre-theoretic or pre-reflective, rather than being the product of complex theoretical argumentation about truth (Dew and Foreman 2014: 57).

Another aspect of science relevant to this discussion is that there is a difference between conditions that hold in the context of discovery and those that occur in the context of justification. Discovery proceeds via a combination of intuitive conjecturing, ad hoc testing, and practical experience. Justification entails conceptual-explanatory hypotheses that explain particular observations and anomalies. Moreover, feedback occurs between these two contexts. Grotesque caricaturing occurs if one collapses the two processes (e.g., Feyerabend 1993: 147–149), elevates one over the other, or ignores the reciprocal interaction between the context of discovery and justification (Norris 1997: 252).

Central to the scientific perspective is that truth claims are assessed against the obdurate matrix of empirical facts or objective reality. As Gorham (2017: 52) says, this request reflects the view that "the ultimate arbiter in science is the empirical world itself." Or as Dew and Foreman (2014: 58) put it, scientific propositions must be grounded in the real world and ontological finality rests with nature itself. This commits science to the pursuit of the truth about nature wherever it leads regardless of whose cultural sensibilities or proprietary feelings are offended (Fishman and Boudry 2013: 923).

Scientifically objective knowledge is thus generated through critical operations designed to help us decide which among the multiplicity of possibilities more accurately reflects the case with respect to the empirical evidence. Logically all claims to knowledge about objective reality cannot be correct. They can all be false, but only one can be true. To determine which claim to knowledge is the most accurate representation of reality, science employs particular epistemological operations. The criteria for scientifically objective knowledge are public verification and testability through peer review (Sidky 2004: 25–32; 2020:57–92).

In other words, the validity of propositions must be assessed independently of the biases, prejudices, and office of the researcher proposing it. This requires that propositions "be capable of test by reference to publicly ascertainable evidence" by qualified others, with the added stipulation that all propositions so tested are to be only provisionally accepted and are subject to review, modification, and even rejection (Hempel 1965: 334). McIntyre (2015: 120) explains:

> The distinguishing characteristic of science is not just reliance on empirical evidence, but openness to revision in those theories that are offered to *explain* that evidence. Science is an open process, where results are shared and theories are freely criticized. And the only goal is to make one's explanation better: to get them closer to the truth.

Similarly, as the evolutionary biologist Douglas Futuyma (1982: 163) put it:

> The hallmark of science is not the question: "Do I wish to believe this?" but the question "What is the evidence?" It is this demand for evidence, this habit of cultivated skepticism that is most characteristic of the scientific way of thought. It is not limited to science, but it isn't universal either. Many people still cling to traditional beliefs in the face of contrary evidence, out of wishful thinking, or desire for security and simplicity. . . . Science challenges not only nonscientific views but established scientific views as well.. . . Our knowledge can progress only if we can find errors and learn from them. Thus, much of the history of science consists of a rejection or modification of views that were once widely held currently accepted beliefs are provisional.

And Carl Sagan (1995: 304) described the role of skepticism in scientific thinking:

> At the heart of science is an essential balance between two seemingly contradictory attitudes—an openness to new ideas, no matter how bizarre or counterintuitive, and the most ruthless skeptical scrutiny of all ideas, old and new. The collective enterprise of creative thinking and skeptical thinking, working together, keeps the field on track.

These attributes set science apart from all other ways of knowing because, as the scientific anthropologist Marvin Harris (2001: 27) stated it eloquently long ago:

> In the entire course of prehistory and history, only one way of knowing has encouraged its own practitioners to doubt their own premises and to systematically expose their own conclusions to the hostile scrutiny of nonbelievers.

For these reasons, as McIntyre (2015: 120) adds, "science is the opposite of ideology, which disrespects truth by trying to substitute wish-fulfillment for facts."

Science works because it entails the systematic and critical evaluation of claims to knowledge through a unique combination of logical analysis and appraisal of empirical evidence, public peer review, and the detection and correction of errors. Sagan (1995: 20–21) put it best:

> Science thrives on errors, cutting them away one by one. False conclusions are drawn all the time, but they are drawn tentatively. Hypotheses are framed so they are capable of being disproved. A succession of alternative hypotheses is confronted by experiment and observation. Science gropes and staggers toward improved understanding. Proprietary feelings are of course offended when a scientific hypothesis is disproved, but such dis-proofs are recognized as central to the scientific enterprise.

Scientifically objective knowledge, therefore, is the knowledge that is obtainable independently by different investigators employing the same set of procedures and observations and the check that the scientific community exerts upon research findings. This is one method through which errors are found and corrected (Futuyma 1982: 164, 167). It is for this reason that scientific knowledge changes and grows over time as researchers uncover and correct errors (see Kuznar 2008: 17–49; Lett 1997a: 41–87; Sidky 2004: 25–32).

Given the nature of the scientific enterprise, all conclusions are provisional and subject to revision (Sidky 2004: 25–32, 2018). There are no absolute truths here as there are in religion or political ideologies and the inherent arrogance on which they are based. Scientists do not appeal to higher powers, paranormal beings, mystical forces, the authority of ancient texts, or the benediction of messiahs or saints, but rely upon the preponderance of evidence when assessing truth claims, which is the best chart toward the truth (cf., McIntyre 2015: 124). Thus, science "claims provisional certainty based upon a process of unrelenting skeptical inquiry in which no premise or assumption is ever considered to be beyond question" (Lett 1997a: 42).

Moreover, as noted, skepticism or doubt is applied with a commitment to finding better theories and is thus a valuable means of seeking out truth, not for the purposes of endorsing a universal rejection of all knowledge because of one's allegiance to a particular ideological position. Postmodern skepticism was a case in point of the latter position. When skepticism is misapplied as the postmodern literati employed it, as "a shield for one's prejudices. . . it can make a mockery of the search for truth" (McIntyre 2015: 124–125).

This relentless search for truth is the reason why science has been so successful and why it surpasses all other ways of knowing if the aim is to obtain factual knowledge about the world. As the anthropologist Russell Bernard (1995: 17) cogently pointed out: "Every phenomenon (including human thought and behavior) to which the scientific method has been systematically applied, over a sustained period of time, by a large number of researchers, has yielded its secrets."

Science deniers and delegitimizers have repeatedly attempted to depict this unique strength of science as its weakness, asserting that science cannot prove any of its theories in an absolute sense and therefore, its accounts are no different from mere opinions. Therefore, scientific truths are merely a matter of convention or agenda-driven agreement among scientists. However, as Barnett and Kaufman (2018: 468) point out:

> This self-correcting nature is not simply the principal strength of science; it is the fundamental core upon which all science is built. The goal of all scientific exploration is not to support a pet theory or confirm a hypothesis. It is to discover the truth. Nothing in science is above being revisited if our understanding of the universe changes.

The science-denial assertion used by various groups in the United States today, taken directly from postmodern thought, is that scientific truths entail "empirical adequacy" and empirical adequacy is not "truth" (Okasha 2016: 55).

In the post-truth era, science-denying religionists are harnessing this very argument to advance the legitimacy of their superstitious premises. I find this development particularly problematic for two reasons. First, fundamentalist religion is posing a threat to democracy and civil society (see Blaker 2003; Thompson and Smulewicz-Zucker 2018). Second, such beliefs have intruded into the discipline of cultural anthropology to transform it into a vehicle for proclaiming the truths of evangelical Christianity. I shall look at this development in chapter 10. Here I want to begin with a general overview of the attack by religionists on science and scientific knowledge (for a more detailed discussion, see Sidky 2020: 57–92).

We may begin with the ideas of Alvin Plantinga, one of the leading theologians and Christian apologists in this country. He argues that because all scientific conclusions are tentative and provisional, they are only "empirically adequate" theories rather than being "true theories" (Plantinga 2009: 154). He, therefore, proposes a substitute or alternate science, what he calls an "Augustinian science," a perspective based on Christian background knowledge, meaning the laundry list of archaic and medieval credulities and superstitions associated with a bygone and defunct worldview. In his words:

> A theory according to which God periodically adjusts the orbits of the planets, or has created life specially, or has intelligently designed certain features of the natural world [all of which would] fall under a general concept of science, but not under any of the cluster of scientific activities or enterprises characterized by methodological naturalism (Plantinga 2009: 159).

What this entails is the crude "strawman argument" employing postmodernist' misrepresentations that a valid or genuine science seeks absolute truths, which is obviously not the case with what passes for science. Plantinga's theistic commitments and supernaturalism prevent him from realizing that the reason science has been so massively successful in every field where it has been systematically applied in a sustained fashion is precisely because it jettisoned the ancient religious superstitions, irrationalism, and medieval delusions, what he calls the Christian "evidence base" and is trying to reinstate.

Science deniers and delegitimizers have also attacked science's naturalistic approach as a futile endeavor because the unobservable parts of reality are not accessible through sensory perception. It follows, therefore, that scientists have to rely on theoretical constructs (i.e., the theory-ladenness argument) to discuss these unobservable phenomena, which are nothing more than "convenient fictions" (Okasha 2016: 55–56). Okasha (2016: 57) states the objection to such an assertion as follows:

> [There is] already substantial knowledge of unobservable reality. For there is every reason to believe that our best scientific theories are true, and those theories talk about unobservable entities. Consider for example the atomic theory of matter, which says that all matter is made up of atoms. The atomic theory is capable of explaining a great range of facts about the world. . . . this is good evidence that a theory is true, i.e. that matter is really made up of atoms which behave as the theory says.

Many theories that entail unobservable entities, however, are empirically successful both by making discoveries that have technological and other earthly applications and by successfully predicting new observations, which would be impossible if such entities were "convenient fictions." This is based on an inference to the best explanation. These things would not be possible if there were not a precise fit between theory and empirical data. If atoms and electrons are convenient fictions then lasers would not work (Okasha 2016: 59). Indeed, a great deal of science involves unobserved entities, such as ice ages, dinosaurs, continental drift, and so on. The assertion that we cannot know unobservable things is hyperbole and implausible because it is tantamount to claiming that the overwhelming body of scientific conclusions does not constitute knowledge (Okasha 2016: 70).

Another objection is that the confidence scientists have in their theories is unwarranted (the underdetermination argument). The reason is that the data are explicable in terms of several mutually incompatible theories (Okasha 2016: 66–67; Williams 2001: 75–77). Kuhn, Feyerabend, and many of the French philosophers said this. However, this is the case in a very inconsequential sense because not all of the possible explanations on offer are ever equally good, in terms of simplicity, explanatory scope, better fit with theories in other areas of science, or predictive power leading to new observations (Okasha

2016: 68). If this was not so, and equally good alternative theories existed for every accepted one, then we would have endemic disagreements among scientists over pretty much everything, which is not the case (Okasha 2016: 68).

SCIENCE AND RELIGION IN A POST-TRUTH ERA

In the post-truth world, science is under attack from various quarters. In particular, emboldened and intolerant religious fundamentalists who have taken over the political arena with a vengeance are proclaiming that science is defunct, and hence their supernaturalism is justified (for a more detailed discussion, see Sidky 2020: 57–92). They are using arguments taken directly out of the postmodernists' science-denial playbook. These ideologues are also capitalizing upon the fatuous assumption shared by a number of practicing scientists that science and religion have separate domains. A strident proponent of this idea was the evolutionary biologist Stephen Jay Gould (1999). He put it as follows:

> Science simply cannot (by its legitimate methods) adjudicate the issue of God's possible superintendence of nature. We neither affirm nor deny it; we simply can't comment on it as scientists. The net, or magisterium of science, covers the empirical realm: what is the universe made of (fact) and why does it work this way (theory). The magisterium of religion extends over questions of meaning and moral value. The two magisteria do not overlap, nor do they encompass all inquiry (consider, for example, the magisterium of art and the meaning of beauty). To cite the old clichés, science gets the age of rocks, and religion the rock of ages; science studies how the heavens go, religion how to go to heaven (Gould 1999: 6).

Gould (1999: 5) claimed that science and religion have their own distinct domains, which he described as the "non-overlapping magisteria," using the acronym NOMA. In this view, there is no conflict between science and religion, and they can happily exist side by side in deferential noninterference. This was never a good idea because it entails an erroneous characterization of science and religion.

Unfortunately and unwisely, several scientific organizations have embraced the NOMA idea, including the American Association for the Advancement of Science (AAAS) and the National Academy of Sciences (NAS). Consider the following statement by NAS:

> Science is limited to explaining the natural world by means of natural processes" and that explanations that entail supernatural or nonnaturalistic phenomena "are

outside the realm of science and not part of a valid science curriculum (NAS 1998: 126, 127).

Eugenie Scott (1999: 29), former director of the National Center for Science Education (NCSE) championed the same idea: "Science is a way of knowing that attempts to explain the natural world using natural causes. It is agnostic toward the supernatural—it neither confirms nor rejects it." The unfortunate problem that Gould and like-minded scientists ignored, as the anthropologist Jacob Pandian (2003: 168) points out, is that science and religion are not, cannot, and have never been complementary enterprises.

By adopting such a condescending position regarding religion, these scientific institutions and individuals cleared a space for religionists to proclaim that their superstitions are outside the scope of scientific appraisal or critique. In post-truth America, this has become more problematic, because now the central objective of the evangelical Christian proponents of so-called "scientific creationism" is to replace science with the Bible in our schools. Religionists do not want to coexist with science peacefully; they aspire to abolish it altogether.

Gould's conception of science is as absurd as his construal of religion. Here is his view of religion:

> Religion just can't be equated with Genesis literalism, the miracle of the liquefying blood of Saint Januarius . . . or the Bible codes of Kabbalah and modern media hype. . . . [If] colleagues wish to fight superstition, irrationalism, philistinism, ignorance, dogma, and a host of other insults to the human intellect (often politically converted into dangerous tools of murder and oppression as well), then God bless them—but don't call this enemy "religion." (Gould 1999: 208)

Sadly, there is overwhelming anthropological and historical evidence demonstrating that Gould's characterization of religion as an agnostic, humanistic philosophy free of supernatural assertions about the material world, paranormal beings, and magical happenings is patently false. What he left out, creationism, superstition, miraculous events, literalism, irrationalism, philistinism, ignorance, dogmatism, or all those things that "insult to the human intellect," are the defining features of the majority, if not all, of the religions that exist today (Coyne 2015: 109–110; Edis 2008: 31).

Moreover, NOMA is contradicted by the fact that religion entails numerous assertions about the nature and origins of life on earth, human nature, and the operation of the world and the universe, infiltrating into the heart of the magisteria Gould treats as the exclusive preserve of his agnostic scientists (Dawkins 1997, 2006; Edis 2008; Fishman and Boudry 2013; Stenger 2007).

NOMA is compatible with postmodern dogma about multiple equally valid epistemic systems, which was all the rage in academia at the time Gould was writing, which makes me wonder to what extent such ideas influenced him. The NOMA perspective falsely restricts the scope of science to the empirical world, thereby conceding that science has limitations and can say nothing about what is outside its specific domain. Moreover, NOMA makes space for and endorses "other ways of knowing" as worthy of belief and respect, including Christian superstitions and an endless array of other egregious paranormal and pseudoscientific nonsense.

It seems that Gould's overlapping magisteria idea is also very amenable to post-truth. This is because it has offered religionists an effective science-denial argument. If science has such limitations, combined with the avowal that science offers provisional or only empirically adequate explanations based on convenient fictions; therefore science is a spurious perspective or merely a story or opinion. These are all ideas for which today's post-truth religionists and science haters must thank the postmodern savants in our universities and colleges (Kakutani 2018: 18; McIntyre 2018: 141–148; Otto 2016: 199; Sidky 2018). It follows, therefore, that religious precepts and their absolute truths are a more valid option than an imperfect endeavor such as science. Praise the Lord!

Of course, this is all religionist wishful thinking. The validity of egregious and patently false superstitions is not enhanced because scientific knowledge is provisional (Slezak 2012: 408). Religion is not and can never be a substitute for science, no matter how strenuously its advocates labor to make it so.

Gould did not anticipate how NOMA provides a convenient out for the purveyors of obscurantist supernatural irrationalism who can now claim that all supernatural phenomena fall under their exclusive jurisdiction and empowers them to make outrageous claims about human nature, reproduction, stem cell research, the well-being of the planet, modern medicine, and so on with impunity. NOMA legitimizes superstitious beliefs by casting them as truth claims beyond or outside the scope of scientific evaluation (cf., Dawkins 2006: 59). Or to put it differently, it endorses the idea that supernaturalism does not require evidentiary justification. Plantinga states his case against science and evolutionary theory as follows:

> It is extremely hard to see how an empirical science, such as biology, could address such a theological question as [to] whether a process like evolution is or isn't directed by God. . . How could an empirical inquiry possibly show that God was not guiding and directing evolution? (in Scott 2008).

Let us break this statement down. First, Plantinga is saying that supernaturalism is immune to any evidentiary challenges from science. Second, theological questions are outside the legitimate domain of scientific inquiry. Third, religionists have access to God's special truths and insights about nature and evolution inaccessible to all others. Fourth, these insights qualify him to pontificate about the theological implications of biological evolution and science. But what credentials does a true-believing theologian such as Plantinga have that qualify him to say anything relevant about evolutionary theory or, for that matter, God that is of relevance to today's world when his imagination is weighed down by the tiresome and arcane superstitions such true-believers advocate? In the post-postmodern post-truth Idiot America, no one needs qualifications to render opinions regarding any matter, including scientific truths.

Science, however, has a great deal to say not only about whether or not God is directing evolution or any other processes or forces in the universe, but also about the existence of such entities as God or the gods (see Sidky 2020). It has, can, and must address the evidentiary basis of religious pronouncements and their factual claims about the world and universe, a point the anthropologist James Lett (1997b) made years ago. Thus, because religion makes all kinds of factual assertions about humans, human nature, the world, and universe, as the philosopher Herman Philipse (2014: 85) points out, religion cannot be exempted from critical assessment by scientific methods.

It should also be noted that not all religionists are content to restrict themselves to the intellectual preserve so graciously allotted to them by Gould. With the appearance of present-day emboldened and bellicose fundamentalism, some religionists reject NOMA. The reason is that it excludes crucial questions about the human condition, the world, and the universe for which they have faith-based, supernaturalistic answers. This is particularly true of the evangelical Christians who have entered the discipline of anthropology and are trying to convert it for their ideological purposes (see chapter 10).

POST-TRUTH RELIGION'S GRIEVANCE WITH SCIENTIFIC NATURALISM

NOMA holds that science is a priori a wholly naturalistic enterprise in its methodology and, by definition, is unqualified to address supernatural questions, such as the existence of gods, ghosts, miracles, revelations, resurrections, all of which are by this definition outside its investigatory scope (e.g., Scott 2001: 246; for a more detailed discussion, see Sidky 2020: 57–92). In other words, when it comes to such matters, science is "agnostic"; it does not confirm or deny the existence of supernatural and paranormal forces and beings (Scott 1999: 29). We may refer to this perspective as "intrinsic" methodological naturalism (Fishman and Boudry 2013).

This characterization of science entails a great deal of condescension and reflects the postmodern sensibilities and political correctness of its sponsors who are desperately trying to respectfully show that there is no conflict between science and religion. Perhaps the idea of "respectful noninterference" was a political strategy on the part of its sponsors to avoid alienating religious people and ensure their support through tax dollars. If so, then their efforts have been an abject failure (Coyne 2015: 113). More importantly, however, this is a false premise because it unnecessarily limits the scope of scientific inquiry and impedes science from following the evidence wherever it leads, and from repudiating erroneous beliefs (cf., Fishman 2009: 814).

The idea of methodological naturalism arose in the context of a legal case about teaching Intelligent Design creationism in public school, called *Kitzmiller v. Dover Area School District* (2005). It was an effort on the part of the scientists involved in the case to deflect the charge raised by the creationists that science has an a priori commitment to "metaphysical naturalism" and disallows the existence of supernatural forces and powers and without justification. The scientists in response were saying that science is naturalistic solely at the level of methodology—it is neutral at the ontological or metaphysical level (Boudry et al. 2010: 228).

Critics of this view within science have pointed out that methodological naturalism is not an accurate characterization of science, it is conceptually flawed, and it unnecessarily imposes restrictions on the scope of scientific research. Moreover, it implies that scientific assertions regarding the supernatural transgress the legitimate boundaries of the scientific enterprise.

There is considerable epistemological confusion over the appropriate characterization of science as an activity committed to intrinsic methodological naturalism. For instance, well-meaning science writers such as Chris Mooney and Sheril Kirshenbaum (2009: 103) accept that methodological naturalism is a fundamental feature of science to make a case that science and religion are not in conflict. They point out that in contrast to metaphysical naturalism, methodological naturalism is not a claim about "the fundamental reality of the world," and therefore does not exclude the possibility of supernatural and paranormal entities and forces, and hence science is not inherently atheistic (Mooney and Kirshenbaum 2009: 104). They add that science and religion are concerned with wholly distinct phenomena, bringing in NOMA, and thus a rapprochement between them is possible (Mooney and Kirshenbaum 2009: 106). They overlooked that religionists are no longer interested in respectful noninterference or a rapprochement. They desire to replace science with the Bible.

Mooney and Kirshenbaum go on to say that it is one thing to exclude supernatural causal forces from scientific explanations (i.e., intrinsic methodological naturalism), and another to assert that science can resolve the debate over the existence of a paranormal being such as God. The latter question, they contend, is entirely outside the legitimate scope of scientific inquiry. In making their case, these writers are adopting the exact position that zealous science-denying theistic philosophers and religious polemicists take, namely that science cannot say anything about the supernatural. The religionist Craig Keener (2011: 121–125), for example, uses this very argument to make a case for the veracity of the miracles in the New Testament by arguing that supernatural forces are outside the purview of science (for a critique, see Sidky 2020: 190–199).

Postmodern dogma, which has poisoned many aspects of intellectual life, enters the discussion as well. Mooney and Kirshenbaum (2009: 101) add that the scientific rational that belief in things for which there is no evidence is unjustified is objectionable because the term "evidence" presumes naturalism. God, they add, is a supernatural entity and not subject to physical laws; therefore, science and methodological naturalism can say nothing about such a being (Mooney and Kirshenbaum 2009: 100). Furthermore, these writers assert that scientists who do make any statements about the supernatural are reaching beyond the limitations of science that "end at the natural world" and are seeking to turn science into an anti-religious doctrine (Mooney and Kirshenbaum 2009: 182).

These well-meaning but mistaken science writers do not understand that methodological naturalism as they conceive it prevents science from its principal objective. That, to reiterate, is "to pursue the truth about the nature of reality on the basis of evidence, wherever it may lead" and to eradicated false beliefs from the public sphere (Fishman 2009: 814; Fishman and Boudry 2013: 923).

Such erroneous assumptions about the nature of science have provided plenty of ammunition to religionists and their many fellow-travelers in the post-truth world for their science denial. Unfortunately, despite all the condescension on the part of the proponents of NOMA, religionists have also made methodological naturalism itself a significant point of contention by again accusing scientists of an unjustifiable a priori philosophical prejudice and dogmatism toward supernaturalism or religion (Boudry et al. 2010: 228). The evangelical Christian apologist Mark Noll (1994: 186) argues, for instance, that scientific cosmological claims about the nature of the universe are merely faith-based assertions analogous to religious beliefs. This entails the fallacious contention first raised by the scientifically ignorant postmodern literati that science is a worldview or faith-based belief system. The comparison is false, as already discussed, because science is a method of discovering the truth, not a particular body of truths (Schick and Vaughn 2014: 160). Another religionist, the Intelligent Design ideologue William Dembski (2003: 91, 96) says that the scientific community has unfairly stacked the cards against creationism by "artificially defining science as limited to material mechanisms" that has "conveniently eliminated design from scientific discussions" (for a detailed critique of Intelligent Design see Sidky 2020:259–294).

Plantinga draws on postmodern anti-science ideas that facts in themselves and objective evidence do not exist and that all belief systems, therefore, have epistemic parity. He then argues that methodological naturalism is not the only path to a genuine science but is instead "a proposed condition or constraint on science" and "not a statement about the nature of the universe" (Plantinga 2009: 151). In other words, empirical phenomena are not the defining condition of knowledge and stating that they are is an arbitrary choice by scientists because of a dogmatic naturalistic bias, which is tantamount to atheism. Plantinga (2009: 151) adds that science is flawed because it excludes any theory that does not conform to methodological naturalism, "whatever its virtue." Clearly, postmodern philosophy has unleashed into the post-truth world all sorts of purveyors of superstitions and irrationalism who are asserting that their perspective is as legitimate as any other and are demanding that they are heard.

Plantinga neglects to provide or suggest any procedures as to how one assesses the "virtue" of such alternative theories. On faith? Revelation? What the gospels say? Ouija boards? An important point to consider, as Lett points out, is that if the supernatural is inaccessible through rational scientific inquiry, then how is it possible for human beings to have any knowledge of such phenomena. In other words, what kind of inquiry could possibly divulge the nature of the supernatural, if rational inquiry cannot? Moreover, if faith and revelation are the paths to such knowledge, then why have human beings using faith and revelation reached radically *different and contradictory* understandings of the supernatural? Virtually every religious person knows that supernatural claims are bogus because religious people reject out of hand nearly all of the hundreds of thousands of supernatural claims that have been made by adherents of other religions around the world over the past many millennia. Almost every religious person is convinced that all the *other* religions are *false* (Lett 2020, personal communication).

It is essential to note, however, that the clash between science and religion is not about methodological naturalism. It has nothing to do with empirical knowledge obtained via the five senses versus religious wisdom regarding some transcendental reality accessible by "other means of knowing." Instead, it is a clash of rationalism and irrationalism, or a conflict between rationality and superstition (Coyne 2015: xii; Lett 1997b: 54).

HOW SCIENCE REALLY WORKS

The methodology of science is more accurately characterized as an empirically grounded guideline based on the historical pattern of the uniform successes of naturalistic explanations and the consistent failure of supernatural postulates (Boudry et al. 2010: 230). The correct description of such a principle is "provisional" methodological naturalism. It is not an a priori presupposition but is a conclusion of science founded upon an inference to the best explanation given all the available scientific data (Fishman 2009: 830; Fishman and Boudry 2013: 924; see Carrier 2005a; Edis 1998, 2008: 28–32; Fishman and Boudry 2013; Gauch 2009; Isaak 2002).

In other words, science does not reject supernatural phenomena by philosophical fiat before appraising the evidence (Carrier 2005: 211). Scientists assume that nature is lawful, that things do not come into existence from nothingness, and that supernatural and psi phenomena are unsubstantiated in relation to empirically grounded a posteriori conclusions from scientific evidence (Fishman and Boudry 2013: 926–927).

The very fact that scientific findings are incompatible with a majority of supernatural, mystical, spiritual, and paranormal claims is a reliable indication that science provides evidence against such claims. Thus, using science to refute religious beliefs is not distorting science; it is doing what science is meant for, the eradication of erroneous beliefs about the world and universe (Fishman 2009: 814). The assertion that supernatural and paranormal claims fall outside the scope of scientific assessment, as claimed by proponents of intrinsic methodological naturalism claim, is therefore erroneous and unjustified.

Science has, does, and can assess supernatural hypotheses. As Fishman and Boudry (2013: 924) observe:

> Science can (and in fact has already evaluated) supernatural claims according to the same explanatory criteria used to assess any other "non-supernatural" claims. These criteria include explanatory virtues such as explanatory power (goodness of fit to the evidence), simplicity/parsimony (data compression unification), and non-ad hoc-ness (introduction of unsupported auxiliary hypotheses merely to save a hypothesis from disconfirmation). To the extent that a supernatural explanation satisfies these explanatory criteria better than rival naturalistic explanations, it should be provisionally favored. To the extent that it does not, it should provisionally be rejected.

However, the problem for religionists and paranormalists is that such systematic evaluations have consistently failed to provide confirmation. In other words, "supernatural claims do not fall beyond the reach of science; they have simply failed" (Boudry et al. 2010: 227). Or, as Coyne (2015: 113) puts it: "Over its history science has repeatedly investigated supernatural claims and, in principle, could find strong evidence for them. But that evidence has not appeared." Why has science been unable to find evidence for the supernatural? Fishman (2009: 831) offers the following:

The best explanation for why there has been so far no convincing, independently verifiable evidence for supernatural phenomena, despite honest and methodologically sound attempts to verify them, is that these phenomena probably do not exist. Indeed, the absence of evidence, where such evidence is expected to be found after extensive searching, is evidence of absence.

While there is always the possibility that we may yet encounter evidence for the supernatural, this is very unlikely to be the case. As the philosopher, Graham Oppy (2018: 14–15) observes, there is enough firmly corroborated science for the unreality of such things as ancestral spirits, astral intelligences, demon, fairies, ghosts, gods, vampires, witches, werewolves, yeti, zombies, karma, or psi to rule out the likelihood that a future science will recognize these things.

HOW SCIENCE ASSESSES NON-FALSIFIABLE CLAIMS

Purveyors of irrational points of view, whether religious or paranormal, take refuge behind the opinion that science can say nothing about their non-falsifiable claims. This is a weakness they think works in their favor. The claim, however, is untrue (Fishman 2009: 814; Fishman and Boudry 2013: 923).

Non-falsifiable propositions, whether they are supernatural, paranormal, or pseudoscientific, are open to critical scientific appraisal in relation to their observational earthly consequence. The issue is not whether such propositions are disprovable, but whether they are probable (Dawkins 2006: 54). Many paranormal, supernatural, and pseudoscientific claims have observational consequences. For example, that prayer heals the sick, God is all benevolent and would not allow evil in the world, the earth came into existence during the Bronze Age, irreducibly complex molecular structures are the handiwork of the theistic god, or that there was once an immense deluge that inundated the entire planet.

In cases of uncertain evidence, the credence of a proposition is assessed using a rule of inference known as "conditionalization," which tells us how to update our beliefs (Meacham 2016). Conditionalization is used extensively in Bayesian statistics. As Okasha (2016: 33) says, "The idea is that any rational scientist can be thought of as having an initial credence in their theory or hypothesis, which they then updated in light of new evidence by following the rule of conditionalization." We can thus assign a hypothesis a place on a range of probabilities going from complete skepticism, to a 50-50 agnosticism, to certainty (Fishman 2007: 818; Howson and Urbach 2006: 6–9, 91–130; Okasha 2016: 30).

These considerations fall within what is called the "Bayesian confirmation theory" that many consider a more accurate depiction of the way scientists assign or revise degrees of confidence in a hypothesis based on new evidence and a given prior probability. This means evaluating propositions according to the following three criteria: (1) prior probabilities, (2) the existence of disconfirming evidence, and (3) the availability of alternative non-paranormal explanations (Fishman 2009: 825). The Bayesian perspective is an alternative to the classical approach in science that prevailed during most of the twentieth century under the influence of the philosopher Karl Popper and the statistician Ronald Fisher (Howson and Urbach 2006: xi).

The assessment of an unfalsifiable claim to knowledge begins with criterion number 1, prior probabilities. Applicable here is Carl Sagan's (1980) reiteration of David Hume's (1902 [1748]: 112) stipulation regarding the occurrence of miracles, which is that "extraordinary claims require extraordinary evidence" (cf., Truzzi 1978: 11). The more extraordinary a claim, the lower its prior probability based on our background knowledge and the heavier burden of proof upon the person making a claim to offset the low initial probability of the proposition being true (Fishman 2009: 817). The low probability of a fantastic or extraordinary claim based on what we already know about how the world operates is a good reason for skepticism. A skeptical stance is initially justified even if there is no direct evidence against the claim.

The availability of disconfirming evidence, criterion number 2, is another way to evaluate a hypothesis. One expects to find evidence if a proposition is correct and to find none if it is false. Consider claims about the existence of paranormal beings of mythology or parapsychology. The philosopher of science Michael Scriven (1966: 156) put it as follows:

> Ancient myths chiefly concern creatures of whose existence no *disproof* could be given, but that lack scarcely affects our view that there is not now, nor was there ever, a centaur, a unicorn, a Zeus, a Circe.

The complete lack of evidence for a phenomenon provides justification to doubt its existence. The philosopher of science Norwood Hanson (1971: 323) made the following observation regarding the God hypothesis:

> If looking and not finding does not constitute grounds for denying the existence of God, then looking and not finding does not constitute grounds for denying the existence of goblins, witches, devils, five-headed Welshmen, Unicorns, mermaids, Loch Ness monsters, flying saucers, Hobbits, Santa Claus . . . etc. But there are excellent grounds for denying the existence of such entities. They consist not simply in the failure to find and identify such remarkable creatures. Rather, these grounds consist largely in the fact that there is no good reason whatsoever for supposing that such creatures *do* exist.

What is involved here is not a formal, deductive demonstration, such as a mathematical proof for the existence of the highest prime number, which entails calculation. Instead, it is proof based on the inductive description of gathered evidence, which requires looking for actual evidence and relying on what we know about the world (Hanson 1971: 310–311).

Assessing a proposition according to criterion 3 is to compare it to plausible alternative hypotheses that are more consistent with other empirical explanations and observations. Such alternatives justify skepticism regarding a paranormal explanation. Science has provided alternative empirical explanations for many phenomena once considered to be supernatural, such as comets, meteorites, bat sonar, paranormal causes of disease, the idea that nature is the handiwork of a supernatural designer, and much more (Fishman 2009: 824). The existence of more plausible and parsimonious alternate and empirically grounded explanations are always ample reasons to justify skepticism toward a truth claim on offer.

As a final thought, the totality of our scientific theories in physics, chemistry, biology, molecular genetics, neuroscience, archaeology, scientific anthropology, and geology, is the best there is (Pinker 2018: 393–395). "Science," as the philosopher Peter Slezak (2012: 406) puts it, is the only game in town: "There is no alternative to our best theories other than the worse ones." Christian metaphysics or the metaphysics of the myriad other supernatural and pseudoscientific perspectives cannot offer better understandings of cosmology, quantum physics, molecular biology, the structure of DNA, epidemiology, the evolution of life on earth, the origins of culture, the rise of complex societies, and so forth.

Chapter 8

The Problem of Pseudoscience in Post-Truth America

As indicated in the previous chapters, postmodern academics and iconic irrationalist philosophers, such as Feyerabend, and to some extent Kuhn, in their efforts to denigrate science encouraged and endorsed pseudoscientific viewpoints, paranormalism, and other forms of irrational beliefs as marginalized voices that needed a hearing. Why? Because pseudoscientific claims undermine the authority of science and erode trust in the reliability of scientific knowledge and expertise. The epistemic relativists are, in part, responsible for the present-day proliferation of pseudoscientific beliefs and assertions. This chapter examines the problem of pseudoscience and its place in the alternative post-truth epistemology.

What is pseudoscience? Epistemic relativists would say that this a pejorative turf-protecting term used by scientists to refer to the multitude of equally valid epistemic systems to which various groups and individuals subscribe. It is pejorative, they would add, because there are no differences between what passes as "science" and pseudoscientific perspectives. In post-truth America, this type of reasoning has empowered purveyors of a wide variety of nonsensical and irrational beliefs to demand that their voices be heard and the validity of their beliefs recognized and respected. This post-truth society and culture has lost respect for "leveling evidence from science," as Otto (2016: 199–200) puts it, has no clue about the role and function of science anymore, considers truth to be a matter of perspective, and substitutes emotions for empirical evidence.

History shows that when societies have become detached from reality, they are incapable of understanding and addressing serious treats and worldly problems and often venture into error and folly. Carl Sagan (1995: 208) put it this way: "When governments and societies lose the capacity for critical thinking, the results can be catastrophic—however sympathetic we may be toward those who have bought the baloney." For reasonable people, these are challenging circumstances where, as Barnett and Kaufman (2018: 467) observe, "fighting for truth is a battle against an amaranthine flow of true believers armed with ignorance and misinformation." We are amid a pandemic of credulous thinking. The irony is that as the sociologist of religion, Damian Thompson (2008: 15) points out: "At a time when our techniques for evaluating evidence is subtler than ever, counter-knowledge [pseudoscience] is not only fooling the public but also corrupting intellectual standards across a range of disciplines."

America is inundated with pseudoscientific beliefs (Beyerstein 1995; Kaufman and Kaufman 2018; Shermer 2002a). The list of what is currently on offer is extensive. Here are just a few examples: Ufology (the study of UFOs), crop circles, alien abductions, ancient astronaut theory, the face[s] on Mars, astrology, fortunetelling, crystal power, psychic surgery, numerology, spiritualism, channeling, mediumship, séances, ghost beliefs, spirit possession, poltergeists, extra-sensory perception (ESP), faith healing, homeopathy, aura analysis, the anti-vaccination movement, climate change denial, Scientology, and Intelligent Design Creationism. Or consider the rejection of scientific medical information on COVID-19 by the Trumpians in favor of Donald Trump's "natural ability" to second guess medical experts by offering pseudoscientific remedies, such as injection of household cleaners and the placement of UV lights inside the human body (Brink 2020). Or more recently, consider Trump's endorsement of the beliefs of Stella Immanuel, a snake oil seller who insists that masks are ineffective against the spread of COVID-19 and claims that scientific medical researchers are using alien DNA to develop a vaccine to make people immune to religious beliefs (Stracqualursi 2020). This is why it is perhaps with justification that Kurt Andersen and Charles Pierce refer to this country as Fantasyland or Idiot America.

In this chapter, I wish to answer the following question: Are the epistemic relativists correct that there is no difference between what passes as "science" and those theories and doctrines labeled pseudoscientific or pseudoscience? This, after all, is one of the foundational constituents of the alternative post-truth epistemology.

We may start with some preliminary definitions because pseudoscience is a slipper notion easier to identify than to define (Ruse 2018: 241). In his book *Pseudoscience and the Paranormal* (2003), professor of neurology Terence Hines describes pseudoscience as "a doctrine or belief system that pretends to be a science" (Hines 2003: 13). According to anomalous psychologists, Christopher French and Anna Stone (2014: 278) pseudoscience refers to "theories, assumptions, and methods that, although adopting the superficial trappings of science, are not truly scientific." More simply, pseudoscience means pretended science. The philosopher Michael Ruse (2018:

241–242) refers to it as claims purporting to be knowledge but are driven by ideological beliefs rather than by the empirical world. There is more to the definition than is provided here, and I shall get back to this issue later in this chapter. For now, we may think of pseudoscience as it appears in the post-truth world as "counter-knowledge" based on "alternative facts" (cf., Thompson 2008: 1).

One could ask what is wrong if people hold such beliefs? What is the harm? The philosophers of science Massimo Pigliucci and Maarten Boudry (2013: 3) point out some grave issues:

> In the form of creationism and its challenges to the study of evolution, pseudoscience has done great damage to public education in the United States and elsewhere; it has swindled people of billions of dollars in the form of "alternative" medicine like homeopathy; it has caused a lot of emotional distress, for example, to people who are told by mystics and assorted charlatans that they can talk to their dead loved one. Conspiracy theories about AIDs, which are widespread in many African countries and even in the United States, have literally killed countless human beings throughout the world. Denialism about climate change, which seems to be ineradicable in conservative political circles, may even help to bring about a worldwide catastrophe. Dangerous cults and sects such as Scientology, which are based on pseudoscientific belief systems, continue to attract followers and wreak havoc in people's lives.

Americans spent over $30 billion out of pocket in 2012 alone on bogus complementary healthcare (Barnett and Kaufman 2018: 473). Numerous people have died because of their trust in sham alternative medical cures and supernatural remedies, and many others have lost their life savings by believing in pretended psychics, diviners, and miracle workers (Ruse 2018: 252–255; Smith 2010: 21–32). Horrifyingly tragic is that 300,000 people in South Africa died of AIDS between the years 2000 and 2004, according to Harvard University estimates, because the government of President Thabo Mbeki refused to allow western antiretroviral drugs, a decision based on bogus science. As an alternative, his Ministry of Health suggested that AIDS is curable using lemon juice and garlic (Boseley 2008; Dugger 2008; McIntyre 2019). In his book *Denying AIDS: Conspiracy Theories, Pseudoscience, and Human Tragedy* (2009), Seth Kalichman provides a detailed examination of the ghastly consequences of pseudoscientific AIDS denialism and its devastating impact on public health in South Africa.

But there is another significant concern. We are led into major error when we have no basis for assessing contending claims to knowledge, substitute ideology for science by political fiat or wishful thinking, rescind appeal to empirical reality, and hold beliefs simply because we feel they are true for us. A grim example of what happens when travelling down this path is Lysenkoism during the Stalinist period in the former Soviet Union. The historian Michael Gordin (2012: 81) has argued that this case, which was considered by Western scientists to be the most egregious form of pseudoscience in the twentieth century, galvanized their reactionary construal of pseudoscience. Let's begin here because there are important lessons to be learned.

At the forefront of this venture was Trofim Denisovich Lysenko (1898–1976), who eventually became director of Genetics for the Academy of Sciences in the Soviet Union (Dejong-Lambert 2012; Graham 2016; Joravsky 1970). He was an agronomist not a genetic scientist, but he was a well-versed and cunning political ideologue who pontificated about science not unlike many present-day scientifically illiterate U.S. politicians, including Donald Trump.

Using Marxist rhetoric, Lysenko convinced Joseph Stalin (1879–1953), the general secretary of the Communist Party and premier of the Soviet Union, that evolutionary genetics developed in the West was incompatible with Marxist philosophy (Medvedev 1969; Soifer 1994). For Lysenko, the science of genetics was nothing more than the ideological instruments of the capitalist establishment to justify class oppression and rationalize the privileged position of the bourgeoisie. Through the efforts of Lysenko, the ideas of both Darwin and Mendel were expunged from the Soviet sciences. In 1948, Stalin outlawed Mendelian genetics altogether (Staski and Marks 1992: 106).

Lysenko's own genetic theory, or his "proletarian science" (Lecourt 1977), was a variant of Jean-Baptiste Lamarck's (1744–1892) theory of inheritance of acquired characteristics. Lamarck believed that species evolved and changed through time as a result of adjustments to the effects of the environment in which they lived and that the traits acquired in life by parents could be passed on to the next generation. The idea that acquired characteristics are hereditary predates Lamarck. His contribution was to apply it to the origin of species (Gould 2002: 177–178; Zirkle 1946: 91–92). Lamarck's prestige was high among Soviet Marxists primarily because his work figured prominently in the book *The Dialectics of Nature* (1876), written by Friedrich Engels, the world's number two Marxist. Engels adopted a Lamarckian perspective as a result of the influence of the work of the famous nineteenth-century American anthropologist Lewis Henry Morgan, who espoused a Lamarckian form of evolution (Service 1985: 49).

Outside the Soviet Union, Lamarck's views had long been discarded as false, in favor of the theory of evolution through natural selection proposed by Charles Darwin (1809–1882). The Darwinian view was merged with Gregor Mendel's (1822–1884) principles of genetics in the 1930s and 1940s, to form the Synthetic Theory of Evolution, which has since been expanded in relation to finding in molecular genetics (see Ayala and Fitch 1997; Kutschera and Niklas 2004; Staski and Marks 1992: 105–106). Lysenko, however, convinced Stalin that he had developed a science of genetics based upon, or compatible with, Marxist philosophy using the principle that nature is perfectible by human agency.

Appointed director of Genetics for the Academy of Sciences, Lysenko was given control over biological scientific research in the Soviet Union. He thus managed to substitute authority and ideology for science, or imposed authority and ideology upon science. This vulgar and scientifically illiterate bureaucrat had his rivals, some of the finest minds and leading scientists and geneticists of the time among them, executed, put in jail, or threatened into silence (Futuyma 1982: 162). He also managed to expunge genetics and scientific biology from Soviet education to its great impairment, circumstances that lasted until the 1960s (Gordin 2012: 79–95; Gorham 2017: 140).

Through the application of his theory, Lysenko promised to transform Soviet agriculture for the better. He would do this by creating new and improved varieties of crops by exposing grains of wheat to different environmental influences, which, he argued, would transform their genetic properties. In just one generation, Lysenko declared, winter wheat could be changed into spring wheat by merely altering the temperatures in which it grew. He even maintained that he could transform one species into another, for example, wheat into rye, by planting it in the appropriate environment. Lysenko dismissed the Darwinian idea that species competed with one another for survival as a bourgeois prop to rationalize class inequality in capitalist societies. Nature was based, not on competition, he argued, but on altruism. He, therefore, recommended that seeds should be planted in clusters so that all except for one would "sacrifice themselves for the good of the species."

After gaining control over biological research and agriculture in the Soviet Union beginning in the 1930s, Lysenko destroyed them, and agricultural production slid further and further into a disaster. Lysenko never had any evidence to support his bogus science, but his political clout made him invulnerable. He was not deposed until after Stalin's death and Khrushchev's resignation in 1965 (Futuyma 1982: 162).

Due to Lysenko's perversions, not only were the Soviet biological sciences and science education set back many decades compared to the West, but more tragically, his pseudoscience resulted in a series of disastrous crop failures during the 1930 and 1940s. An even greater tragedy occurred when Mao Zedong employed Lysenko's sham science in Communist China. According to Windschuttle (1998: 7, 200):

> [Mao] used Russian theory to draw up eight rules for Chinese farming, one of which commanded that seedlings should be planted much closer together than before. The theory that they would die if crowded was relegated to the competitive assumption of bourgeois science whereas the Great Helmsman's proletarian

theory claimed plants of the same "background" would fraternally share light and food.

In China, Lysenko's sham science was in part responsible for one of the worst famines in human history between the years 1958 and 1963, resulting in the death of up to forty million people during Mao's Great Leap Forward (Becker 1996; Windschuttle 1998: 7).

Lysenko's efforts are highly reminiscent of attempts by present-day U.S. politicians and their corporate sponsors and religious allies to manipulate science by insisting on the uncertain and tentative status of established scientific findings regarding climate change, evolutionary theory, contraception, and embryonic stem cell therapy (Gorham 2017: 141). To this list we can add Trump's appalling stance on COVID-19 that has led to thousands of needless deaths.

The disaster caused by Lysenko is a somber example of what happens when political fiat or wishful thinking are substituted for scientific research. It should be a warning to contemporary U.S. politicians who are striving to undermine science, wish to extricate the input of scientific research from policy decisions, or threaten scientists with federal prosecution, for example, James Inhofe, Republican senator from Oklahoma (Pilt 2010). Lysenko consulted his sacred book, Karl Marx's *Das Kapital*, while Inhofe relies on the Bible. Quoting Genesis 8: 221, Inhofe reassures Americans that climate alarmists forget that: "God is still up there, and He promised to maintain the seasons and that cold and heat would never cease as long as the earth remains." He confidently adds: "The arrogance of people to think that we, human beings, would be able to change what He is doing in the climate is to me outrageous" (Grim 2015). Thus, in Idiot America archaic and medieval credulities and supernaturalism are guiding policy decisions that have potential negative consequences for everyone on this planet.

What can we learn from Lysenko's fiasco? In his book *Science on Trial* (1982), the evolutionary biologist Douglas Futuyma (1982: 162) offers the following assessment:

> A grim story indeed, but what do we learn from it? That reality stubbornly refuses to be bent to our desires or ideologies. Genes cannot be altered to suit our ends, as devoutly as we may wish them to be. Truth cannot be established by the Communist Party, nor by the vote of a democratic society or a board of education. Reality does not yield to wishful thinking.

To answer the question raised at the start of this discussion: Yes, there is a difference between science and those theories and doctrines labeled pseudoscientific. Why? First, pseudoscience is not the same as "erroneous science." Lots of scientific hypotheses turn out to be wrong. Second, it is also different from bad science due to incompetence or carelessness. As Lilienfeld (2018: xv) points out:

> Pseudoscientific claims differ from incorrect scientific claims, and in many ways are far more pernicious, because they are deceptive. Because they appear at first blush to be scientific, they can fool us. To most untrained eyes, they appear to be the real thing, but they are not.

Recall that in post-truth America people are primed to accept nearly any pseudo-profound bullshit, if it bolsters prejudice and superstitions or enhances profits.

Third, pseudoscience is also different from scientific fraud (McIntyre 2019). This includes such acts as plagiarism, falsifying evidence, and fabricating experimental results in the pursuit of personal or professional status, tenure, promotion, or to obtain research funding.

What sets pseudoscientific perspectives apart from science is their approach to evidence (Lilienfeld 2005). It is important to note that there is no consensus among philosophers of science over the precise criteria for demarcating science and pseudoscience (see the volumes edited by Pigliucci and Boudry 2013 and Kaufman and Kaufman 2018). However, this does not mean that the issue should be put aside, as the philosopher of science Larry Laudan (1983: 125) advised, stating that the term pseudoscience is meaningless and only useful as a rhetorical tool. In his book *The Pseudoscience Wars*, the historian Michael Gordin (2012: 3, 79, 206) takes a similar position. However, lots of philosophers of science disagree, stressing that defending the scientific perspective by making a distinction between sense and nonsense is imperative given the deluge of intransigent purveyors of pseudoscientific theories and esoteric postulates confronting the general public and educators (Mahner 2013: 29; Pigliucci 2013: 26).

The demarcation problem is complex and need not detain us further here. For this discussion, we can move forward by keeping a few ideas in mind. Let us begin with the general criteria offered by Pigliucci and Boudry (2013: 2):

> If a theory strays from the epistemic desiderata of science by a sufficiently wide margin while being touted as scientific by its advocates, it is justifiably branded as pseudoscience.

First, pseudoscientific theories forward extraordinary claims in the absence of the necessary extraordinary evidence. Its proponents are unconcerned that their claims have an especially high burden of proof. Usually, the evidence provided comes in the form of anecdotes, myths, folklore, testimonials, and eyewitness reports that are always problematic and unreliable. As the philosopher and physicist Victor Stenger (2012: 235) put it, "The plural of anecdote is not data." There are a host of human cognitive and perceptual errors that along with the constructive nature of memory that make anecdotal and eyewitness reports particularly unreliable (French and Wilson 2003; Hines 2003: 238; Smith 2010: 142).

Second, in contrast to science that presupposes a natural, causal, and lawful world (Mahner 2013: 38), pseudoscientific theories often postulate the operation of paranormal energies, supernatural forces, and otherworldly beings. Third, pseudoscientific propositions are framed to be proof exempt with ad hoc postulates to address contradictory evidence rendering them unfalsifiable (Sagan 1995: 21). Hence, such hypotheses do not get adjusted or changed. For example, believers in psychic powers rationalize scientific disconfirmations of their cherished hypotheses by attributing the failures to the "psi experimenter effect," that is, that paranormal phenomena disappear in the presence of skeptical scientific observers. The psi proposition is thus retained despite the strength of the counterevidence. In scientific research, however, disconfirmation leads to the alteration or discarding of hypotheses. For this reason, pseudoscientific knowledge does not grow, it does not yield new information, and nothing concrete is ever learned (Coker 2001).

Fourth, proponents of pseudoscientific explanations often attempt to place the burden of proof on the nonbeliever. For example, prove that extraterrestrial beings or ghosts do not exist. However, the burden of proof is entirely and always upon the proponent of an extraordinary claim, and the more extraordinary a claim is in relation to what we know about the world the greater the burden of proof on those making the claim (Fishman 2009: 817).

Finally, pseudoscientific perspectives depend on an anything-goes approach to knowledge, use persuasion through rhetoric rather than valid evidence, ignore rational standards, and argue from logical fallacies, such as the argument from ignorance, reduction to absurdity, appeal to authority, special pleading, and the least plausible hypothesis, among others (Coker 2001). Subjective validation and appeal to emotion and sentiment replace justification in relation to objective empirical evidence (Coker 2001; Gardner 1957: 12–14; Sidky 2004: 25, 397). Schick and Vaughn (2104: 4) describe the underlying premise of pseudoscientific approaches as follows:

> There's no such thing as objective truth. We make our own truth. There's no such thing as objective reality. We make our own reality. There are spiritual, mystical, or inner ways of knowing that are superior to our ordinary ways of knowing. If an experience seems real, it is real. If an idea feels right to you, it is right. We are incapable of acquiring knowledge of the true nature of reality. Science itself is irrational or mystical. It's just another faith or belief system

or myth, with no more justification than any other. It doesn't matter whether beliefs are true or not, as long as they're meaningful to you.

By contrast, science explores the nature of reality, and the ultimate arbitrator is whether or not there is evidentiary justification for believing a claim about some aspect of existence (Fishman 2009: 830). Claims can be assessed in terms of their evidentiary support or whether they have an epistemic warrant. In other words, one way to get around the semantics of demarcation is to use evidentiary justification to assess claim as "bad, poor, or even stupid theories" (Truzzi 1996: 574). It is not the best solution, but a workable one. There are lots of pseudoscientific claims that fail this measure, such as astrology versus astronomy, evolutionary biology verse creationism, therapeutic touch versus scientific medicine, ancient astronaut theory versus scientific archaeology, and so forth (cf., Mahner 2013: 35).

Pseudoscientific beliefs arise from and are an expression of archaic irrational modes of thought that predate science by millennia and have been the source of all sorts of false, fanciful, and patently false beliefs about humans and the nature of the world and universe (cf., Sagan 2001: 385). Many pseudoscientific ideas fall in the category of what philosopher Stephen Law (2016) calls "X-claims." These refer to false beliefs about incorporeal agents, miraculous powers and forces, extraordinary events, magical healings, and holy relics. Such ideas and perceptions stem from particular human perceptual and cognitive biases and proclivities. People everywhere rely on X-claims to explain phenomena that they cannot otherwise explain, and they also comprise the foundational tenets in many religions, including mainstream ones (Law 2016: 16, 23). X-claims are almost always based on testimony and subjective experience and are systematically unreliable. The human cognitive and perceptual apparatus is particularly vulnerable to cyber-attacks by X-claims that create false impressions and conclusions.

The cognitive underpinnings of X-claims include a range of factors and I shall only mention a few (see Blancke and Smedt 2013; Blanco and Matute 2018; Bukens 2013; Shackel 2013; Sidky 2020: 121–172; Trivers 2011). There is group-think, which becomes operational when enthusiastic people with similar beliefs and attitudes interact. Hindsight bias leads a particular outcome to fit a prediction after the fact. Then there is selective memory, which refers to our tendency to recall events that stand out and forget those that are uninteresting. Memory conformity occurs when multiple spectators of an unusual or anomalous event, such as a crime, sightings of UFOs, apparitions of the Virgin Mary, ghosts, or monsters, discuss the incident among themselves before offering a formal statement.

A potent cognitive predisposition is the confirmation bias, which has been discussed in previous chapters, that leads people to seek out any confirmatory evidence for their beliefs while systematically ignoring information that disputes them (Goode 2012: 296; Smith 2010: 144). There is also the backfire effect when disconfirmation of one's deeply held convictions leads to a doubling down on those beliefs. Moreover, there is cognitive dissonance, which arises when someone holds two sets of conflicting beliefs and uses clever rationalizations of those beliefs to resolve the conflict, rather than changing them (Festinger et al. 1956: 3).

Our theory of mind renders the possibility of the existence of all sorts of nonmaterial paranormal beings, such as ghosts of dead people, primordial ancestors, and deities. Also, our hyperactive agency-detection cognitive module makes us continually scan the environment for possible signs of agency and under certain circumstances can also cause the perception of disembodied agents, such as ghosts, spirits, angels, and so forth. Our innate pattern-finding attributes makes us prone to find apparent meaningful connections in random data or meaningless noise, called *apophenia*, and leads to the perception of shapes, like faces, in random stimuli, called *pareidolia*. We thus think we have detected hidden codes in holy books, posit conspiracies by connecting random bits of data, hear ghostly voices in electronic static, and see human-like faces on Mars, and so on (see Shermer 2002b; Sidky 2020: 121–173). These cognitive biases have far-reaching implications in explaining why humans are predisposed to pseudoscientific and paranormal beliefs and are a rationality defeater for them (cf., Law 2016: 32).

Pseudoscience and irrational modes of thinking are always harmful. The Lysenko fiasco is but one example. History has shown that societies caught up in pseudoscientific fantasies, "alternative ways of knowing," a hatred of science and scientific knowledge, and associate irrational belief often go down the path to perdition. A horrifying case in point is Nazis Germany, run by a regime bolstered by pseudoscience. The Nazis touted a philosophical perspective analogous to postmodernism, including the adoration of one of the apostles of postmodern savants, the philosopher Friedrich Nietzsche (Hitler's favorite philosopher), from whom the postmodernists acquired their distrust of rationality, truth, and democracy.

Like the postmodernists, the Nazis were vehemently opposed to Enlightenment ideals and everything associated with them, including science, rationality, and democratic principles. Central to Nazi ideology were the beliefs of the many anti-science, anti-Enlightenment ideologues and the irrationalism touted by the *völkisch* or "people's" groups active during World War I and the following decades. These bands were enthralled with and advocated German nationalism, spiritualism, astrology, and other occult practices. One of their key ideologues was Julius Langbehn, who espoused a burning hatred of science, positivism, rationalism, empiricism, materialism, technology, secularism, democracy, and skepticism. These ideas contain eerie parallels with postmodern philosophy. Langbehn also endorsed pan-Germanism (*Pangermanismus*) and the superiority of the white German race.

Especially significant for the Nazis were the works of the paranormalists Guido von List and Lanz von Liebenfels, who embraced the schema of "root races" expressed in the charlatan Helena Blavatsky's bogus paranormal theology called Theosophy. They transformed the idea of root races into the doctrine of Ariosophy, in which they presented race-mixing as the cause of all the ills of the world. This dogma, furthermore, provided guidelines for the purification of the German Aryan blood through the elimination of the *Untermenschen* or inferior races (Goodrick-Clarke 2005; Kurlander 2017: 3–61; Newman 2005: 73; Regal 2009: 28–29). Thus, the intellectual climate that propelled Hitler and his goons into power was one of paranormalism, irrationalism, and zealous anti-science viewpoints (Holton 1992: 124). Even before the Nazis seized power, they were calling for a replacement of science with a German-made Aryan "alternative."

When the National Socialists seized power in 1933, they exerted massive efforts into developing officially sanctioned counter-knowledge and counter-sciences. These Nazi "alternative" forms of knowledge included forms of astrology, a mystical physics, and Aryan archaeology and anthropology, all in the service of the Third Reich's racist program of genocide (Holton 1992: 124; Regal 2009: 28–29). Nazi racism was a pseudoscientific perspective, legitimized by scientific-sounding jargon but grounded in mythologized history involving the lost continent of Atlantis and the fictional northland of Thule as the mystical homeland of the superior white Aryan race. An important fact here is that this ideology tapped into racist and paranormal beliefs that have been around for millennia before modern science was developed and have often been justified religiously as part of God's grand design (Fagan and Hale 2001: 85; Pinker 2018: 397).

As physicist Rory Coker (2001) has put it, everywhere, toleration of pseudoscience "encourages people to believe anything they want. It supplies specious arguments for fooling yourself into thinking that all beliefs are equally valid." The psychologist Thomas Gilovich (1991: 6) has cogently stated that tolerating such flawed thinking and superstitions has a high cost because it endangers our ability to see the world accurately:

> There [. . .] is a price we pay when we tolerate flawed thinking and superstitious beliefs. [. . .] Thinking straight about the world is a precious and difficult process that must be carefully nurtured. By attempting to turn our critical intelligence off and on at will, we risk losing it altogether, and thus jeopardize our ability to see the world clearly. Furthermore, by failing to develop our critical faculties, we become susceptible to the arguments and exhortations of those with other than benign intentions.

Similarly, the philosophers Theodore Schick and Lewis Vaughn (2014: 13) observe:

> A democratic society depends on the ability of its members to make rational choices. But rational choices must be based on rational beliefs. If we can't tell the difference between reasonable and unreasonable claims, we become susceptible to the claims of charlatans, scoundrels, and mountebanks.

Also, as Sagan (1995: 38) put it:

> If we don't practice these tough habits of thought, we cannot hope to solve the truly serious problems that face us—we risk becoming a nation of suckers, up for grabs by the next charlatan who saunters along.

Yet, as mentioned throughout this discussion, for close to forty years, the very people in American universities and colleges who were entrusted to be the guardians of truth and clear thinking not only glorified and embraced such thinking, they encouraged it. Thompson (2008: 18, 19) concurs, pointing out that the spread of pseudo-profound bullshit in the 1980s and 1990s coincided with:

> postmodern claims, first advanced by the French philosopher Jean-François Lyotard, that orthodox science was essentially a language game played by a white male elite. This worldview found powerful reinforcement in the phenomenon of political correctness, in which the boundaries of knowledge are gerrymandered around people's sensitivities. . . . The left has helped spread [pseudoscience] by insisting on the right of ethnic, sexual and religious minorities to believe falsehoods that make them feel better about themselves.

In his book *Fantasyland: How America Went Haywire* (2017), Andersen says something similar:

> The very Americans who ought to be important fighters in the long war in defense of reason, professors and the graduate students whose minds they shape, instead became enablers of Fantasyland [post-truth] (Andersen 2017: 308).

These custodians of wisdom and knowledge denied that science was a unique way of knowing and embraced and encouraged all types of pseudoscientific perspectives. Recall Feyerabend, who saw no difference between science, which he called a "superstition," and pseudoscientific views, such as magic, astrology, voodoo, and creationism. He was also an enthusiastic supporter of the works of the "vulgar charlatan" and paranormalist Carlos Castaneda, to be discussed in chapter 10 (Stove 1991: 11). Because Feyerabend denied that science had a special status, he believed that magic and related beliefs maligned by science and rationality were not poetic fancies but superior perspectives. This philosopher also thought that voodoo has an empirical reality and even sought the aid of shamans to cure his illnesses, including his fatal brain tumor (Andersen 2017: 193).

I have also discussed how Kuhn's ideas permitted the Harvard University psychiatrist John Mack (1997) to justify his claim that alien abductions are real (unless he made this claim for publicity purposes to generate book sales). More generally, from Kuhn's thesis followed that if there is no single way of knowing, the common authority of evidence is invalid; therefore all the other perspectives rejected by science are equally plausible and acceptable. This was tantamount to an endorsement of spiritual worldviews and beliefs in miracles, magic, ghost and spirits, and other archaic superstitions (Otto 2016: 185–186). But such corrosive effects were attributes not just of the works of these two thinkers; rather it was the case with the thinking of all the postmodern savants in social sciences and humanities departments in American colleges and universities. They all pontificated about the evils of science, advocated epistemic relativism, urged the distrust of expertise, and encouraged people to believe whatever made them feel good about themselves, thereby audaciously encouraging irrational modes of thought.

A case in point is the work of the political scientist and postmodern writer Jodi Dean who in her book *Aliens in America* (1998) expresses the typical enthusiasm for falsehoods and absolute derision for reason and rationality (Andersen 2017: 311). There are no "widespread criteria for judgments about what is reasonable and what is not," she says, and denies the existence of a shared "concept of reason, and a set of criteria by which claims to reason and rationality are judged" (Dean 1998: 9, 11).

Predictably, like her colleagues who share this philosophy, Dean advances the idea of multiple truths, each with its own claim to legitimacy, and is thrilled to defend the veracity of the "voices" of those who say they have seen flying saucers or were abducted by extraterrestrial beings. She adds that those in positions of power deploy terms like "reasonable" and "rational" to silence and control people, and portrays herself a leftwing activist and champion attracted to "critical positions" and a defender of the "unreasonable" and the "irrational" (Dean 1998: 9–10). Dean revels in the fact that those touting irrational ideas are no longer "on the fringe." In her words:

> Thanks to the developments in communication networks, the "irrational" can get their message out. They can connect with those myriad others also dismissed by science. They can network and offer alternatives to the official deployment of reason (Dean 1998: 9).

In Dean's view, science comprises a hegemonic instrument of oppression, and its notion of truth is merely an expression of power. She adds,

> The so-called consensus reality is exclusionary; it is based on the silencing and discrediting of real, everyday people, people who want to be heard. . . . As long as they are dismissed and objectified, as long as they don't count as citizens whose voices and opinions are worth taking seriously, then truth will be only a play of power (Dean 1998: 45).

For Dean, therefore, disbelief in science is that path to social emancipation. This is epistemic relativism in the service of irrationality. These remarks, to paraphrase David Hume, are so absurd that they elude the force of all argument (Stove 1991: 31).

Perhaps it is with justification that Andersen (2017: 311) writes: "If there were a University of Fantasyland, she'd be a strong candidate for the provost." Such intellectual trends all led to post-truth America. Why? Andersen correctly puts it as follows:

> [Once the notion that] there are many equally valid realities and truths, [and] the idea of gates and gatekeeping was discredited not just on campuses but throughout the culture, all the barbarians could have their claims taken seriously . . . the anything-goes relativism [did not remain sequestered on campuses]. . . and when it flowed out across America, it helped enable the extreme Christianities and consequential lunacies on the *right*—gun-rights hysteria, black helicopter conspiracism [vehicles operated by the secret agents of the New World Order], climate change denial, and more. The term *useful idiot* was originally used to accuse liberals of serving the interests of true believers further left. In this instance, however, postmodern intellectuals—postpositivists, poststructuralists, social constructivists, epistemic relativists, cognitive relativists, descriptive relativists—turned out to be useful idiots for the American right. . . .Neither side has been aware of it, but large factions of the elite left and the populist right have been wearing different uniforms on the same team—the Fantasyland [post-truth] team (Andersen 2017: 196–197).

The skeptic, humanist, and author Arthur C. Clarke (2003: 185) was appalled by this cultural trajectory:

> The United States (and much of the world, East and West) appears to be sinking into cultural barbarism, harangued by the fundamentalist ayatollahs of the airwaves, its bookstores, and newsstands poisoned with mind-rotting rubbish about astrology, UFOs, reincarnation, ESP, spoon-bending, and especially "creationism."

Clarke (2003: 185) was particularly angry about the nonsensical pseudoscientific ideas espoused by creationists. The science writer John Rennie (2002) has listed an array of such nonsensical and deceptive creationist claims, my favorite one is: "If humans descended from monkeys, why are there still monkeys?"

However, it is incorrect to label creationism merely a pseudoscience (contra Scott 2001). It is something more insidious. Those making pseudoscientific claims aspire to achieve the respectability of science by adopting scientific-sounding nomenclature. Creationists while impudently using the trappings of science want to demolish and replace it with the archaic superstitions of the Bible. The most recent variant of creationism goes under the label of "Intelligent Design Creationism" a pseudoscientific dogma based upon and validated by postmodern thought, as I shall discuss shortly (for a more detailed epistemological assessment, see Sidky 2020: 259–264).

"Intelligent Design Creationism" is the pseudoscientific division of the crusading evangelical Christian movement in the United States. Its singular objective is to supplant science and make the Bible the focal point of American culture and education (Forrest and Gross 2004; Pandian 2002: 2373). Like other pseudoscientific perspectives, this enterprise has no overarching research agendas to produce new knowledge or to test innovative theories. It exists solely to deceptively demonize science, attack evolutionary theory, and forward a religious agenda founded upon archaic superstitions touted by ignorant Middle Eastern tribal people who died thousands of years ago (cf., Forrest 2002: 80).

Intelligent Design lacks a positive theory, and the purported scientific explanation for the evolution of life that it offers is the bogus antiquated assertion: "God did it" (Sober 2006: 105). Its supernatural premise makes it impossible to translate it into a scientific research program. The reason for this is simple, as mathematician David Shotwell (2003: 49) explains, the supernatural "provides no direction for research, suggests no testable hypotheses, and gives no reason to expect one result rather than another from any observations or experiment."

More specifically, there are two main explanations for why this approach fails as a scientific effort. First, the statement that it is the Lord's doing "explains nothing because it explains too much" (Mahner 2012: 1450). If everything is explained by saying God did it, then inquiry cannot go any further, leaving us in the dark, which as David Hume (1987 [1758]: 66) would have put it is necessary for "priestly power, and to those pious frauds, on which it is commonly founded." Thus, as the philosopher of science Martin Mahner (2012: 1451) puts it, such "an explanation that explains everything explains nothing." Second, such an omni-explanatory proposition is problematic because the principles and mechanisms of the supernatural are unknown. Explaining one unknown phenomenon by appealing to something that is even more unknown, that is, the mysterious operations of the theistic God, involves the logical fallacy of *ignotum per ignotius* (explaining an indefinite by an even greater unknown). In other words, such an explanation substitutes one mystery with another mystery (Fishman and Boudry 2013: 941). The entire project is a sham based on negative arguments and rhetoric (Pennock 1999: 212).

Creationists aim to accomplish their objective using political pressure and to amass votes rather than by offering for appraisal alternative methodologies and data superior to those of science (Bridgestock 2009: 45; Forrest and Gross 2004; Pennock 1999). They call their strategy to sway public opinion in favor of their superstitious beliefs, "The Wedge" (Forrest and Gross 2004). In other words, because their perspective lacks any scientific merits, the proponents of Intelligent Design justify their enterprise in terms of popular appeal and public relations.

William Dembski (2003: 89), a mathematician who is one of the leading philosophers of the movement claims that the design argument must be valid otherwise it would not have such widespread popular support that it is on its way to becoming a mainstream view in the United States. This entails the logical fallacy of argument by popular consensus. Dembski acknowledges this but makes the case anyway. But sadly lots of people believe in lots of absurd and bogus ideas, sometimes with terrifying consequences. This is what led to Lysenkoism, Fascism, and Nazism. So there is no compelling argument here. Popular consensus never compensates for the problematic epistemic status of spurious claims.

Dembski (2003: 90) tries to bolster this appeal to consensus by saying that Intelligent Design must be credible because the public wants it taught in schools, but does not want witchcraft or flat-earth geology as part of the curriculum. This ludicrous argument also does not carry any weight. We must not forget the regrettable fact that this post-truth public also believes that demons exist, evil spirits cause diseases, UFOs are extraterrestrial spacecraft, witchcraft is real, prayers can cure cancer, demons impregnate women while they sleep, aliens abduct people daily, Elvis lives, vaccines cause autism, and that the U.S. government and the Israeli Secret Service were responsible for the 9/11 attacks. The absurdity of this has not escaped Charles Pierce, the witty commentator on American culture. In his book *Idiot America* (2009), Pierce the says the following about such a political savvy challenge to evolutionary theory:

> [It] makes as much sense as conducting a Gallup poll on gravity or running someone for president on the Alchemy party ticket. It doesn't matter how many

people believe that they ought to be able to flap their arms and fly; none of them can. It doesn't matter how many votes your candidate got; he's not going to be able to turn lead into gold. . . . a politically savvy challenge to evolution is as self-contradictory as an "agriculturally savvy" challenge to Euclidean geometry would be (Pierce 2009: 9).

He sees this as another symptom of a much broader pattern of irrationalism and nonsense that is now characteristic of American culture:

Idiot American is a strange, disordered place. Everything is on the wrong shelves. The truth of something is defined by how many people will attest to it, and facts are defined by those people's fervency. Fiction and nonfiction are defined by how well they sell. The best sellers are on one self, cheek by jowl, whether what's contain in them is true or not (Pierce 2009: 161).

I have addressed the failure of Intelligent Design Creationism elsewhere (Sidky 2020: 259–294). Here I want to specifically look at the role of postmodern ideas in the development of this bogus theory. The philosopher Robert Pennock shows exactly how that philosophy has delivered to Christian fundamentalists the requisite tools to question the validity of academic traditions with which they disagree and undermine scientific materialism in hopes of replacing it with a supernaturalistic perspective centered on the theistic God. Their tactics are right out of the postmodernist playbook.

Ideologues of Intelligent Design Creationism maintain, for instance, that they intend to "deconstruct" the philosophical barriers posed by biological naturalism and relativize its precepts (Pennock 1999: 211, 2010: 759). Sound familiar? Science can be rejected, they argue further, because its claims have no greater epistemic validity than those of other myths and fairytales (Pennock 2010: 760). This is the common postmodern claim that knowledge is and can never be anything but a narrative of those in power who have silenced other equally valid stories. Power determines what constitutes knowledge, the argument goes, not some independent body of objective evidence. Or alternatively, knowledge is the ideology that serves the interests of some powerful group and nothing more.

It is the same with the creationist claim that Darwinism is a religion imposed on society through indoctrination, which expresses the postmodern premise that sciences is just propaganda or a faith-based system. Science has nothing to do with reality, religionists declare, facts are convenient fictions, and evolutionary theory is just an imaginative yarn. Because every tribe has its own valid truth, as postmodernism has disclosed, the argument goes, therefore, the truth of the ancient tribes expressed in Genesis are equally valid (Pennock 2010: 762). Creationists have also coopted the epistemic plurality clause espoused by the academic relativists. They use it to argue that believers in science accept the validity of evolutionary theory because it is useful in relation to their epistemic system and beliefs in Genesis are useful in terms of their own equally valid epistemic system.

Pennock (1999: 211) also notes that the law professor Phillip Johnson (1940–2019), the architect of the Intelligent Design movement and its pseudoscientific Discovery Institute, openly acknowledged the importance of the precepts offered by Kuhn, Rorty, Derrida, and Feyerabend in his effort to delegitimize science. Johnson also said that the original title of his book *Darwin on Trial*, where he introduced the "Intelligent Design Theory," was the postmodern sounding "Darwin Deconstructed." This supports McIntyre's (2015: 106) point that while at the time postmodern theories were widely reviled outside the academy and by many within it, they "proved to be incredibly influential when it came time for conservative critics of science to seek intellectual cover for their attack on evolution and global warming."

However, there is a twist. Creationists—like the right-wing populists and white power ideologues who are also using postmodern theories in their own battle against science—do not share the other tenets of postmodernism and use epistemic relativism pirated from the academics only about human knowledge, claiming that science is invalid because its contention that naturalistic methods lead to objective truths is bogus (Pennock 1999: 210). However, these religionists depart from the postmodern savants in a significant way because for them, epistemic relativism has no bearing on their supernatural truths and their effort is to overthrow scientific naturalism and replace it with "theistic realism," which is their metanarrative. As Pennock (1999: 212–213) explains:

> Postmodernists accept relativism and seem happy to dispense with notions of subjective human viewpoints. Creationists, however . . . believe that although human reason by itself is impotent, there remains one way to get a "God's-eye view" of the world, namely, from God himself. God's divine revelations saves us from relativism by providing us with absolute truths in Scripture.

Pennock (2010: 777) lays responsibility for these circumstances on the dalliance of irresponsible academics in American universities and colleges with radical epistemic relativism. As he puts it:

> [Intelligent Design Creationism] shows in a striking manner how radical postmodernism undermines itself and its own goals of liberation. If there is no difference between narratives—including no difference between true and false stories and between facts and fiction—then what does liberation come to? . . . Those original goals—the overthrow of entrenched ideologies that hid and

justified oppression—that motivated the postmodern critique were laudable. But the right way to combat oppression is not with a philosophy that rejects objectivity and relativizes truth, for that [eviscerates] oppression of its reality.

Much earlier, the philosopher Paul Boghossian (1996: 14–15) made the same observation concerning the self-defeating aspect of the postmodernists' approach to social justice and liberation:

> If the powerful can't criticize the oppressed, because the central epistemological categories are inexorably tied to particular perspectives, it also follows that the oppressed can't criticize the powerful.

The cases examined in this chapter clearly indicate the unpleasant consequence of the flirtation of a group of irresponsible and self-serving academics with a fundamentally incoherent ideology that they forwarded under the disguise of scholarship. Their enterprise was not only an abject failure but it also contributed to a pervasive anti-intellectualism and scientific illiteracy that has provided the intellectual tools for purveyors of alternate ways of knowing, profit hungry corporations, religious extremists, and anti-democratic populists to forward their agendas.

Chapter 9

Postmodern Anthropology
Epistemic Relativism and Incoherence as an Experimental Moment?

As stated earlier, American cultural anthropologists working during the late 1980s and 1990s, who were in a perfect position to investigate the spread of postmodern irrationalism in academia, did nothing of the sort. Instead of analyzing such beliefs as anthropologists, many became converts, endorsers, and proselytizers of what we have seen were nonsensical and fundamentally incoherent philosophical precepts obtained from a segment of Parisian intelligentsia. Cultural anthropology thus did its part to feed into the type of broad anti-intellectualism that today characterizes post-truth Fantasyland, United States, which is the main focus of this study.

It should be noted at the outset, that the discussion here is primarily about the subfield of American *cultural* anthropology. Contemporary anthropological linguistics, biological anthropology, and archaeology are all mainly scientific. For this reason, the latter have been far more successful as fields of study in generating broadly useful data than cultural anthropology. Their success is due to the fact that they are all far more scientific. Few scholars outside of cultural anthropology have found much utility for what this subfield generates, namely, ethnography, but many non-anthropological scholars are impressed by the findings in anthropological linguistics, biological anthropology, and archaeology. The field of anthropology should recognize, confront, and correct the marked disparity in the intellectual value of its four subfields (Lett 2020, personal communication).

Today, postmodern cultural anthropology is mostly defunct as are some of its versions in other scholarly fields. However, there were clusters still hanging on to such premises well into the twenty-first century. For example, the volume *Anthropology and Science: Epistemologies in Practice* (2007) edited by Edwards, Harvey, and Wade, is packed with all the familiar specious bits of postmodern anti-science dogma. I shall briefly examine its introductory synthetic first chapter. The authors describe science as a "culturally specific form of reasoning," and its "facts" the product of social process. They position anthropology against "the pretensions of modern science," to interrogate rather than confirm the prevailing scientific orthodoxy and its rationalist orientation and "universalizing theory." The idea of multiple epistemic systems, all treated as comparable to Western science, is used to reveal the limits of scientific rationalism for understanding "live worlds." Further, they see the objective of the discipline to dismantle scientific ideas that naturalize racial, gender, and, sexual divisions. The tools for this task are drawn from discourse analysis and employed "to investigate how cultural ideologies" intrude upon science and scientific knowledge.

There is nothing new here, just the routine parroting of the specious conjectures by various eccentric French philosophers palmed off as new and innovative insights. Unfortunately, there are others as well who still treat postmodern dogma as credible (e.g., Herzfeld 2017; Lukas 2013: 641). Also postmodern writings continue to appear in introductory textbooks without any sort of adequate critical appraisal (e.g., Moore 2019: 34–354; Ortner 2006: 119–127).

The discussion here is intended to highlight how American postmodern cultural anthropologists contributed to the already widespread anti-intellectualism and science illiteracy. What follows, therefore, is a brief exposition of how science denial, anti-intellectualism, and irrational modes of thinking were received by a group of self-serving anthropologists caught up in the latest modish bunkum from Paris making the rounds in American colleges and universities. These academics utterly succumbed to the seductive allure of French postmodernism and immediately adopted its premises. This was not an unusual turn of events. American scholars have demonstrated a long-standing inclination to simply discard everything and embrace the newest and most fashionable perspectives or intellectual fads from Europe (Cerroni-Long 1999: 9). A generation or so earlier, anthropologists forsook all for Claude Lévi-Strauss's highly problematic structural anthropology (see Hénaff 1998; for an assessment see Sidky 2004: 246–275). The same happened when translations of the works of Foucault and Derrida finally became available to the mostly monolingual anthropologists in the United States (Woolin 2004: 8).

Postmodern thought had the greatest impact on those already committed to subjective interpretive approaches in American cultural anthropology. In part, postmodern anthropology involved an emendation of Clifford Geertz's (1988: 10) nonscientific interpretive or hermeneutic perspective with its emphasis on the insider's point of view, the notion of culture-as-text, and the idea of ethnography as fiction. Geertz's claim to fame was his effort to equate culture with systems of meaning and making systems of meaning the only legitimate domain for anthropological investigation (Sidky 2004:

327–333). Geertz's views are spelled out in his articles "Thick Description: Toward and Interpretive Theory of Culture" (1973), "Blurred Genres: The Reconfiguration of Social Thought" (1980), and other essays in his books *The Interpretation of Culture* (1973) and *Local Knowledge* (1983). Geertz who started out as an English major was adamant that anthropology was a literary endeavored. Anthropology, as he put it, "[is] not an experimental science in search of law but an interpretive one in search of meaning" (Geertz 1973: 5). Postmodern anthropology drew on Geertz's interpretive slant, especially his shift of focus from social structure "to mental or cultural phenomena," and his metaphor of cultures-as-text (Marcus and Fischer 1986: 28).

The anthropological rendition of postmodern theory involved the wholesale pirating of completely unaltered and inadequately understood French postmodern precepts. These were terrible ideas on their own right, as already discussed, and their anthropological manifestations were even shoddier. These included an intense revulsion for reason and truth, epistemic plurality, fixation on language and writing, the idea that everything is a text, and the premise of the nonexistence of objective reality or facts. Added to this was a massive dosage of moralistic platitudes, sanctimonious posturing, and a great deal of intellectual dishonesty. Hence, there was nothing new here, no further elaboration of ideas, no updating, no novel concepts, and no independent innovations. It was simply the appropriation of the facile postmodern version of epistemic relativism and applying them to the sorts of conventional things anthropologists did. Its exponents, however, boldly described their enterprise "as nothing other than "*relativism, rearmed and strengthened* for an era of intellectual ferment, not unlike, but vastly more complex than, that in which [the discipline] was formulated" (Marcus and Fischer 1986: 32).

The type of universal epistemic relativism these anthropologists proposed was different from the concept of cultural relativism traditionally used in anthropology, which if applied appropriately, refers to domain specific relativism, that is, looking at and understanding features of cultures in their context. In this view, truths are consensual truths or truth by coherence. It does not lead to the conclusion that all knowledge universally is relative to epistemic systems and nothing else. This kind of relativism also does not justify the idea of the *incommensurability* of cultures, contra to such assertions. In the same way that a common reality would permit a Ptolemaic and Copernican astronomer to understand each other, anthropologists are able to understand the people whose culture they are investigating. In my research on shamanism, my informants and I were able to share ideas even though we were operating in terms of our respective epistemic systems. To reiterate, there has never been a case where an anthropologist has returned from the field to report that the culture he or she encountered was so unfamiliar, so impenetrable, that it could not be comprehended.

For the anthropologists in question, however, postmodern revelations were cosmic in scope ushering a new dawn leading to, as one writer put it, "a pragmatic understanding of epistemology" and the realization that "truth" is a mirage, and science and rationality are culturally constructed instruments of oppression (Herzfeld 2001: x, 2, 5, 9, 10, 22). They characterized their orientation as the "rearrangement of the very principles of intellectual perspective" (Herzfeld 2001: 2). Others described their undertaking as "an experimental moment in the human sciences [sic]" (Marcus and Fischer 1986). An added insight was that the once "axiomatic separation of theorizing scholar and ethnographic subject" or "the observer" and "the observed" is a falsehood (Herzfeld 2001: 2, 10). As Marilyn Strathern (1987: 264–265), a lauded British postmodernist prodigy, put it:

> The observer/observed relationship can no longer be assimilated to that between subject and object. The object(ive) is joint production. Many voices, multiple texts, plural authorship.

Facts, according to the wisdom of the French literati were inseparable from the observer who grapples with them. Thus, ethnographic texts were to be jointly produced by the authors and their informants, consultants, co-authors, and so forth, which means that these ideologues wrote as much about themselves as the "other."

Truth, reason, objective knowledge, and science received the standard treatment, being identified as the embodiments of everything detestable and obscene. The works of earlier anthropologists who had ventured down that path were disparagingly dismissed as a form of oppression and domination. The new savants would have none of that:

> These subjects, who must be spoken for, are generally located in the world dominated by Western colonialism or neocolonialism; thus, the rhetoric both exemplifies and reinforces Western domination. Moreover, the rhetoric itself is an exercise in power, in effect denying subjects the right to express contrary views, by obscuring from the reader recognition that they might view things *with equal validity*, quite differently from the writer (Marcus and Fischer 1986: 1–2).

Anyone concerned with such abysmal pursuits as looking for facts, data, or attempting the systematic appraisal of knowledge were "betraying their enduring entanglement with the logic of Enlightenment theories" (Herzfeld 2001: 183–184). Scientific anthropology in particular was scorned because it was "grounded in the politics of religious and economic domination" (Herzfeld 2001: 184). Why? Well, because science entails a commitment to a rational empirical perspective, the recognition of a distinction between different ways of knowing, and the requirement that propositions must be validated against empirical evidence. The postmodernists' epistemological egalitarianism did not permit any of this.

Expunged from their repertoire were the canons of verifiability and replicability and the idea that objective knowledge is possible. This is how one enthusiast expressed it:

> Postmodern realists [sic] see no way across the gap between appearance-sensation-experience and reality except in terms of an impressible act of imaginative production. Reality, according to postmodern theories, is not only obscured from sight; it is intrinsically invisible, like a black hole (Shweder 1991: 335–336).

Here again these devotees presumed that they alone, through some hermeneutical aptitude and wizardry, were capable of crossing that gap between "appearance" and "reality," an imaginative act beyond the capacity of all others (i.e., they did not address the reflexivity thesis).

With respect to the awkward issue of validation, Clifford (1986: 25), another pessimistic purveyor of the philosophy said this:

> The writing and reading of ethnography are overdetermined by forces ultimately beyond the control of either an author or an interpretive community. These contingencies—of language, rhetoric, power, and history—must now be openly confronted in the process of writing. They can no longer be evaded. But the confrontation raises thorny problems of verification: how are the truths of cultural accounts evaluated? Who has the authority to separate science from art? realism from fantasy? knowledge from ideology? Of course such separations will continue to be maintained, and redrawn; but their changing poetic and political grounds will be less easily ignored. In cultural studies at least, we can no longer know the whole truth, or even claim to approach it.

These ideologues were under the misguided impression that a philosophy that denied objective reality, relativized truth, and extolled a crude anti-intellectualism and an abhorrence of knowledge was the path to liberation and social justice in the world (cf., Pennock 2010). As Stephen Tyler (1986: 135) another sage of the movements observed: "Post-modem ethnography aims not to foster the growth of knowledge but to restructure experience." What resulted from this perspective was a full-fledged truth denial anti-intellectual ideology doled out in American institutions of higher learning, in this instance from departments of cultural anthropology.

The formulations of postmodern anthropology were canonized in the mid-1980s in two books *Anthropology as Cultural Critique: An Experimental*

Moment in the Human Sciences (1986) by George Marcus and Michael Fischer and *Writing Culture: The Poetics and Politics of Ethnography* (1986), a volume edited by James Clifford and George Marcus. Marcus and Fischer (1986: 263) inaugurated the new agenda by declaring that anthropology was in the grips of "a crisis of representation." Clifford (1986: 2–3) confidently proclaimed the collapse of anthropological paradigms. Marcus (1986b: 263) added that "the larger theoretical project of twentieth-century social and cultural anthropology is in disarray." The reigning scientific paradigms were declared to be defunct, and anthropology was pronounced to be an entirely literary enterprise. Marcus and Fischer (1986: vii) added that "hopes for a natural science of society [are] challenged by theories of interpretation that say that people must be treated differently from nature." The also introduced their version of anthropology as a field of study:

> The explicit discourse that reflects on the doing and writing of ethnography itself is what we call interpretive anthropology. It grew out of the cultural anthropology of the 1960s gradually shifting in emphasis from the attempt to construct a general theory of culture to a reflection on ethnographic fieldwork and writing (Marcus and Fischer 1986: 15–16).

Ethnography "as a written product of the fieldwork experience itself" thus became the central concern of these anthropologists (Marcus and Fischer 1986: 20). The reasoning was as follows: the way ethnographic knowledge is obtained must be scrutinized and then this was linked to the fact that there was much inequality in the world. This is a gross *non-sequitur*, but recall that the philosophic position being used entailed a rejection of logic and rationality. From this the conclusion was reached that the way knowledge of the world was obtained and how ethnographies were written created the inequalities that exist in the world (Gellner 1992: 39). A skeptic would point out that what they were actually saying was that clarity of thinking and factual knowledge—detestable things that they spurned—created all the ills of the world (Gellner 1992: 39). Stated in these terms, the preposterousness of this view is evident. However, these savants, like the French writers they mimicked, couched their incoherent, logically flawed, and absurd assertions in clever and convoluted rhetoric embellished with plenty of ominous aphorisms, and delivered in a high decibel vitriol, that shrouded the nonsensical and incoherent nature of their assertions.

These writers were less concerned with the interpretation of cultures than they were about the interpretation of how ethnographies were written. Geertz, it might be noted, had made the same proclamation three years before the publication of the book *Writing Culture*. Geertz (1983: 3) maintained that:

the growing recognition [among anthropologists] that the established approach to treating [cultural] phenomena, *laws-and-causes social physics*, was not producing the triumphs of prediction, control, and testability that had for so long been promised in its name.

Building on Geertz's notion of culture-as-text, and the idea of ethnography as fiction, Clifford (1986: 6) declared:

To call ethnographies fictions may raise empiricist hackles. But the word as commonly used in recent textual theory has lost its connotation of falsehood, of something merely opposed to truth. It suggests the partiality of cultural and historical truths, the ways they are systematic and exclusive. Ethnographic writings can properly be called fictions in the sense of "something made up or fashioned." . . . But it is important to preserve the meaning not merely of making, but also of making up, of inventing things not actually real.

This is all stuff right out of Latour's comments regarding the texts he produced, as discussed in chapter 3. Clifford (1986: 7) added:

The maker . . . of ethnographic text cannot avoid expressive tropes [metaphors], figures, and allegories that select and impose meaning as they translated it. In this view . . . all constructed truths are made possible by powerful "lies" or exclusions and rhetoric. Even the best ethnographic texts—serious, true fictions—are systems, or economies of truth. Power and history work through them, in ways their authors cannot fully control.

The mysteries or rather mystifications piled on. Reality itself was construed as cultural construct residing in texts. This view differed from Geertz's metaphor of cultures as "acted out" texts embodied in behavior existing "out there" to be interpreted. For the postmodern writers there was nothing out there, and there were no texts until the ethnography had been fabricated. Thus the tenuous and illusory linkage between Geertz's interpretive anthropology and empirical reality dissipated in the postmodernist reformulation of it. This is the reason that the postmodern writers later disowned Geertz because his works made references to "the real world" (Gellner 1992: 44, 48). Tyler (1986: 29) described the new conception of ethnography:

Because it is participatory and emergent, post-modern ethnography cannot have a predetermined form. . . . Whatever form the text takes-if any at all-it will stress sonorant relativity, not only between the text and the community of discourse of which it is a part-the usual sense of "cultural relativity" but within the text itself as a constitutive feature of the text.

The pseudo-profound bullshit dispensed by the French postmodern sages were thus put into practice by shifting the focus of cultural anthropology to writing about other cultures, that is, doing ethnography. In this vision, anthropology was about note-taking and inscribing. Their undertaking, therefore, was all about how to write ethnographies. Its practitioners consider themselves to be essayists, and their singular task was the production of ethnographic texts and the analysis of how such texts are written.

However, while ethnography became a primary preoccupation, it was kind of ethnography devoid of any theoretical schemes, but inspired by a self-assured moral cause, the critique of the Western worldview and science through the creation of "space" for the voices of "the other." This was what they considered emancipation, justice for all, and so forth. In other words, they were mimicking the pointless efforts of Foucault, Derrida, Lyotard, Latour, and the other savants toward the same objective. There is not a single original thought in the entire corpus of postmodern anthropology. Like their counterparts in other social science and humanities departments these writers were merely "disciples of or commentators on the French masters" (Sokal and Bricmont 1998: 3). References to the "voices of the other" were how they understood the epistemic plurality clause, which dictates that there are multiple alternative epistemic systems, each one as valid as the next, except science. These ideologues transformed anthropology into a mode of morally charged social and political advocacy/critique with the task of challenging evocations of science and logic associated with the privileged elite of politically dominant cultures.

But there is more. These savants also declared the death of epistemology (cf., Rabinow 1986: 241–242). Why? Because epistemology holds that there is a right and wrong way of approaching the acquisition of knowledge and it is necessary to find a justifiable way of making distinctions between different ways of knowing (Gellner 1992: 38). This is something these writers repudiated. In effect, they were declaring that they possessed a special or "alternative way of knowing," to use post-truth jargon, one that did not require empirical appraisal or logical coherence, but an approach that was superior to all other methodologies. These are all exactly what purveyors of alternative ways of knowing in post-truth United States are claiming today. However, nothing these anthropologists wrote and nothing that they produced through their experimental ethnography offered an iota of evidence that any of their presumptions were true. Nor is there any proof anywhere that any "other" or "others" were emancipated by the incoherent and incomprehensible texts and poems these anthropologists have bequeathed us.

It is remarkable that these academics actually believed that epistemic relativism was path to emancipation. As already discussed, this is probably one of the most ludicrous ideas ever conceived in Western philosophy because it is it false and its corollaries are incoherent. To say it again, these included the premise that reality is unknowable, all truths are consensual, one interpretation is as good as another, or in post-truth vernacular, "if it is true for us it is true." This kind of relativism encourages subjectivism, literalism, dogmatism, mysticism, irrationalism, absolutism, and lends itself to authoritarianism as is perfectly clear in post-truth America today. Moreover, it was a perspective that prompted intellectual dishonesty, bolstered anti-intellectualism, and aided scientific illiteracy (cf., Sokal and Bricmont 1998: 207). In many ways postmodern anthropologists may be counted among the originators and initiators of misinformation, counter-knowledge, and alternative facts that have facilitated magical thinking, irrationalism, and supernaturalism in today's post-truth world.

The strategy the purveyors of the new kind of cultural anthropology used to legitimize their enterprise was to juxtapose their edified outlook with the obsolete and obscene mainstream anthropology, which they characterized as "laws-and-causes social physics," or anthropology based on "Newtonian models" (Geertz 1983: 3; Herzfeld 2001: 43). I still don't know what these assertions means. Did anyone every do Newtonian anthropology? Or laws-and-causes ethnography? But here is the intellectual dishonesty, science has never been the principal perspective in American cultural anthropology. If anything, this field has been dominated almost exclusively by nonscientific or unscientific paradigms, despite the frequent use of the honorific "scientific" by many, including Geertz, and Marcus and Fischer in the title of their unfortunate tome. Once we ignore the honorific use of the term "scientific" and focus on the research protocols actually employed, it turns out that there was very little science to found. For the greater part of its existence, American cultural anthropology has been an entirely humanistic, interpretive, and meaning-oriented affair, although the words "science" and "scientific" peppered the anthropological literature. What Franz Boas, the prodigious originator of the discipline in the United States, and his students were engaged in was pure inductive atheoretical data gathering, or the careful "detailed study of local phenomena" (Boas 1940: 277). In Boas's incorrect understanding once all the facts were in they would speak for themselves (Boas 1940: 641, 644; Radin 1939: 301; White 1987a: 91, 1987b: 204–205).

The assertions by Marcus and his associates about paradigmatic collapse was a sham. There was a small contingent of researchers engaged in ecological and materialist studies who appeared in the late 1950s and into the 1970s, but they were never the dominant perspective. The circumstances under which cultural anthropology has languished for so long have not been created by too much science or too many scientific paradigms, but by too little science, and too few scientific theories. Had these luminaries bothered to familiarize themselves with the history of their discipline, instead of rejecting "disciplinary origins and traditions" (Marcus 1992: viii–ix), they would have realized that the tedious debate over the possibility or impossibility of a science of culture goes back at least to when anthropology first began as an academic discipline over a century ago (Harris 2001a, 2001b; Johnson and Johnson 2001: vi; White 1949).

The postmodernists paragons were not really on to something remarkable. What was new was the politicized rhetoric in which the old science/antiscience debate was couched. What was also different was the arrogant self-righteous moralism these writers ascribe to their perspective, which entailed the dictum that if you don't conduct research the postmodern way you are an oppressor of "the other," a colonialist, misogynist, racists, or much worse (cf., Gellner 1992: 48).

Where did all of this leave the ethnographer? By pronouncing efforts to certify or validate knowledge as politically evil and a form of domination, and spurning the idea that it is possible to attain a clear understanding of another culture, these luminaries were confronted with a terrible quandary. Gellner (1992: 48) captured the dilemmas nicely:

> The problem of knowledge, and in particular the problem of knowing alien conceptual system, give rise to deep and unsolved dilemmas. One can use these difficulties to castigate all those who had previously . . . came back with clear and intelligible data, and present one's own unintelligibility and inward-turnedness, peppered with all the great names in the history of ideas, as so much deeper. It also takes much less work. There is also the wider consideration that this hermeneutic awe of the Other is presented somehow linked . . . . to intercultural egalitarianism: unless you speak as we do, you are a colonialist, if not worse. It is presented as a precondition of liberation and equality. The links are spurious, but they are assiduously insinuated.

If objective knowledge did not exist, and the observer and observed were inseparable, what was there for the ethnographer to inscribe? The answer was engagement in the fabrication of texts that expressed multiple voices and idiosyncratic meanings gathered from of the authors' elucidating their own cognitive pains over the impossibility of knowledge. Here are Tyler's (1987: 102) views of the dilemma:

> Ethnography is the endorphin of culture, an intertextual practice which, by means of an allegorizing identity, anesthetizes us to the other's difference. Its other is a same, made so by a process of double occultation, for the ethnographic text can represent the other as difference only inasmuch as it makes itself occult, which is the condition of modernism. Postmodern ethnography must be another kind of intertextuality whose projects is not to reveal the other in univocal

descriptions which allegorically identify the other's difference over our interest. It must be instead, a fantasy of identities, plurivocal evocation of difference making a unity in fantasy that mimics on every page the rationalism that seems to inform it, and reveals between every line the difference it conceals in every word, that it might speak not for the other "for us," but let the other's voice be heard, too, and not just "for us," but "for us both."

Endorphin of culture? Double occultation? First, it is unclear what Tyler is really trying to say or not say, if anything at all. Recall that abuse of language, incomprehensibility, and nonsensicality were the point of such texts (Benson and Stangroom 2006: 48). Second, such an ethnographic enterprise required many adjustments and emendations to how such texts were to be written. It required that

> objective truth . . . be replaced by hermeneutic truth. Hermeneutic truth respects the subjectivity both of the object of inquiry and of the inquirer, and even of the reader or listener. In fact the practitioners of the method are so deeply, . . . imbued both by the difficulty and undesirability of transcending meanings . . . that in the end one tends to be given poems and homilies on the locked circles of meaning in which everyone is imprisoned (Gellner 1992: 35).

There was no knowledge to be found here, but a lot of anguish and personal reflections (Salzman 2001: 136). Postmodern discourse in anthropology, as Fox (1992: 55) pointed out, was characterized by the "routinization of indignation" and the "politicization of theory," and angst concerning the hopelessness of the problem of knowledge.

As it turned out, the grandiose mandate amounted to writing "narrative ethnographies of the particular," in other words, cleverly and experimentally written, subjective, idiosyncratic stories from the "bottom up" (Abu-Lughod 1991: 150–151). The "voices of the other" was the motto of the day. Thus, the highly lauded and aggressively touted anthropological enterprise promising earthshattering insights into the human condition simply led down the same dreary dead-end road of particularism—Boas's ill-advised "detailed study of local phenomena"—with equally disappointing and dismal results (see Sidky 2004: 113–164, 326–335).

In actuality, what this shift involved was the substitution critical thinking and systematic and rigorous analysis with impressionistic anecdotal accounts or storytelling and writing poetry. Say whatever you want, it is still anthropology. Or is it? This is where more instances of intellectual dishonesty and irresponsibility come in. Narratives and anecdotes do not enhance knowledge. They are thick with bias and fulfill strictly ideological functions aimed at swaying audiences through rhetoric and appeal to emotion rather than evidence (Dawes 2001: 113). That is how the French savants instilled their ideas and that is how their American emulators in anthropology did so as well. The pseudo-political project of these writers hinged upon clever and ideologically tailored stories with "spaces" for "the voices of the other." The aim of their enterprise was to use marginal knowledge of marginal communities to question and destabilize "received values" of the dominant Western cultures (Herzfeld 2001: 5). This was their idea of radicalism, emancipation, and egalitarianism. All of it on paper, of course. Embracing "local knowledge" and the so-called "other's point of view" became bold statements of political radicalism and militancy. Doubters beware.

One of the major problematic features of the enterprise these writers were advocating was that empirical data and validation of research findings no longer played a role in their work. Here one should mention Carlos Castaneda, author of *The Teachings of Don Juan: A Yaqui Way of Knowledge* (1968), and its numerous sequels, that is treated as paradigmatic by today's paranormalists in anthropology (see chapter 10). Castaneda wove an elaborate tale about his apprenticeship under a shaman or "sorcerer" named Don Juan and his personal entry into the magical world and alternate realities of the Yaqui. One anthropologist referred to this work as "both ethnography an allegory" (Goldschmidt 1968: vii). Here allegory means post-truth. Not surprisingly, all the standard ingredients of postmodern dogma are to be found in Castaneda's writings: "subjective truths," "separate realities," "alternative facts," as well as the tendentious idea of "ethnography as fiction" that decouples anthropological research from empirical facts (on the epistemological issues see Silverman 1975). It is not unexpected, therefore, that postmodernists and their nonacademic doppelgängers, the New Age mystics, magicians, gurus, wizards, and pseudoscientists lauded and copied Castaneda's efforts in search of their own shamanic visions and mystical exultations.

Marcus and Fischer (1986: 40) commended Castaneda's work as an "alternative textual strategy," which they lamented was rejected prematurely because it did not offer the reader a way of monitoring and evaluating the sources of the data presented. Verification of research was altogether absent here. Given their epistemological stance, these postmodern savants failed to mention or, as is more likely, were unconcerned with the fact that Castaneda plagiarized the work of ethnographers who had actually done field research (e.g., Wasson 1957, 1958) in order to construct his bogus yarn about flying magicians, shape-shifting, and the rest (DeMille 1976, 1990; Beals 1978; Harris 2001b: 319–326). Facts can be made up, that is what the French savants taught their devotees. It seems that cultural anthropology in Idiot America was already on its way to post-truth as early as the mid-1980s.

The postmodern luminaries in cultural anthropology were widely received by many of their colleagues and graduate students because their message held the promise of liberation from the evils and fetters of "modernity." Their discourse was replete with statements about liberating "the other," and liberating themselves. But astonishingly, this is a form of liberation hitherto unparalleled in human history—it was liberation on paper, in texts. According to the rhetoric: "To be subordinate or equal is to be written about as subordinate or equal. We can create a morally acceptable world just by writing appropriately" (Sapire 1989: 565).To reiterate, I have yet to find a single case of anyone being liberated because of these purported emancipatory texts.

From a sarcastic perspective, there was a far more practical reason for the popularity of this enterprise. It was not its chimerical promises of liberation and feigned radicalism. It was because those who engaged in this egalitarian enterprise were "liberated" from the burdensome chore of having to learn scientific research methodologies and of having to undertake the wearisome task of actually conducting empirical fieldwork (Fox 1992: 49). Moreover, these anti-science celebrities who repudiated the rules of logic, empirical facts, validation, and standards of proof and disproof were unfettered from the responsibility of knowing anything and at the same time felt empowered to espouse nonsense without having to be accountable for or defend the coherence and rationality of their arguments because their statements were immune to appraisal (Reyna 1994: 576).

But how does one pass off such efforts as sound scholarship? Based on the cases in my department, the career strategy for tenure, promotion, accolade adopted by these sanctimonious self-appointed champions of the oppressed "other" entailed a tenacious denigration and demonization of opposing intellectual perspectives, intimidation of colleagues with whom they had theoretical differences, and considerable shrewd politicking with university administers and board of trustees, an activity for which they had great aptitude. University administrators, often impressed or intimidated by their zealous self-righteous moral one-upmanship, not wishing to appear politically incorrect or culturally insensitive to the plight of minorities and the oppressed, in turn, lavished them with favors, preferential treatment, tenure, and promotion.

Thus unencumbered by the conventions of scientific research and standards of scholarship, and recipients of academic rewards, they happily rendered moralistic judgments and spoke truth to evil on the basis of subjective, intuitive, impressionistic procedures, bolstered by the thought that their "moral" perspective alone was enough to suppress ethnocentrism and prejudice and guarantee greater insights. Their message said nothing about the phenomena in question, but rather directed the readers on how to react emotionally to those phenomena (D'Andrade 1995: 4). They did not want to comprehend the world, but rather to advocate a particular vision of it that accorded with some private political and moral agenda based upon the values of one stratum of Euro-American society to which these writers belonged. As

I have already discussed, postmodern philosophy was a quasi-religious moralistic ideology with a cult-like following masquerading as scholarship. In retrospect, the rhetoric about empowering the other was merely self-serving and highly immoral.

It was self-serving because, as Sangren (1988: 411) pointed out, these texts did nothing to overcome the sociopolitical inequalities around the world, but they did enhance careers in the universities where their authors worked and were tenured. Their rhetoric of de-legitimation undermined academic authority figures, bolstered their personal institutional standing, while their demonization of "totalizing theories " and malicious portrayals of other perspectives denied opponents the opportunity to voice their viewpoints. Thus, as Sangren (1988: 414) points out:

> This amounts to a kind of desire for authority without responsibility.... Space is created for young scholars by ruling out the validity of earlier scholarship (and those who practice it); one is free to experiment and to criticize, delegitimate, demystify, deconstruct, explode, subvert, transgress, etc., any sort of "other," real or fabricated, that suits one's purposes, without bearing responsibility for defending one's positions; and an openly acknowledged freedom to engage in mystification and creative self-empowering fabrication unaccountable to any challenge of logic or facts is simultaneously and summarily appropriated for experimental writers and denied to totalizing "others."

One would think, given all the hype, bluster, and hubris about the excellence of postmodern theories and the declared purported amazing experimental moments, that these scholars would have bequeathed us with vast and perceptive insights about the human condition, social justice, equality, and so forth. Where are these superb and sublime texts that we may consult them? Where are the brilliant breakthroughs of the experimental moment? Where are the cases of liberating anyone in the real world? Sadly, there are none. This is because in the end this entire ethnographic enterprise boiled down storytelling and poetic orations. They weren't even good stories and poems because, alas, none of these sages possessed Geertz's literary aptitude and command of the English language.

Did the postmodern view of knowledge represent "the rearrangement of the very principles of intellectual perspective" (Herzfeld 2001: x, 2, 5, 9, 22), as one infatuated true-believer put it? No. Was its case against science in anthropology compelling and based on evidence? No. What the postmodern savants offered was disinformation and an intellectually dishonest enterprise that accomplished nothing aside from bewildering their students about the role and function of science. This was something that as scientifically illiterate Americans they needed the least.

There was a great deal of callous disregard about the consequences of the dogma these erudite anthropologists were prescribing. Tim O'Meara's (1995: 427) warning, which fits our present circumstances today even more than it did twenty-five years ago, was this:

> I hold that epistemological relativism is evil. It is an instrument of subjugation, not liberation. No matter how righteous the cause, it is dangerous as well as false to claim a special "way of knowing" about the physical world that produces "knowledge" which is immune to empirical testing and logical contradiction. Well-meaning people should stop handling that venomous snake-which they apparently do not understand and certainly cannot control-before it turns fascist and bites us all.

Why didn't these savants grasp the irrationality and incoherence of what they were peddling? Why didn't they consider the consequences of their teachings? If we are generous we might attribute their certitude to various difficult to control cognitive biases. In the anthropology departments that they were able to take over and dominate and during the conferences they attended, group-think was probably a factor, meaning people of like mind encouraging each other into greater zeal and passion about what they believe (cf., French and Stone 2014: 119–120). They indeed lauded and cited each other's works endlessly, published in journals under their editorial control, hired their own ilk, and were remarkably unconcerned about the cogency or coherence of their narratives. Sokal demonstrated this in a dramatic fashion, we may recall, when he put the ideas of the masters of this school of thought to the test. We could also suggest that the Dunning-Kruger effect was operating in these academic units. The savants overestimate their own intelligence and competence leading them to the conviction that they could not be wrong (Dunning 2011; Kruger and Dunning 1999). How else does one explain the irresponsible way these luminaries conducted their scholarly endeavors?

If these cognitive factors were not at work, then it puzzling why these purported "experts" in human society and culture overlooked the fact that when members of a society are unable to differentiate between true and false claims—which is what they were encouraging—they become prone to accept the declarations charlatans, scoundrels, and mountebanks (cf., Schick and Vaughn 2014: 13). That is how post-truth American appeared.

Further, why didn't these specialists in human behavior know that "science and democracy are intertwined" because both empower people by encouraging critical thinking and reasoned debate crucial to the democratic process (Ambasciano 2018: 172)? Why else do right-wing reactionaries and conservative forces exert enormous amounts of effort and resources to abandon facts and "delegitimize science" and its significance in human life (Snyder

2017: 65). The alternative to the explanations above is worse, it means that these virtuosos were intellectually dishonest and knowingly inculcated bogus ideas in their students and through their publications.

But none of these issues matter because these professors operating in this country's highest academic institutions—in this case departments of anthropology—formulated and disseminated an elaborate anti-intellectual dogma that disparaged truth, denigrated knowledge, encouraged irrational thinking and lauded and fostered the progression of pseudoscientific beliefs. For this there is no excuse no matter how vigorous the special-pleading on offer may be.

Chapter 10

Paranormal and Theistic Anthropology

From Postmodernism to Post-Truth Supernaturalism

Postmodern anthropology is mostly defunct. However, postmodern ideas continue to impact the discipline in various ways. In its initial incarnation, the savants in this field were interested in a kind of reflexive critique. However, their enterprise morphed into present-day perspectives that advocate and extoll particular ideological stances. These included what I call "paranormal anthropology" and "theistic anthropology," both of which I find particularly problematic and objectionable. The reason is that the purveyors of these approaches, to borrow a phrase from the philosopher and New Testament scholar Robert Price, are dignifying credulity as a method (Price 2010: 274). Their enterprise is not about the discovery of new knowledge about the empirical world—they already possess the purported truths they wish to advocate—but to advance particular faith-based religious or supernaturalist agendas.

I will first discuss paranormal anthropology because theistic anthropology more or less piggybacked on developments in this area to justify inserting faith-based beliefs into the discipline. Unfortunately, while there are some colleagues in other subfields of the discipline, such as archeology, who are striving to address the challenges posed to their area of study by pseudoscientific and paranormal perspectives, cultural anthropologists have embraced and are propagating such approaches. A case in point is Jeb Card's book *Spooky Archaeology: Myth and the Science of the Past* (2018), where he systematically addresses the difficulties presented to that field by alternative archaeologists, Ley Lines enthusiasts, lost continent seekers, and other hacks and cranks.

Regrettably, cultural anthropology has played a significant role in encouraging paranormalism and pseudoscientific outlooks in the context of researching the magical principles and mystical practices of faraway cultures.

As early the 1960s, the attitude was that the paranormal beliefs and practice of indigenous people had to be respected and treated no differently than science and reason (Andersen 2017: 196–197). Under the influence of postmodern thought, such beliefs were exalted further as instances of marginalized perspectives falsely denigrated by science and rationality but which had equal epistemic parity with science (itself a mere story). These understandings of the world are, therefore, to be revered and given space so that the voices of their proponents, gurus, shamans, and messiahs could be heard in the name of the postmodernist emancipation of the "other." Andersen (2017: 193–194) who is not an anthropologist, offers the outsider's perspective about what these anthropologist were up to:

> Anthropology decided that oracles, diviners, incantations, and magical objects should be not just respected but considered equivalent to reason and science. If all understandings of reality are socially constructed, those of the Kalahari people . . . are no more arbitrary or faith-based than those of professors.

He makes the following observation regarding Carlos Castaneda's work that I mentioned earlier:

> [The sorcerer Castaneda encountered] fed him hallucinogens—jimsonweed, peyote, psilocybin mushrooms—and told him he would reveal the secrets that make up the lot of mans knowledge. Under the influence of drugs, Castaneda says he turned into a crow, talked to coyotes, and communed with spirits. . . . Castaneda, enthusiastically endorsed by [Margaret] Mead, reported on the so-called primitive people to persuade Americans that magic was real.

I cannot find any reasons to disagree with this assessment. Castaneda said that his experiences were not hallucinations but that they indeed took place in "an alternate reality." Here we have both epistemic and ontological relativism right out of the tendentious postmodern philosophy books. Castaneda's message was that there is more to reality than meets the eyes. Further, that the world is more mysterious than we know, spirits are real and ever-present, and that there is profound wisdom in sacred knowledge of indigenous cultures that are beyond the boundaries of empirical understanding.

This message resonated and still resonates heavily with popular audiences in Fantasyland, United States, including the followers of the New Age movement and groups of neo-shamans seeking enchantment in the modern world, all of whom are disillusioned by science and technology and a materialistic world view. They want their own shamanic visions and magical flights to the beyond. These perspectives, as I have already discussed, where the non-academic counterparts or doppelgängers of postmodernism. The postmodern philosophers encouraged and celebrated the public expression of such irrational and nonsensical views as part of their mission. This, we might recall, is how postmodern radicals construed emancipation and justice for all.

Yes, there have always been a few honest fieldworkers who rejected the idea that paranormal forces and beings have an ontological reality independent of the observer in a particular culture. They looked on ghosts, demons, angels, and goblins as aspects of a given culture's consensual reality rather than constituting a facet of a universal reality of all cultures (e.g., Murdock 1980: 54; Spiro1982: 52; Lett 1997b). However, such individuals have always been a minority.

Indeed, one could argue that in cultural anthropology paranormal beliefs have not been the exception but the rule. Consider Joseph K. Long's book *Extrasensory Ecology: Parapsychology and Anthropology* (1977). In this volume he vouches for the ontological reality of "ghosts, astral projection, and poltergeists," the probability of levitation, and the genuine nature of psychic surgery (Long 1977: vii, 248, 375, 384–385). Scientific anthropologist James Lett (1997b: 117) rightly described this book as "perhaps one of the most regrettable examples of the irrational approach to the paranormal within cultural anthropology."

Even revered figures in American anthropology were staunch paranormalists. Margaret Mead, to name one, was an ardent advocate of such beliefs. She spread the truth about such matters in her public lectures and essays (Lett 1997a: 67; Mead 1977: 48). Her status as an icon in the field—a veritable disciplinary mother goddess to her acolytes—gave credence to the supernatural bunkum she espoused and was already all too common in popular culture in Idiot America. More than that, Mead used her prestige as an academic superstar to gain membership for the pseudoscientific Parapsychological Association into the American Association for the Advancement of Science (Lett 1997b: 113). The noted physicist John Wheeler was justifiably appalled by this and remarked that giving parapsychology a place on the same platform as science dignified what he described as "pathological" pseudoscientific enterprise (Gardner1989: 185–192).

In general, however, anthropologists have often evaded or ignored the question of whether or not spirits actually exist or addressed the ontological status of supernatural beliefs (cf., Lett 1997b: 103–104; Sidky 2015: 11–12). This stance is referred to a methodological agnosticism and is associated with the principle of cultural relativism (i.e., looking at cultural items in their own contexts). A good representation of this viewpoint is to be found in the work of the noted British anthropologist Edward Evans-Pritchard (1965: 17) who maintained that

> [the anthropologist] is not concerned, *qua* anthropologist, with the truth or falsity of religious thought. As I understand the matter there is no possibility

of *knowing* whether the spiritual beings of primitive religions or of any others have any existence or not, and since that is the case he cannot take the question into consideration.

Methodological agnosticism disallows the critical scrutiny of religion in terms of scientifically meaningful categories in accordance with the tradition of systematic skepticism. For instance, as the American anthropologist Richley Crapo (2003: 8–9) says:

> If we resort to simply deciding that belief in things that are not accepted by the contemporary scientific community as "real" should be called "supernatural beliefs," then we adopt a truly ethnocentric method, one that amounts in essence to equating "supernatural" with "(scientifically) false."

The sad fact is, contrary to what writers such as Crapo maintain, all things supernatural, paranormal, religious, transcendental, or any other label one wishes to use are indeed scientifically false (see Sidky 2020). As Lett (1997b: 111) bluntly put it, every paranormal and supernatural belief in every culture, regardless of whether their sponsors are shamans, priests, rabbis, mullahs, or psychics, is demonstrably untrue (see chapter 7).

Other anthropologists have approached the idea of spirits and related phenomena through a non-paranormal perspective, using psychological, sociological, or symbolic analytical frameworks. Such approaches are meaningful to the researcher, rather than making sense in terms of the indigenous explanatory models of reality and conceptions of reality. In other words, while the insiders' supernatural views of people in different cultures were considered anthropologically interesting and worthy of exploration and analysis, they were seldom taken as a valid alternative to the Western scientific construal of reality (Young and Goulet 1994: 10). At least not until the writings of the French postmodern philosophers became available to the mostly monolingual American cultural anthropologists.

A departure from the earlier perspective and also from the cultural relativistic framework occurred during the 1980s under the influence of postmodern dogma regarding the nature of reality, its claims regarding the bogus character of scientific investigation, and the ideas of "multiple truths," and "multiple ways of knowing." If these things were true, then it followed, that no one could say what is false. All types of "theories" could now be entertained on a level playing field. All previous studies were now branded as "reductionist" because they treated supernatural beliefs and paranormal experiences as explicable in terms of psychological, cognitive, ecological, or some other material factors. Parnormalist and theistic anthropologist criticized such approaches because they treated religious and supernatural beliefs as "epiphenomena." Given these assumptions, field researchers during this time period adopted an alternate approach, or an alternative way of knowing, to put it in present-day post-truth jargon. Their goal was to obtain alternative hermeneutic truths, which entailed being respectful of both of the object of inquiry and of the inquirer. Again, facts were deemed to be inseparable from the observer reporting them so the ethnographers engaged such in such work had to document their own inner soliloquies and provide information about themselves (cf., Gellner 1992: 25).

The coterie of writers that are of interest here are those who began writing about their subjective paranormal experiences, ghostly encounters, and spooky feelings while engaged in field research. Advocates referred to this approach as "experiential ethnography," "extraordinary anthropology," or more recently, "paranthropology." I prefer to call this perspective "paranormal anthropology" for reasons that shall become clear below. I would have used the term "spooky anthropology" had not Card thought of it first.

Using their hermeneutic approach, these intrepid seekers declared that they had found an innovative method to understand reality that had evaded all others before them. They were thus able to grasp the reality of the spirit world or know that spirits, ghosts, and other incorporeal agents exist, something they say that other approaches have failed to do (Goulet and Miller 2007: 5; Koss-Chioino 2010: 131). Moreover, in doing so, they said that they had "completely redefined what is considered valid ethnographic experience and research" (Koss-Chioino 2010: 132; Goulet and Miller 2007).

This is the same sort of hubris exhibited by other postmodern savants in anthropology, who referred to their endeavor and "the rearrangement of the very principles of intellectual perspective" (e.g., Herzfeld 2001: x, 2, 5, 9, 22). So, more of the same. The paranormalists also reaffirmed other tidbits of standard and dubious postmodern dogma. They held that science and scientific knowledge would no longer be privileged, all voices and claims to knowledge were to be equally heard and respected, and anthropology would no longer defend modernity against the "spiritual knowledge of other cultures" (Hufford 2010: 256). What astonishing claims!

The roots of paranormal anthropology go back to Castaneda. Sadly, originality of thought has never been the forte of these intrepid trailblazers and experimental ethnographers. They consider Castaneda's approach as the first "experiential ethnography" of the paranormal by a social scientist (Marton 1994: 273). It should be noted that his way of doing ethnography was not an immediate hit because, we might recall, it turned out that Mr. Castaneda was a fraud. He basically fabricated his paranormal adventures using the ethnographic findings of other anthropologists (De Mille 1976, 1990).

By the 1980s, however, circumstances had changed, and none of this mattered. Recall that Baudrillard (1986: 142) had said that objective "truth doesn't exist." Latour (1985: 99, 186, 258) had shown that truth is established as a result of dialogic agreement among people. Kuhn and Feyerabend were saying that truth is irrelevant in developing theories or knowledge. And Foucault (1984: 75) had argued the scientific knowledge could no longer be privileged and any alternative perspectives or claims should be extolled as long as they emanated from among the powerless, the marginal, the incarcerated, and the insane. Finally, Marcus and Fisher (1986) had transformed Geertz's ideas of ethnography as fiction and the premise of culture as text to declare that ethnographies were made up or fictive constructions and affirmed that objective empirical accounts of culture are impossible and immoral. This is why writers inspired by the French philosophers as a group experienced so much anguish about their field experiences. But that did not matter so much because if ethnography is the outcome of dialogical interactions between anthropologists and informants then ethnographers' subjective, intuitive experiences of ghosts and spooky things, and imagination could be treated as valid data (Goulet and Young 1994). Now, Castaneda's writing acquired new significance and became sources of inspiration for these radical but anguished ghost-seeking postmodern fieldworkers. Remember how the postmodern savants George Marcus and Michael Fischer (1986: 40) praised Castaneda's work as an "alternative textual strategy" utterly unconcerned about his plagiarism, fake facts, or the issue of validation.

The first ethnographers to act on this new realization were Michael Harner and the late Bruce Grindal (Glass-Coffin and Kiiskeentum 2012; Glass-Coffin 2010: 208; Grindal 1983; Hellweg et al. 2015). As a result of his field experiences, Harner now professes his belief in the reality of the spirit world and says that for him that realm is as tangible as the world of people. He arrived at this insight through personal experience after ingesting powerful hallucinogenic drugs while doing field research among the Jivaro of Ecuador. That is when he personally met the beings and beasties of the paranormal world of his host culture and became a true-believer (Harner 1999: 1–2).

Along similar paranormal lines, Grindal (1983: 60) offered an astonishing paranormal account of seeing a Ghanaian man's return from the dead, or an actual resurrection. Grindal (1983: 60) had an anomalous experience—a lot of people have these. I have had them as well, although my encounters did not lead me to become a true-believer in ghosts and other spooky things (Sidky 2017: 101, 2020: 125). Grindal admits that he had his experience while in an "altered state of consciousness." However, he interpreted this event in paranormal terms, rather than psychologically as a hallucination or delusion. To the contrary, he said that what he experienced was something beyond the limits of ordinary empirical understanding (Hellweg et al. 2015: 205–216).

In true postmodern fashion, Grindal apprehended his experience in terms of the intersubjectivity of the event with his informants, whereby his intuitive grasp of their explanation of the occurrence informed his ultimate understanding of the resurrection event. His conclusion was: the canons of empirical research must be set aside if we are to achieve a genuine understanding of what is real (Gridal 1983: 76). Some laud Grindal's essay as an exemplary model "for anthropological methods across the sub-disciplines" of anthropology (Hellweg et al. 2015: 207). The way to understand the mysterious preternatural world of "the other," it seems, is beyond empirical analysis and can only be grasped through private, intuitive and subjective procedures (Jackson 1989: 52; Stoller 1986: 55).

Here the anthropologist is not simply suspending judgment, which is a corollary of the principle of cultural relativism (i.e., looking at beliefs and practices in their particular contexts), but rather suspending disbelief, which is a corollary of ontological relativism (i.e., accepting as real the construal of reality by members of the cultures being studied). This is the same problematic incoherent radical epistemic skepticism also found in the tracts of many other luminaries, including the founding figures of postmodern philosophy.

These anthropologists reject cultural relativism because, they say, framing beliefs in spirits and other paranormal phenomena in terms of cultural relativism removes such precepts from "serious consideration" (Glass-Coffin and Kiiskeentum 2012: 113). Moreover, this stance is disrespectful. Such matters must be respected, appreciated, and taken seriously. What "respect" and "take seriously" really mean is often never fully clarified (cf., McCutcheon 2001: 4–5). Here is how paranormalist Paul Stoller described respect in his book *In Sorcery's Shadow: A Memoir of Apprenticeship among the Songhay of Niger* (1989). This writer proudly claimed that he essentially adopted the entire range of Songhay superstitious beliefs. Among the various paranormal experiences he had, Stoller (1989: 148) recounts a frightening panic attack, which he defined as an entity encounter. He goes on to say how the magical incantations he learned from the locals thankfully saved him from this supernatural assault. Stoller (1989: 229) described what he took away from his field experience as follows:

> As anthropologists, we must respect the people among whom we work. [...] For me, respect means accepting fully beliefs and phenomena which our system of knowledge often holds preposterous. I took my teachers seriously. They *knew* that I used divination in my personal life. They *knew* that I had eaten powders to

protect myself. They *knew* that I wore objects to demonstrate my respect for the spirits. They *knew* I had an altar in my house over which I recited incantations.

Really? Here, respecting, appreciating, and taking religion "seriously"—an aphorism that these anthropologists endlessly recite—as religious studies scholar Robert Segal (1983: 110) pointed out long ago in relation to his area of study, amounts to taking the stance of the devotee over that of the skeptic on metaphysical issues and entails an understanding of religion with endorsement. In short, it is something close to religious "conversion" (Wiebe 1984: 158). This sort of cross-cultural gullibility and paranormalism among anthropologists is most regrettable. Nevertheless, today these writers insist on the validity of their approach and claim that such matters must be taken "seriously" and describe their task "to bear first-person witness to the reality of unseen world" (Glass-Coffin and Kiiskeentum 2012: 125), that is, that spirits and the spirit world actually exist outside the consensual reality of any given culture.

There are many highly problematic issues with this style of anthropology, starting with the assumptions made regarding spirits, ghosts, and goblins. For paranormal anthropologists, the idea that spirits and "other realities" exist is based entirely upon the ethnographer's personal subjective experiences in the field and is taken as axiomatic (Koss-Chioino 2010: 140; Turner 1994: 87, 2010: 218). As paranormal anthropologist Edith Turner (1998: 84) has put it, "spirits actually exist." That is it! That is all that is offered as evidence, a subjective impression. What Turner and like-minded companions misunderstand is that this is the *claim* not the *proof* of what is being asserted. Proof requires evidence. Hearsay won't do. For Turner, however, this is the only "parsimonious anthropological explanation" for such paranormal encounters in the field that accounts both for the anthropologist's experience and that of the members of the host culture (Turner 1994: 83, 87). But is this the most parsimonious explanation? Or have we sauntered into the swamp of gullibility?

Actually, no, it is not the most parsimonious explanation. Turner is parroting the same banal reason for the existence of spirits, ghosts, and spooky things, repeated by believers the world over. Paranormal anthropologists assert that the ubiquity of spirit encounters—a percentage of people in all cultures have anomalous experiences—and spirit beliefs is compelling evidence that spirits have an ontological reality independent of the human mind (Hufford 2010: 142–143; Koss-Chioino 2010). Not so. Recall that the scientific perspective requires that we must always consider plausible alternative hypotheses that are more consistent with other empirical explanations and observations before settling on supernatural ones (see chapter 7). By ejecting scientific methodologies, these ghost-seekers and visionaries fail to consider that the explanation for such weird experiences is not in mysterious jurisdictions and hidden realities for which there is absolutely no evidence, but in humans themselves. I mean human biopsychological and cognitive dispositions that make occasional paranormal impressions inevitable for some people across space and time (Bridgstock 2009: 50).

Indeed, research in clinical and cognitive psychology and human behavior has shown that the human perceptual apparatus, while reliable most of the time, has limitations and operates in a way that guarantees that we will have "ostensibly paranormal experiences" (French 2001: 4). As psychologist James Alcock (1985: 538–539) points out:

> Often our brains can mislead us, and can lead us to believe that we have had a paranormal experience even when no such thing has happened. Indeed, even if there is no such thing as a paranormal phenomenon, human information processing works in such a way that we are all likely from time to time to have experiences that seem for all the world to be paranormal.

Such experiences are the cost of possessing the type of cognitive and information processing capacities conferred upon us by evolution that is capable of rapidly processing large amounts of incomplete data and yielding conclusions for action (Gilovich1991: 2; Sidky 2020: 93–110, 121–140).

The evidence that such experiences are brain based and not otherworldly is extensive (Persinger and Makarec 1987; Stenger 1990: 106; Zusne and Jones 1989: 69). As the physicist and philosopher Victor Stenger (2012: 242) put it, the fact that no paranormal claim has withstood scientific scrutiny compels us to conclude that such phenomena do not exist. In other words, widespread experiences of seeing ghosts or apparitions, having spooky and weird sensations, or encounters with the unseen worlds, and so forth are due to something rather trivial, namely that "the central nervous system of all human beings exhibits some common functional properties" (Brugger 2001: 210). Oh, but let us not forget that postmodern cultural critics disregard scientific evidence and evolutionary theory as modernity's "totalizing theories" or "hegemonic discourse," or something like that.

Paranormal anthropologists are too enthralled with their supposed ghost sightings and glimpses into the beyond to be concerned about rational parsimonious explanations. They simply take the existence of spirits as a given. As cultural and medical anthropologist Bonnie Glass-Coffin (2010: 206–207) states it explicitly, experiential anthropology requires that we accept the reality of "unseen worlds" and take at face value "spiritual and cognitive maps" that differ from our own. Why? Well, by doing so fulfills a political agenda shared by these writers, that is to challenge Western assumptions about the nature of reality, and repudiate modernity—which they hold in great contempt—and thereby create a "truly decolonized ethnography" (Glass-Coffin and Kiiskeentum 2012: 115; Glass-Coffin 2010: 206–207). Thus, paranormal anthropologists have politicized ontological relativism and their notion of liberation is to write ghost stories, a sort of supernatural emancipation on paper. An astonishing achievement, indeed.

But there is more. These writers boldly declare that visionary experiences and spirit encounters will no longer be rendered as "artifacts of primitive cultures," stigmatized, or dismissed as naïve, retrograde, and pathological as conventional anthropologists have done (Hufford 2010: 146). But have they been so depicted? Instead, such experiences are to be fully embraced and their ontological and epistemological implications explored and acknowledged. This is not "going native," they say, but rather a way of experiencing the spiritual reality of others first hand (Wilkes 2007: 75–76). What the differences between these two conditions are is never specified.

One writer even takes a conspiratorial angle, suggesting that conventional anthropologists are afraid of "rendering the uncanny at face value" because of what it might reveal about the facts of life and history (Goslinga 2013: 388). Such statements are good indicators of how scientifically illiterate such writers are. Scientists have not shied away from grappling with such phenomena and claims. As Fishman and Boudry (2013: 924) observe, "Science can (and has already evaluated) supernatural claims according to the same explanatory criteria used to assess any other 'non-supernatural' claim." Unfortunately for believers, the results of such systematic evaluations have unvaryingly been negative. "Such claims," Boudry et al. (2010: 227) point out, "do not fall beyond the reach of science; they have simply failed." To reiterate Fishman's (2009: 831) observation:

> The best explanation for why there has been so far no convincing, independently verifiable evidence for supernatural phenomena, despite honest and methodologically sound attempts to verify them, is that these phenomena probably do not exist. Indeed, the absence of evidence, where such evidence is expected to be found after extensive searching, is evidence of absence.

Similarly, as Jerry Coyne (2015: 113) says something similar: "Over its history, science has repeatedly investigated supernatural claims and, in principle, could find strong evidence for them. But that evidence has not appeared." Hence, a reasonable conclusion, he adds, is "that the absence of evidence is indeed evidence of absence" (Coyne 2015: 204).

For paranormal anthropologists such as David Young and Jean-Guy Goulet (1994: 14, 19) adopting the explanatory model of the host culture for paranormal experiences is necessary. It demonstrates the depth to which the ethnographer has penetrated an alien culture and the degree to which his psychic and cognitive patterns have harmonized with those of the members of that culture, thereby opening up alternate realities. Really? Or is this being too besotted with postulated unseen agencies and hidden realities and a gross amount of sheer gullibility? But, for the paranormalists the implications of this realization are momentous. As they say, access to these previously impenetrable aspects of human experience leads one to question taken-for-granted assumptions about the nature of existence and the realization that the structure of reality may be quite different from the observer's own culturally constructed views about what is real. How does this constitute a novel finding? Mystics, self-styled ambassadors from heaven, poets, psi believers, addicts, and schizophrenics and lunatics have been telling others about these sorts of experiences and feelings for millennia.

However, for the paranormalists in anthropology, emic accounts of the reality of other cultures have greater validity than the defective culture-bound rationalist perspective espoused by Western science because they have tapped into the "really real." The problem with such statements is that nowhere is there any evidence offered in support of even one of these claims. Their ghost beliefs are a priori assumptions. The kinds of things they report are merely subjective impressions, anecdotal reports, and opinions, which constitute some of the worst types of evidence there is. This is because of the many human cognitive and perceptual biases involving anecdotal and eyewitness reports that often results in distorted accounts and even resulting in testimonies about things that have never happened (Holt et al. 2012: 28; Loftus 1993; Smith 2010: 182). Like the proponents of pseudoscientific perspectives, these anthropologists are forwarding extraordinary claims without the requisite extraordinary evidence. Simply saying it is true because I saw or felt something is insufficient. This is not even a new philosophical problem. Long ago, the ever-insightful Thomas Paine (1880 [1794]: 3) made a point about subjective reports of otherworldly encounters and supernatural experiences that applies here: As he put it:

> Something has been revealed to a certain person, and not revealed to any other person, it is a revelation to that person only. When he tells it to a second person, a second to a third, a third to a fourth, and so on, it ceases to be a revelation to all those other persons. It is a revelation to the first person only, and hearsay to every other, and consequently they are not obliged to believe it.

Paranormal anthropologists are asking us to accept hearsay about the reality of the other worldly beings and forces as first-person testimonials. This assertion is not compelling.

None of these observations are relevant, however, because these writers adamantly and unanimously reject science and rationality as a way of knowing. For them, science is an invalid, ethnocentric, Eurocentric, immoral, and even worse, "cognocentric" (meaning dedicated to the acquisition, growth, logical analysis, and advancement of knowledge). As such, they consider it an inappropriate goal for anthropology (Turner 2010: 218). All naturalistic, scientific explanations of spirit beliefs are deemed to be unfortunate, misconceived, misleading, and disrespectful (Koss-Chioino 2010: 133). Moreover, the empirical procedures used by science-oriented researchers, it is maintained, constrain the full apprehension of reality, which involves phenomena beyond the limits of ordinary perceptions and empirical understanding. It is also, let us not forget, a form of domination and neocolonialism. This is where their subjective acuities, with which they are endowed but all others lack, come into play.

This sort of epistemic relativism is seductive, but it is an incoherent and false premise, as discussed in the previous chapters. But the stance these writers take against science is understandable because of the nature of the subject matter under discussion. As Grindal (1983: 76) put it, paranormal phenomena do not lend themselves to rational analysis, objective corroboration, filming, tape-recording, and so forth, all of which he considers "moot issues." In other words, paranormal anthropologists consider themselves exempt from conventional evidentiary and methodological criteria of research and are asking for a license to espouse whatever they feel without accountably.

Given that you cannot prove the existence of spirits scientifically, the argument goes, these anthropologists by necessity must jettison science and rationality as part of the reviled "Enlightenment episteme" (Glass-Coffin and Kiiskeentum 2012: 115). Moreover, to "experience the real" requires that we open ourselves to new possibilities through subjective and private approaches (Goulet and Miller 2007: 5; Jackson 1989: 55; Stoller 1986: 52). They describe this approach as "subjective-cognitive engagement" to attain knowledge impossible to acquire "through normal means of objective observation" (Hunter 2012: 37, 2018). Experiential anthropologists, like the conventional postmodern savants, envision themselves as embattled champions of truth, intrepid pioneers of spiritual illumination helping to usher in a revolutionary and profound understanding of the world, and courageously fighting "an entrenched scientific establishment that is conservative, close-minded, and culture-bound" (Lett 1991: 309).

Finally, for these individuals, the "perceived realities of the unseen worlds" experienced firsthand represent a transformative occasion and a source of personal spiritual growth, which, as I see it, is religious conversion (e.g., Glass-Coffin 2010: 209, 212; Goulet and Miller 2007: 2). Lots of people in lots of places have such conversion experiences. How is the anthropological variety any different or more significant? Perhaps they carry more weight because its expositors are educated professors with credential such as PhDs employed by prestigious institutions.

All sorts of problems arise here. This enterprise is no longer about description and analysis or translation, but rather about a kind of understanding based upon embracing and "surrendering to the unknown" (Glass-Coffin 2010: 215), whatever that means! This is advocacy for native spirituality or endorsement of indigenous superstitions. For this reason, their narratives say more about their personal cognitive frames and cultural gullibility rather than about the subject matter their stories are supposed to illuminate. One could easily make the case that this as a form of mysticism defined here as "the immediate spiritual intuition of non-verifiable truths that are believed to transcend ordinary understanding" (Lett 1991: 326).

What one finds here is embarrassing credulity and maybe a bit of duplicity. What these writers are promoting, simply put, are "alternative ways of knowing," "subjective truths," "alternative facts," and "counter-knowledge." It is a deceitful way of justifying positions that lack rational and evidentiary warrant and to express beliefs presented as being exempt from all scientific challenges. Such views are versions of the onerous present-day post-truth stuff that is also pivotal to current right-wing bunkum. In other words, that facts and opinions are indistinguishable, for every fact there is an equally valid "alternative fact," truth is in the eye of the beholder, and "if it's true for you, it's true." Paranormal anthropology has a secure home in Fantasyland, United States or Idiot America.

Aside from encouraging and promoting irrationalism and corrupting the standards of critical thought and honest intellectual inquiry, paranormal anthropology has had two unfortunate effects. On the one hand, it has emboldened fundamentalist Christians to advance their archaic and medieval superstitions. For example, the Christian apologist Craig Keener cites this anthropological literature as the basis of the methodology he uses in his massive two-volume work *Miracles: The Credibility of the New Testament Accounts* (2011). In that work, he claims that the resurrections of the dead are common and solidly documented occurrences worldwide, religious miracles are genuine empirically documented supernatural events everywhere, and hence the gospel fables are true (Keener 2011: 220–227). I have addressed Keener's work elsewhere and it is unnecessary to elaborate here (see Sidky 2020: 190–200).

On the other hand, paranormal anthropology has spawned something called "theistic anthropology," which is of concern to the present discussion. What is theistic anthropology? As one of its expositors explains, this approach assumes the ontological validity of religious truths (Bielo 2015: 39). This perspective is founded upon the various postmodern notions that have already been discussed. First, that science has been delegitimized—it has not, this is merely religionist and postmodernist wishful thinking—therefore their superstitious beliefs now have equal or greater validity. Again, post-truth stuff. Also widely shared among these writers is the postmodernists' hatred of modernity and the Enlightenment, as well as the rejection of science and scientific approaches to the study of human phenomena. They all have the same goal as that of the much-cited postmodern maven Susan Harding. For her, this research track is a means "to problematize the [modernist] apparatus, its representations, and its constitutive power as hegemonic discourse which directly defines and dialogically generates its 'other,' and then investigate [it] in that context" (Harding 1991: 391–391).

Theistic anthropologists also cast-off the axiomatic separation of the observer and observed, insisting on the "absolute inseparability of 'experience' and 'construal'" (Bielo 2015: 39; Kahn 2011: 83). This is an aspect of their effort to deconstruct modernity's "totalizing opposition between 'us' and 'them'" (Harding 1991: 393). Such an approach opens the possibilities of establishing the validity of alternate epistemic systems, in this case, specifically evangelical Christianity. What is on offer is a perspective suited to what its proponents call "the post-secular age" and a post-reflexive era, where theology has thankfully returned (Robbins 2006: 288; Kahn 2011: 76). As Philip Fountain and Sin Wen Lau (2013: 228–229), two other proponents of this viewpoint, put it: "The widely heralded 'return of theology' to the humanities and social sciences is one of the most remarkable new features of contemporary academia." Here we are in post-truth land. It appears that fundamentalist Christianity has now superseded postmodernism in the exact fields of study, the social sciences and the humanities.

Also rejected is the ethnographic strategy of bracketing out of faith or belief during field research. Joel Kahn (2011: 79), another religionist, argues that the tactic of methodological agnosticism during field research when one encounters "those whose experience one might at first find fantastical" is untenable. He adds:

> A common strategy is to require that faith-based truth claims are "bracketed out," treating secular and religious discourse as "nonoverlapping magisterial." This secularizing strategy is, however, problematic on a number of counts (Kahn 2011: 76).

You might recall the discussion earlier that some religionists are unhappy with Gould's NOMA. The rejection of methodological agnosticism is understandable because these writers are true-believers with an agenda to make anthropology a Christian discipline and an instrument for proselytizing the Lord's words. Thus, they wholeheartedly reject Gould's nonoverlapping magisteria because they consider it tantamount to a condescending and insulting bracketing-out strategic agnosticism (Kahn 2011: 80). For them, this attitude is ultimately an ethnocentric endeavor that "does violence to all modes of experiencing and being in the world" (Kahn 2011: 82). They will have none of that. Why? Because they wish to move beyond modernity's restricted one-dimensional construal of selfhood and open the possibility that mystical experiences have a central place in modern culture. But hasn't that been the assertions of our New Age gurus, vatics, wizards, and home-grown evangelical ayatollahs since at least the 1960s?

More importantly, this non-agnostic methodological stance is essential to these writer because through it they are able to avoid the thorny problem of treating experiences of the divine as something ordinary or "epiphenomenal" when they encounter people who say that their religious experiences are sublime and beyond "human experiencing altogether" (Kahn 2011: 81). The methodological stance theistic anthropologists are advocating will allow all the marginal voices of what Harding (1991, 2000) called "the repugnant cultural other" of secular modernity to be treated with the respect they deserve. We are on the path to liberating the "other" once more, but this time in a spiritual sense, and once again on paper.

The term epiphenomena, which these writers repeat endlessly, require a comment. It is another word for and has the same function as what the Romanian philosopher and historian of religion Mircea Eliade called "reductionist" or "reductionism." These terminologies have become catchphrases among religious studies researchers who use them to dismiss perspectives that depart from their deferential treatment of religious phenomena as things explicable solely in their own terms (Segal 1983: 98; Sidky 2020: 28).

Thus, through such a respectful approach, the world can be re-enchanted once more and religious experiences maligned by science, and rationalism are no longer deemed as poetic fancies, but superior perspectives. It should be said that these true-believing writers are solely concerned with religious experiences related to the god of Christianity, not those associated with an all-inclusive egalitarian cadre of supernaturals, such as Quetzalcoatl, Baʿal, Amun Ra, Jupiter, Ahura Mazda, Shiva, or Dorji Drakden.

Also unacceptable for these theist writers is the modernist notion of the secular rational self, or the sense of selfhood offered by scientific naturalism, that casts people into a disenchanted world and compels to think that there is:

> nothing transcendent, that the world is not an enchanted one, that things do not happen for reasons beyond nature, that time is unidirectional and the short span of my existence finite, and that my body occupies a place in empty and potentially infinite space in the same way as do all other material objects (Kahn 2011: 78).

Fountain and Lau (2013: 230) explain why the secular self is objectionable: "All secular social theory, whether modern or postmodern, is inherently nihilistic and bound within an ontology of perpetual violence which can only lead to perennial conflict." It seems that these writers at some stage in their intellectual progression also turn negatively on the philosophical precepts of postmodernism that have facilitated their approach, just as the proponents of Intelligent Design Creationism have done, as already discussed.

Rejection of the secular self also means that these writers reject the "disciplinary bias" that anthropology is a completely secular analytical project (Cannell 2006: 1). The only reason anthropology has until now been averse to engaging Christianity at home, they add, is because the field developed in the anti-religious environment of post-Enlightenment. This unjustified and arbitrary secular bias, Fountain and Lau (2013: 229) say, also explains "anthropology's long-standing resistance to 'taking seriously the religious experiences of others' . . . [which] inhibits our ability to engage in serious conversations about and with theology" (Fountain and Lau 2013: 229).

One of the works they often cite to bolster their perspective is Edward Evans-Pritchard's (1962) paper presented to an audience of believers after his conversion to Catholicism because he raised some of these issues (Hann 2007: 385). Once anthropology makes such an attitude adjustment, the argument goes, it will become possible to envision once again a religiously charged and mystical world where personal faith has a value and the respect it deserves. The shift to the engagement of Christianity also permits these anthropologists to conduct field research in their own countries (Hann 2007: 383). This is both easier and safer than doing field research in faraway places and unfamiliar cultures.

While religionists in anthropology have claimed Evans-Pritchard as one of their own, this constitutes a disingenuous appropriation. I have discussed this issue with one of Evans-Pritchard's students, Anthony Walker one of my former mentors. As he put it:

> Evans-Pritchard never sought to convince colleagues or students of the necessity for a professional anthropologist to have either religious belief or nonbelief in order to comprehend the religious phenomenon. In his essay "Religion and the Anthropologist" (reprinted in his *Essays in Social Anthropology*), he adopts more or less an entirely historical perspective that makes no mention at all of his own religious perspective or of his conversion to Roman Catholicism while in Libya. Consequently, there is no justification for evangelical Christians or other Trumpists to use Evans-Pritchard's example as ammunition for their cause! (Anthony Walker 2020, personal communication)

Theistic anthropologists see things differently with respect to personal supernatural beliefs. As Bielo (2015: 39) explains: "The core of the approach is that anthropologists can affirm the ontological reality of religious worlds through their research, not bracket off, ignore, abstain, or limit themselves to role play." Really? Are nontheistic anthropologists interested in obtaining reliable data about the human conditions simply role-playing? He adds that his tactic "directly challenges some core social science tenets: to rely strictly on empirical data, to maintain a critical distance from what you are studying, to be skeptical of your own subjective experiences." This is merely parroting what the postmodern aficionados in cultural anthropology were pontificating ad nauseam in the 1980s.

Theistic anthropology is based on the works of paranormal anthropologists, such as Edith Turner (1998), Jean-Guy Goulet, and others discussed above. Their works are considered paradigmatic exemplars because they take the religions of others seriously and are trying to develop methods that offer the possibility that religious phenomena are ontologically real, instead of considering them as epiphenomena with no basis in reality (Bielo 2015: 41; Cannell 2006: 3). Turner's (1992: 2) claim to fame among this cadre of religionists is her insistence that paranormal or supernatural is "real" because she saw "with [her] own eyes a large afflicting substance, some six inches across, emerge from the body of the patient under the doctor's hands." Such contentions are naïve and verge on the absurd. Shamans and healers, including the many I have worked with, have an extensive repertoire of sleight-of-hand techniques or conjurations they use to impress their clients and, I might add, ethnographers and Western tourists as well. There is nothing magical or paranormal about any of this. Such gullibility is astonishing but understandable in post-truth Idiot America. I wonder what Turner's reactions would be to the antics of the bogus Filipino psychic surgeons? Or what she would think about how easily any stage magician, James Randi for example, can replicate these marvels? Perhaps she would say nothing because of her respectful and nonjudgmental hermeneutic approach.

Theistic ethnographers also consider Jean-Guy Goulet's (1994: 114, 117) work relevant to their own efforts because of his "open-minded approach." For example, Goulet says that the Dene of northwestern Alberta, Canada, with whom he worked, "have the ability to travel to and from the 'other land' through dreams and visions . . . and are firm in their conviction that individuals, including ethnographers, who have not directly experienced the reality of dreams and visions do not and cannot understand Dene religion." Thus, he advocates a deep and experiential tactic to such serious matters. Unfortunately, religionists, mystics, magicians, shamans, and their assorted fellow travelers often make such claims as an affirmation of their special magical dexterities and sublime knowledge.

The point of theistic anthropology is not scholarship but to bring Jesus into anthropology or reconfigure the discipline into a Christian enterprise in the same way that Intelligent Design Creationists, who have also pirated postmodern tenets and are trying to replace science with a biblical perspective.

Drawing on theologian John Milbank's book *Theology and Social Theory: Beyond Secular Reason* (1990), Joel Robbins (2006: 287), an avant-gardist of this approach, advocates a type of dialogue between anthropology and theology in which ethnographers must imagine:

> that theologians might either produce theories that get some things right about the world they currently get wrong or model a kind of action in the world that is in some or other way more effective or ethically adequate than their own.

However, Robbins does not say how true-believing theologians could possibly get anything right when their imagination is weighed down by the tiresome medieval credulities and arcane superstitions they advocate. The author and skeptic Arthur C. Clarke put it best regarding theology and moral codes:

> The greatest tragedy in mankind's entire history may be the hijacking of morality by religion. However valuable—even necessary—that may have been in enforcing good behavior on primitive peoples, their association is now counterproductive. Yet at the very moment why they should be decoupled, sanctimonious nitwits are calling for the return to morals based on superstition.

Ultimately, Robbins (2006: 288) aims to bring into anthropology theology's aim of finding "God's design for this life underneath the cultural trappings" of the world. I cannot count how many times I have heard such avowals from all sorts of true-believing self-appointed ambassadors from heaven, as David Hume called them. It is remarkable, however, to hear such declarations from academic anthropologists. Hann (2007: 385–386) makes an important observation worthy of careful attention, namely that the scholars pushing for anthropology of Christianity endorse the idea of "Christian exceptionalism" or the belief that they alone possess the one true faith that gives them privileged insight into the condition of the troubled denizens of the modern world (e.g., Keane 2006). Thus, these professed anthropologists are in the company of the hordes of other post-truth religious extremists who along with their white supremacist allies are bent on making America white again. They have taken over the political arena with a vengeance and are seeking to establish the theocracy of Jesus or Caliphate of Christ (see Blaker 2003; Hedges 2006; Sharlet 2010; Stenger 2003: 10). This is religion disguised as scholarship. It seems that theistic anthropology also has a secure home in Idiot America.

To wrap up this discussion there are two underlying assumptions theistic and paranormalists make that needs clarification: (1) that religious phenomena are amenable solely to subjective/interpretive emic analysis, and (2) that religious phenomena are intrinsically different from all other aspects of the human experience. The first assumption is highly dubious because the insider's perspective is of limited analytical and explanatory utility (Murphy and Margolis 1995: 4; see Sidky 2004: 360–361, 2015: 140–158). This shortcoming arises from the following factors. First, believers do not have automatic, privileged access to the true nature of their own beliefs and behaviors (Segal 1983: 114). Second, attaining the insider's view—call it "going native," experiencing the spiritual reality of others first hand, or whatever—is impossible. As the philosopher of science Graham Oppy (2018: 33) correctly points out, no one is so well-placed to be able to assess the insider's perspective precisely. The anthropologist William Klausner (1994: 18) cogently addressed this problem years ago:

> There are limitations to culture conversion, no matter how close one's identification, engagement, attachment, and empathy. As in religious conversion, one often becomes more Papal than the Pope and loses one's perspective and objectivity. However, loss of detachment and objectivity does not mean one has actually assumed the essence, as well as the form, of a new cultural identity.

Third, the assumption that religious phenomena are intrinsically different from everything else is disingenuous and false. This view posits that religion comprises a mysterious, nonquantifiable, incomprehensible, and non-falsifiable inner world, a subjective experience, or a pure inner impulse. The sources of these ideas are the works of the historian of religion and quasi-mystic Mircea Eliade (1963b: xiii, 1969: 70) and the interpretive anthropologist Clifford Geertz (1973: 4; cf., Frankenberry and Pennock 1999; Sidky 2008: 25–40, 2015: 7–8). From this stance, all the outsiders can do is describe, empathized with, "respect," appreciate, and "take seriously" and nothing more (cf., McCutcheon 2001: 4–5). Religious beliefs and spiritual consciousness, to state it differently, are treated as autonomous self-generating independent variables that have sociopolitical effects, but themselves have no causes (McCutcheon 2001: 85). If this is taken to be the case, then it follows that religious phenomena are solely amenable to subjective, interpretive, respectful, and nonjudgmental or hermeneutic approaches and fall outside the scope of scientific analysis.

This stance is a science stopper wherever it is applied, and that is its purpose. It, therefore, articulates nicely with postmodernist anti-science assertions and the barrage of post-truth nonsense that is daily an affront to rational people. However, this assumption is nonsensical. Scientific anthropologists and other social scientists have conclusively demonstrated that no aspects of human behavior, experience, or any other human phenomena, including shamanism, mysticism, paranormal beliefs, and religion exist apart from historical forces, social influences, the effects of culture, and even human biology (McCutcheon 2001: 10).

In his book *An Unnatural History of Religions*, Leonardo Ambasciano (2018: 176) calls the approach in question the "unnatural history of religion," an endeavor characterized by a subjective approach and an anti-scientific and fideistic partiality, that is, a perspective that construes faith as something independent of reason or rationality. Moreover, such a view creates what the philosopher and cognitive scientist Daniel Dennett (2006: 258–264) refers to as "the academic smokescreen" that has served to impede the scientific analysis of religion as a naturalistic phenomenon. Religionists have adopted this stance because it avoids risking the disclosure, as McCutcheon (2001: 14) puts it, "that religion—like all other aspects of human social life—may well turn out to be all too ordinary." That is too painful and will not do. This is why these sanctimonious true-believers take the position that religious phenomena are intrinsically different from other aspects of human experience.

But, those who adopt this view are, in effect, suspending "their critical faculties and their capacity for disbelief" and side-stepping rational argumentation (McCutcheon 1997: 445). Thus, the study of religion becomes merely "a reporter repeating the insider's [or their own] unsubstantiated claims" (McCutcheon 1997: 449, 2001: 73). This abysmal failure is particularly lamentable given the fact that in the present post-truth world, religious fundamentalisms and archaic delusions are on the rise and pose a threat to civil society and deliberative democracy. Long ago the philosopher of religion Donald Wiebe (1984b) attributed this to a "failure of nerve" because the scholars in question have renounced critical ontological investigation and analysis in favor of phenomenologically and hermeneutically based subjective approaches (McCutcheon 1997: 448).

Like their paranormalist compatriots, theistic writers and purported ethnographers also insist that they are exempt from scientific evidentiary standards and assessment because of the nature of the sublime truths and ontological realities with which they are concerned. By jettisoning scientific tenets, these religionists feel that they have glorified and legitimized supernaturalism and its associated archaic and medieval credulities and superstitions. They fail to realize that simply asserting that their work is outside the scope of scientific appraisal does not shift the burden of proof they must bear or excludes their claims from scientific scrutiny. They have not carried that burden well because there is no evidence anywhere in the bourgeoning literature being produced by these writers to support any of their contentions. To reiterate a point raised earlier, their purported scholarly enterprise is merely an exercise that dignifies credulity as a method and has an ideological motivation. As James Lett (1997b: 111) put it bluntly:

The simple fact of the matter is that every religious belief in every culture in the world is demonstrably untrue. Regardless of whether they are mediated by shamans or priest, regardless of whether the intent is manipulative or supplicative, the one constant that runs through all religious practices all over the world is that all such practices are founded upon nonfalsifiable or falsified beliefs concerning the paranormal.

Moreover, as discussed in chapter 7, science can also show with a high degree of certainty the extreme improbability of all non-falsifiable paranormal or supernatural conjectures.

Theistic anthropologists are evangelical Christians who want to create Christian anthropology or an enterprise for giving witness to the risen Lord. What else could affirming the ontological reality of religious worlds denote? It is an embarrassing development in my discipline for which postmodernists are to blame.

Paranormal and theistic anthropologists both rely on alternative ways of knowing, alternative facts, and private subjective insights—which is what they call "ethnographic" research—to prove the existence of imaginary worlds and unseen realities, phenomena for which there is no evidence anywhere across space and through time. Their work represents the conjunction of postmodernist bunkum and post-truth nonsense. The only difference between the two enterprises is that the first group is concerned with establishing the veracity of ghosts, spirits, ethereal beasties, goblins, poltergeists, and mystical worlds, while the second group seeks to prove the truth of the gospels of Jesus Christ.

Chapter 11

From Postmodernism to Post-Truth United States

The legacy of the Left's assault on science and rationality is a terrible one. In her book *A House Built on Sand: Exposing Postmodern Myths about Science* (1998), the philosopher and historian of science, Noretta Koertge, details the negative impact of postmodernism on scientific literacy in various fields of study in the United States. The education researcher Carl Bereiter in the early 1990s pointed out the deleterious impact of postmodernist science denial on science education. He described such effects on otherwise "mainstream" science educators as follows:

> Reluctance to call anything a fact, avoidance of the term *misconception* (which only a few years ago was a favorite word for some of the same people); considerable agonizing over teaching the scientific method and over what might conceivably take its place; and a tendency to preface the word *science* with *Eurocentric*, especially among graduate students (Bereiter 1994: 3).

The same dogma also facilitated the spread of pseudoscientific beliefs as "the voices" of the marginalized needing to be heard that also cast doubts on the legitimacy of the scientific enterprise. Postmodernism's contribution to science illiteracy and the proliferation of irrational beliefs in the United States is alone sufficient to warrant the strongest condemnation of the entire philosophical perspective and its conceited votaries. However, the most far-reaching impact of postmodern thinking outside university campuses, as Otto (2016: 203) notes, is that it "informed and enabled a much more massive attack on science by religious ideologues and powerful industrial interests in the years to come."

As early as 2011, at a time when disparaging the scientific establishment had already become a routine for nearly all Republican politicians playing to their emboldened conservative constituents, there were those who maintained that the tactics used by conservatives and right-wing ideologues was "straight out of the left-wing playbook" (Warner 2011). Others, however, such as the science writer Chris Mooney, rejected the idea that the academic Left empowered right-wing science denial, asserting that there is nothing postmodern in the latter's stance and stressed how unlikely it is for Republican senators to have read Foucault of Derrida (Mooney 2011). Faithful true-believers, mostly professors in the humanities, also adamantly deny that postmodern academics and their war on science had anything to do with the rise of post-truth. Some have ventured only as far as to blame the postmodernists of complicity and complacency in the development of post-truth politics (Conway 2017). A few do admit that postmodern epistemic relativism has undermined the concept of truth, but offer ad hoc excuses, namely, that postmodernism was not a monolithic philosophy and not all the thinkers associated with the movements adopted extreme views about truth, or that a concrete causal link between postmodernism and post-truth cannot be established and hence such a linkage is unlikely (Hanlon 2018; Illing 2019). Along these lines, professor of sociology, Andrew Perrin says that the indictments of postmodernism exaggerate the theory's effects and are based on caricatures of a philosophy that is more nuanced and profound. Instead, he attributes post-truth to "naked partisanship and media fragmentation driving politics" (Perrin 2017).

However, others see an unmistakable linkage between the decades-long science deligitimation enterprise on campuses across the country and the emergence of the alternative post-truth epistemology that rebukes science and scientific knowledge and defies conventional standards of evidentiary validation. This is because postmodern thinking spread beyond academia and came to influence popular discourse and politics in pervasive and unexpected ways (Otto 2016: 178). Many who deny associations between postmodern dogma and post-truth politics underestimate postmodernism's indelible influence on mainstream intellectual life and popular culture. In his book *Sociology of Postmodernism* (1990), the sociologists and cultural studies professor Scott Lash described the pervasive effects of postmodernism outside academia:

> "Postmodernism" has become a household word. Major newspapers in more than one country have run series of articles on it. There have been countless TV shows addressing the problems it poses. Hair stylists and employees in boutiques where young people buy clothes or records from Los Angeles to Berlin will have heard of postmodernism and may well have an opinion of it. Better-spoken taxi drivers in the world's major metropolises will be able to drive the visitor to their city's districts where the new postmodern architecture is to be found. . . . Just about all the topical academic periodicals with any sort of connection to things cultural have published a special issue on postmodernism.

New series of books coming out of various publishing houses have featured, embarrassingly, the word postmodernism, sometimes in the majority of their titles (Lash 1990: 1).

Political scientist Gregory Smulewircz-Zuker (2018: 212) makes a relevant point that initially postmodern anti-science invectives had a minimal political impact outside of the social sciences and humanities departments. Its direct lasting effect was on the academic Left itself, whose proponents now find themselves politically irrelevant and in an agenda-less intellectual morass. As long as postmodern rhetoric and diatribes were "confined to the isolated and bloodless corners of academe" their wider social effects were fairly limited (Wolin 2004: 313). Also, at first, while postmodernist cynicism tarnished the idea of truth in classrooms and lecture halls, the effect was somewhat innocuous so long as there was still some blurry cultural consensus that truth had precedence (D'Ancona 2017: 96). None of these conditions lasted for very long. Postmodern beliefs leaked out into the popular culture and in the post-truth era popular consensus about the precedence of truth has vaporized.

How did this happen? It was the outcome of the forty years or so when the literati in American universities inculcated students with their relativistic dogma and anti-science tirades. True-believing professors spread this dogma in departments of social science, education, political science, English, gender studies, American studies, Black World studies, and other humanities. As Kurt Andersen explains in his book *Fantasyland*: first, postmodern thought became entrenched in universities and colleges; second, from there, it spread to the outside world by three generations of indoctrinated students, some ten million educated Americans, and seeped into the minds of an already scientifically illiterate public (Andersen 2017: 309).

Whether or not any or all of these students became true converts or attained a deep understanding of the subtilties of postmodern dogma is not the issue. The take-away from the university classrooms was not a solid comprehension of postmodern philosophy itself, which many students probably found impenetrable because most of it was incoherent nonsense, but its clear-cut anti-science message. Oxymoronic scientific creationists, as discussed earlier, rely on postmodern precepts that science is merely one fable to forward their superstitions while at the same time they reject other aspects of the philosophy, such as its epistemological egalitarianism about all truth claims being equally valid.

As Otto (2011: 132) says, the message that stuck in the minds of the recipients of postmodern wisdom in universities was that "science is just a story," power certifies what passes for truth, and that people in authority can get away with falsehoods by selective culling pieces of scientific evidence to support whatever they wished. Moreover, "this cynical doublespeak seemed to confirm the idea that was at the very heart of what would become the neoconservative movement: [namely] that winners write the history books" (Otto 2011: 132).

The noted historian Richard Evans also sees a causal connection between postmodernism and post-truth politics. He points out that the apostles of post-truth and Trump's key advisors and sycophants at the time, Kellyanne Conway, Steve Bannon, and Sean Spicer graduated from U.S. universities during the zenith of the postmodern intellectual fad. There can be no doubt that they were influenced by the anti-science rhetoric of their professors. He adds: "If I am wrong, and postmodernist disbelief in truth didn't lead to our post-truth age, then how do we explain the current disdain for facts?" (in Forstenzer 2018: 19, and Swain 2017).

The philosopher Joshua Forstenzer has investigated how the work of one particular postmodern luminary, Richard Rorty, might have contributed to post-truth politics and the dismissal of traditional epistemic norms in public discourse. This inquiry was prompted by the fact that, as Forstenzer puts it, "post-truth politics echoes significant aspects of Rorty's wider philosophical project, a project he once called 'postmodernist bourgeois liberalism'" (Forstenzer 2018: 16, 17). In question here are Rorty's epistemic relativism, his recurrent assaults on science, knowledge, facts, rational justification, and his idea that truth claims are dependent on the particular persons making them. All of these are recapitulated in the post-truth rhetoric of ideologues espousing authoritarian goals and oppressive political agendas (Forstenzer 2018: 26). Forstenzer concludes as follows:

> Rorty's philosophical project bears some intellectual responsibility for the onset of post-truth politics, insofar as it took a complacent attitude towards the dangers associated with over-affirming the contingency of our epistemic claims (Forstenzer 2018: 4).

Many of the students trained in postmodern anti-science went on to become conservative political and religious leaders, policymakers, journalists, journal editors, judges, lawyers, and members of city councils and school boards. Sadly, they forgot or rejected all of the lofty ideals of their teachers about social justice and multiculturalism, except that science is bogus and truth is "a matter of perspective and agenda" (Kakutani 2018: 43). These cadres of people with little interest in the message of social equality, epistemological egalitarianism, or feminism coopted the central lesson of postmodernism to assert the legitimacy of their own not so egalitarian dogmas (McIntyre 2015: 19–20,106; Sidky 2018: 41–42).

It turned out that the Left's mendacious flirtation with the eccentric views of a few offbeat Frenchmen generated ideas that were highly compatible with and provided one the most robust arguments for right-wing populism and its authoritarian agendas (cf. Kakutani 2018: 18; Smulewircz-Zuker 2018: 205). The irony is that critical theorists in the humanities and social sciences touting epistemic relativism to achieve social justice and equality ended up in the post-truth era as tacit accomplices of anti-democratic right-wing populists, sinister conspiracists, and evangelical ideologues who deny the truth of evolution, global climate change, and the validity of scientific research because it refutes their medieval and archaic superstitions (cf., McIntyre 2015: 106). To state it differently, the academic Left supplied the Right with the precise tools it needed to advance not so egalitarian or benevolent agendas (Andersen 2017: 309; Smulewircz-Zuker 2018: 205).

In the post-truth world where we have landed, anyone touting any beliefs at odds with various scientific findings has a license to demand that his or her views be given equal time and deference (Kakutani 2018: 18; Sidky 2018). This is the postmodernists' multiple equally valid truths idea in action. Another of their legacies is that facts do not matter. A disturbing characteristic of contemporary post-truth public discourse, as Nichols (2017: 25) points out is a "solipsistic and thin-skinned insistence that every opinion be treated as truth." Why is this of grave concern? Philosopher Timothy Snyder (2107: 65) explains:

> To abandon facts is to abandon freedom. If nothing is true, then no one can criticize power, because there is no basis upon which to do so. If nothing is true, then all is spectacles. The biggest wallet pays from the most blinding light.

What is significant is that religious fundamentalists are no longer advancing their claims simply as faith-based perspectives, or pseudoscientific beliefs, versus science as in earlier times, but rather as one story versus another story, which is how the postmodernists portrayed the scientific enterprise (Pennock 2010: 138).

To some, at first glance, the causal linkage between postmodernism and the present-day widespread anti-intellectualism and hostility toward science may appear only partial and inferential. Also, it may also seem implausible that Trump's populist devotees and right-wing followers would allow themselves to be influenced by college-educated elitist professors. However, it is important to remember that such ideas have come down to them not through presentations by snobbish intellectuals in universities and colleges, but indirectly by way of vulgar politicians, bloggers, YouTube videos, website publishers, and Alt-Right ideologues who have adopted simplified versions of academic anti-science discourse tailored to suit the mentality, intellectual capacity, and educational level of their followers and audiences.

In this regard, Kakutani (2018: 45–46) points out that the Right appropriated "some dumbed-down corollaries" of postmodernist views, such as its repudiation of objectivity and truth, an idea that was long the exclusive preserve of the Left. McIntyre make a similar observation: "Even if right-wing politicians and other science deniers were not reading Derrida and Foucault, the germ of the idea made its way to them namely that science does not have a monopoly over the truth" (McIntyre 2018: 139–141). For these reasons, Smulewircz-Zuker (2018: 214) refers to the post-truth purveyors of such beliefs and theories as "vulgar postmodernists," who resemble their academic counterparts, but minus a sophisticated epistemology. These postmodern notions are now part of popular culture and are being used by Trump's cronies and sycophants to excuse his barrage of falsehoods.

A case in point is Trump's personal lawyer Rudy Giuliani's assertions during an NBC New Meet the Press in August 2018 interview in defense of his patron: "Truth isn't truth . . . It is somebody's version of the truth." In another interview with CNN's Chris Cuomo, Giuliani also stated that nowadays, facts are "in the eye of the beholder" (Kenny 2018). It is highly unlikely that a boorish opportunist such as Giuliani or his boss have read any postmodern tracts. Even if they did, there is a good possibility that they would not understand any of it. What we have here is a very dumbed-down postmodernism at work in contemporary American politics.

While what post-truth politicians are touting is dumbed-down, however, it contains the main elements of postmodernist dogma, namely, denial of facts, the impossibility of factual knowledge, the notion of knowledge as "elitist" (Derrida), a virulent anti-intellectualism, suspicion of experts, hostility toward Enlightenment principles (Nietzsche and his twentieth-century French devotees), distrust of democracy, the ideas of "fake news" and elitist media (Baudrillard's idea of *simulacrum*), multiple truths (Foucault), and the extolling of pseudoscientific beliefs (Kuhn, Feyerabend and all of their postmodern emulators). Understanding these vulgarized ideas does not require that one read or fathom the foundational postmodern tracts. Recall that even the postmodern literati themselves did not fully comprehend the eloquent sermons contained in these texts.

It is implausible that today's political ideologues, populists, right-wing agitators, religious fundamentalists, and conspiracy theorists invented these ideas on their own. They merely coopted what had been in circulation for forty years on university and college campuses across the country. There are too many convergences between postmodern philosophical ideas and post-truth rhetoric to dismiss this association as spurious. It is also significant that a number of postmodern gurus (see below) themselves have now acknowledged how their enterprise went terribly astray by encouraging reactionaries and religionists to use postmodernist dogma in their own battle against science, rationality, and truth.

There is a twenty-first-century twist to all of this that sets apart the non-academic recipients of epistemic relativism from the snobbish academic postmodernist crowd. The domain of these "vulgar postmodernists" is not the classroom or universities but the Internet. Lewandowsky and associates (2013a: 624) have shown that individuals who reject science tend to rely heavily on the Internet for information (see Diethelm and McKee 2009; McKee and Diethelm 2010). In this virtual space, science deniers are able to reinforce their mutual beliefs and paranoia regarding truth, science, biased elitist scientists, and other oppressors imagined or otherwise (McKee and Diethelm 2010: 1310–1311). These circumstances, combined with the widespread public scientific illiteracy engendered by academic postmodernist thinking and corporate America have created the perfect environment for bashing science and extolling pseudoscientific nonsense and irrationalism. Hence, post-truth may be called "the digital" version of postmodernist skepticism about truth and knowledge (Ambasciano 2018: 176).

Thus, it is sad to say that none of the optimistic expert predictions about how the Internet would change the world, bring economic prosperity, lead to a deliberative and tolerant world, and usher a new age of culture and democracy has materialized (Curran 2012: 3; Negroponte 1996). Instead, as professor of communication, James Curran (2012: 11) points out, the cyberspace created by the Internet has produced "a ruined tower of Babel with multiple languages, hate websites, nationalist discourses, censored speech and overrepresentation of the advantaged" (see also Painter et al. 2016: 8–23; Curran et al. 2012). Similarly, Oreskes and Conway (2011: 240–241) write:

> With the rise of . . . the Internet, it sometimes seems that anyone can have their opinion heard, quoted, and repeated, whether it is true or false, sensible or ridiculous, fair-minded or malicious. The Internet has created an information hall of mirrors, where any claim, no matter how preposterous, can be multiplied indefinitely. And on the Internet disinformation never dies. "Electronic Barbarism" one commentator has called it—an environment that is all sail and no anchor. Pluralism run amok.

Along the same lines, Phil Williamson (2016) points out that websites are supplanting newspapers as the primary sources of information for the public and even high-level politicians (Lewandowsky et al. 2017: 359). Angela Nagle (2017: 2), who has discussed the role of the Internet in the rise of the Alt-Right, makes a relevant comment:

> The triumph of the Trumpians was. . . a win in the war against mainstream media, which is now held in contempt by many average voters and the weird irony-laden Internet subcultures from the right and left, who equally set themselves apart from this hated mainstream.

Unlike traditional news outlets, social media is devoid of any quality controls or fact-checking mechanisms. Hence, as anthropologist Jonathan Mair (2017) points out, there are no formal procedures for scientists to correct the misrepresentation of their findings. As the investigative journalist James Ball (2017: 8) adds further, everything on the Internet looks true, or rather, it is nearly impossible to discern the truth from the lies. Any website with a plausible name and design similar to mainstream news sites becomes believable. In other words, he adds, "everything looks equally credible online." He also points out a significant feature of Internet use:

> Online, we have our natural groups we create by accident (our Facebook friends and similar) as well as divisions we create deliberately, such as the political parties or causes we sign up to. We can regularly see what other members of those groups see and share, and they can see what we do too—the architecture and infrastructure of the modern internet could almost have been designed to trigger the instincts that make us likely to believe things which are not true (Ball 2017: 180).

The Internet's purported underlying principles of openness have created an unchecked space or cyber world where deceitful stories, bogus conspiracy theories, racist and fascist extremism, false assertions about elite-controlled mainstream media, fake news, and other patently bogus assertions have greater circulation than stories presented in genuine news sources (see Painter et al., 2016: 8–23; Curran et al. 2012).

The right-wing's efforts to discredit science and scientific knowledge are furthered by the fact that the American public lacks a basic understanding of science and scientific standards and is incapable of appraising the disingenuous, uninformed, and tendentious methods and the irrational and unsubstantiated beliefs upon which the so-called alternative views are based. Under these circumstances all sorts of bogus claims become believable. Thus vast numbers of people are easily bamboozled into accepting the veracity of mythologized history, pseudoscience, and a host of other absurd viewpoints (cf., Fagan and Hale 2001).

A perfect illustration of this is how many seem to have accepted Trump's distrust of experts, his claim that he knows more about COVID-19 than government scientists, and that his personal beliefs about the virus are more accurate than what epidemiologists and health officials are maintaining. For instance, he deemed the death rates predicted by experts as false, that cases were "going very substantially down" when they were rising, that corona virus was "like the flu" contra to the experts who were stating that it was considerably worse, and that sick persons could go to work, while medical authorities were saying otherwise (Egan and Khurana 2020).

What is more remarkable is that most Americans are not even aware that they are being bamboozled or that dangerous circumstances are confronting their society and its democratic ideals. And to cite Carl Sagan (1995: 240) again: "Once we've been bamboozled long enough, we tend to reject any evidence of the bamboozle." There is a point of no return from this deep rabbit hole because once we give quacks and hacks power over us, we seldom get it back (Sagan 1995: 240).

A peculiar attribute of post-truth online political rhetoric is extreme incivility (Lewandowsky et al. 2017: 359). The communication studies professor Brian Ott (2017: 60) points out, for example, that Twitter has encouraged a type of discourse that is "simple, impetuous, and frequently denigrating and dehumanizing," that "fosters farce and fanaticism, and contributes to callousness and contempt." A central feature of such online incivility, as the sociologist Sarah Sobieraj and political scientist Jeffrey Berry observe, is rage:

> [This results in political discourse intended] to provoke visceral responses (e.g., anger, righteousness, fear, moral indignation) from the audience through the use of overgeneralizations, sensationalism, misleading or patently inaccurate information, ad hominem attacks, and partial truths about opponents (Sobieraj and Berry 2011: 20).

The post-truth landscape has another characteristic, namely an extensive fragmentation of sources of information that permit the rapid spread of lies in "ideological echo chambers." These are automatically created custom-designed information environments based on online user algorithms where individuals are exposed only to sites and information that confirms their preexisting attitudes and biases. These echo chambers permeate cyberspace and serve to amplify those beliefs and prejudices and lead people to think that their opinions, no matter how bizarre and baseless, are broadly shared thus making them resistant of alterations or corrections (Rabin-Havt 2016: 195–196; Jasny et al. 2015; Lewandowsky et al. 2017: 359; Pariser 2011).

More significantly, the fragmented characteristic of online media enables vote-maximizing politicians to veer off into extremism on such matters as abortion, gay marriage, transgender identity, and gun control whenever mobilizing their own core constituents is more rewarding than alienating undecided or opposing voters (Glaeser et al. 2005). This fractionated media landscape is thus a crucial factor in the emergence of the alternative epistemic realities that characterize post-truth America (Curran et al. 2012; Del Vicario et al. 2016; Lewandowsky et al. 2017: 359 Deuze and Witschge 2017).

The Internet information echo chambers nourish the confirmation bias that leads people to gravitate solely to outlets that confirm what they already know. The availability of so many information sources, to reiterate, thus make it possible for individuals to selectively interact with like-minded people isolating them from contrary opinions, thereby creating information or news silos (McIntyre 2018: 58–59). As Andersen (2017: 416) observes, there is now:

> a new global cottage industry that knowingly concocts and publishes false news stories, each optimized to be clicked, shared, and viralized.... The direct democracy of the Internet search algorithms is a stark example of Gresham's law, the bad driving out—or at least overrunning—the good.

Consequently, we are now verging upon a bizarre and disquieting epistemic terrain. In the words of Lewandowsky and his colleagues:

> [it is] a world that has had enough of experts. That considers knowledge to be "elitist." [where] it is not expert knowledge but an opinion market on Twitter that determines whether a newly emergent strain of avian flu is really contagious to humans, or whether greenhouse gas emissions do in fact cause global warming, as 97% of domain experts say they do. In this world, power lies with those most vocal and influential on social media: from celebrities and big corporations to botnet puppeteers who can mobilize millions of tweet bots or sock puppets—that is, fake online personas through which a small group of operatives can create an illusion of a widespread opinion In this world, experts are derided as untrustworthy or elitist whenever their reported facts threaten the rule of the well-financed or the prejudices of the uninformed (Lewandowsky et al. 2017: 354).

The Internet has also contributed to the proliferation of an array of postulated bizarre and nefarious plots in the form of conspiracy theories. While conspiracy theories were once mostly restricted to peripheral cultural spaces or "the cultic milieu," (Campbell 2002: 14), cyberspace and the Internet have brought them into the cultural mainstream. As the expert on right-wing extremism Jeffry Bale (2007: 45) has observed:

> despite the unprecedented scientific and technological progress of the past half-century ... millions apparently ... believe in the existence and terrestrial intervention of angels and daemons, alien abductions, murderous Satanist undergrounds, sinister cattle mutilations, mind control devices embedded in televisions, the Chupacabra, ritual Jewish baby-killing and blood-drinking, Vatican-sponsored "crusades" against Islam, and elaborate conspiracies of the most fantastic sort.

Conspiracy theories of this kind are not to be confused with the all too real conspiratorial or clandestine activities that are a regular facet of politics

(Bale 2007: 50), for example, Watergate and the Iran-Contra affair (on the epistemological problems of distinguishing warranted and unwarranted conspiracy theories, see Keely 1999). In contrast to these real-world intrigues, conspiracy theories are intricate fictional stories and anecdotal accounts that may or may not be based on a kernel of truth.

Conspiracy theories are relevant to the present discussion because they are often linked to a broad-based rejection of science and scientific knowledge although such a correlation may not be obvious at first glance. The logic is something like this: NASA faked the Apollo moon landings—therefore climate science (or any other science) is a hoax (Lewandowsky et al. 2013a: 622).

Conspiracy theories exploit a widespread human psychological proclivity to which David Hume (1902 [1748]: 118) called attention long ago, namely an inextricable and irrepressible propensity for the extraordinary and the marvelous. The philosopher Robert Pennock (1999: 277–278) points out in this regard that while humans have a sincere desire to understand how the world operates; yet, at the same time, they are paradoxically fascinated with the supernatural, the mysterious, the paranormal, and the unknown. People thus want to believe that there are other planes of existence and that there is more to reality than meets the eye and are constantly tempted by "cover-ups" and conspiracy theories that do not lend themselves to verification.

Conspiracy claims also thrive on another human psychological propensity, namely our tendency to constantly seek patterns. This leads people to causally connect otherwise random happenings to construct seemingly meaningful patterns and positing intentional agents as their architects and masterminds (Shermer 2011: 208). When these factors combined with another human psychological tendency, the confirmation bias, believers are led to seek, pay attention to, and remember only information that supports their claims and summarily rejecting all evidence to the contrary (Shermer 2011: 209). Hence conspiracy theorists become convinced that there is an overwhelming amount of evidence supporting their claims, whereas there is almost always a more banal explanation for the evidence involved (Schick and Vaughn 2014: 279).

These postulated machinations usually address various sociopsychological needs by providing explanations for particular crises, unexpected incidents, upheavals, perceived sociopolitical ills, anxieties, or disasters in terms of the covert actions of all-powerful, fiendish individuals, organizations, evil and demonic forces, or international networks bent on wrecking a way of life or seeking global domination (Bale 20007: 49–51; Barkun 2013: 3; Sunstein and Vermeule 2009: 205). A case in point is the conspiracy theory engendered by the fear and uncertainty that COVID-19 is a bioweapon that was deliberately released on the world. Depending on the source of the narrative, the virus was created in the Wuhan Institute of Virology, a CIA lab in the United States or the United Kingdom, or even by Bill Gates (Barclay 2020; Dickson 2020;

Field and Krzyzaniak 2020; Yanzhong 2020). The stated motives are similarly varied, for example, to make money from a vaccine, to stop protests in Hong Kong, to undermine the economy, and so forth.

In the United States, such rumors are being propagated by the likes of Trump's Presidential Medal of Freedom recipient Rush Limbaugh and Tom Cotton (R-AR) before Congress and on Fox News (Barclay 2020). Trump's assistant and ideologue Peter Navarro has forwarded the most outlandish version of this conspiracy. He claims that China created the virus in a lab, deliberately sent hundreds of thousands of its citizens infected with the disease as "super spreaders" to Milan and New York. At the same time the Chinese Communist Party purchased two billion masks and gloves around the world to hamper healthcare workers and accelerate the pandemic (Stephanopoulos 2020).

Conspiracy theories simplify complex events by personify their sources, thus offering believers some tangible and easy to grasp reason for a specific event or perceived plight in place of impersonal and indeterminate social forces and factors (Bale 2007: 51; Goertzel 2010: 493). Thus, whole arrays of confusing circumstances that before seemed random, disconnected, hidden, and totally incomprehensible are now neatly explained in terms of some "master plan" of sinister omnipotent agents and organization (Schick and Vaughn 2014: 280). Nearly any event can be explained in these terms. Thinking that they have solved some purported mystery, conspiracy theorists acquire a feeling of power and of being in control for having identified the clandestine enemy and for discovering the truth that has evaded others. For these reasons, conspiracy theories are highly alluring and engross people. Sociologist Donna Kossy (1994: 191) observes:

> Conspiracy theories are like black holes—they suck in everything that comes their way, regardless of content or origin: conspiracies are portals to other universes that paradoxically reside within our own. Everything you've ever experienced, no matter how "meaningless," once it contacts the conspiratorial universe, is enveloped by and cloaked in sinister significant. Once inside, the vortex gains in size and strength, sucking in everything you touch.

Such bogus stories and their outlandish postulates (e.g., Reptilian overlords who drink human blood to preserve their human appearance, the Illuminati are building a New World Order, or the QAnon right-wing conspiracy theory) are attention-grabbing or "sticky," can easily take hold, and spread by leaping from brain to brain like brain infections (cf., Dennett 1995: 344; Heath and Heath 2007). However, while conspiracy ideas spread easily, they are difficult to disprove (Goertzel 2010: 493; Lewandowsky et al. 2017: 355). Why? First, because conspiratorial claims posit the involvement of all-powerful organizations or agents who act in complete secrecy they have a built-in defense against the objection that there is no evidence for the purported machination—"Yes, that is how extensive the conspiracy is!" (Dennett 1995: 349). The second factor that renders falsification difficult is that conspiracy claims arbitrarily intersperse facts and speculations and are often based solely on hearsay and anecdotal information. As psychologist Marius Raab and his colleagues note:

> The complex and anecdotic reasoning immunizes against falsification. Extreme constituents attract attention and polarize the debate; and they also might induce a shift of people's individual explanatory constructs toward a conspiratorial plot. In sum, a flavor of oddness might not be a weakness of such theories, but indeed an integral part and enabler of their persuasive power (Raab et al. 2013: 7).

Thus, the presence of extreme bizarre statements, such as Reptilian aliens posing as our political leaders, or Nazi flying saucers, and so forth, in a pool of given information, seem to persuade people to discount standard information (Raab et al. 2013: 2). In other words, even the most outlandish and implausible conspiracy theory in circulation can be deployed as a rhetorical device to generate emotional responses and reactions among particular groups, exerting powerful social and psychological effects (Goertzel 2010: 494). Moreover, there is some evidence that simply hearing a conspiracy regardless of how implausible it may seem lowers trust in governmental institutions, even if the conspiracies are not directly related to those institutions (Douglas et al. 2017: 540; Einstein and Glick 2015: 679). Along the same lines, as Wood et al. (2012) have shown, even mutually incompatible conspiracy theories are positively correlated with the endorsement of conspiracism, which is bolstered by wider cultural beliefs regarding conspiracy theories in general.

Consider the QAnon conspiracy that has seeped into the Republican party and is endorsed by Trump who has repeatedly retweeted QAnon content (LaFrance 2020). This bizarre narrative alludes to the existence of a nefarious and all-powerful international organization (the deep state) of Satan-worshipping, sex trafficking pedophiles who drink the blood of children for its purported rejuvenating properties. QAnon subscribers, a group the FBI considers a potential domestic terrorist threat, cast Trump as their valiant savior secretly battling to vanquish this sinister global threat (Arnold 2020).

Such lurid but baseless conspiracies engender distrust in governmental institutions, democratic principles, and social norms, and convinces proponents that their votes are meaningless. The ideologues touting the conspiracy theory thus acquire a free hand to forward their own perverted private agendas while proclaiming, "don't believe anything you see or hear," "truth does not exist," and trust me because only I am able to defeat the hidden overwhelming sinister forces at work.

People who believe one conspiracy are more likely to also believe others (Goertzel 1994: 731). Lewandowsky and his colleagues (2013a: 622) have found that the endorsement of a cluster of conspiracy theories—for example that HIV was created by the government, the FBI assassinated Martin Luther King, Jr., the Bush administration and Israeli intelligence masterminded the 9/11 attacks, and the Air Force is hiding evidence of extraterrestrial visitors—predicts dismissal of climate science as well as other scientific findings (see also Lewandowsky et al. 2013b: 623; Lewandowsky et al. 2016).

Overall, conspiracy theories contribute to paranoia and distrust of social institutions, disdain for scientists and politicians, and pose a societal problem because they are often deployed to refute scientific evidence in public forums or legal proceedings with negative consequence, as in the case of public health or environmental policies (Goertzel 2010: 496; Jolley and Douglas 2013).

As already noted, conspiracy theories have always been around, but the contemporary varieties are very distinctive. As Russell Muirhead and Nancy Rosenblum (2019: 2–3) point out in their book *Lots of People Are Saying: The New Conspiracism and the Assault on Democracy* (2019):

> classic conspiracism gives order and meaning to occurrences that, in their minds, defy standard or official explanations. . . . [In contrast] the new conspiracism is something different. There is no punctilious demand for proofs, no exhaustive amassing of evidence, no dots revealed to form patterns, no close examination of the operators plotting in the shadows. The new conspiracism dispenses with the burden of explanation. Instead, we have innuendo and verbal gestures (Muirhead and Rosenblum 2019: 2–3).

They add that present-day conspiracies have two unique attributes: first, they are conspiracies "without the theory"; and second, they have a destructive impetus—to delegitimate democracy (Muirhead and Rosenblum 2019: 2–3). Another way to describe these postulated machinations is that they are decidedly postmodern versions of the conspiracy theories of the past, characterized by a complete disregard for facts, an absence of theories, and an aversion to science, democracy, and all they represent. Also, as Keely (1999: 126) observes, such beliefs possess an "almost nihilistic degree of skepticism about the behavior and motivations of other people and the social institutions," which also gives them a very Nietzschean and postmodern flavor.

Conspiracy theories are potent vehicles for delegitimizing mainstream media and institutions of higher learning, thereby subverting common public consensus, a factor upon which post-truth thrives. As the philosopher Jason Stanley points out in his book *How Fascism Works* (2018):

> What happens when conspiracy theories become the coin of politics, and mainstream media and educational institutions are discredited, is that citizens no longer have a common reality that can serve as background for democratic deliberation. In such situations, citizens have no choice but to look for markers to follow other than truth or reliability (Stanley 2018: 71).

Here, those markers become the post-truth ideologues themselves that people look to for authoritative information. The vulgar postmodernists that make up the Right have displayed a remarkable talent for using bogus conspiracies and manipulating social media to reach and indoctrinate large numbers of citizens and muster up mass opposition to science, truth, gun control, gay rights, and so forth. In this respect, the Right's assault on truth, unlike that of postmodern academics during the 1980s and 1990s, is on a scale so massive that it now imperils democracy and the future of evidence-based governance (Williamson 2016; Smulewircz-Zuker 2018: 214, 217–218).

As discussed above, while some writers downplay postmodernism's indelible influence on post-truth today, such an effect cannot easily be ignored. Moreover, not all postmodernists themselves have been oblivious about these circumstances. Michael Bérubé (2011), professor of literature and cultural studies and a postmodern thinker in retrospect, writes: "When we claimed to be doing 'science studies,' did we know what the hell we were talking about?" He acknowledges with distress how "climate-change deniers and creationists who are taking on science are "using some of the very arguments developed by an academic left that thought it was speaking only to people of like mind." Bérubé (2011) concedes further that science studies went terribly wrong "giving fuel to deeply ignorant and/or reactionary people."

Bruno Latour also has attempted to exonerate himself by expressing concerns about the hijacking of postmodern critical theory by right-wing anti-science ideologues and conspiracy theorists to advance their own causes. Latour (2004: 227) says:

> Entire Ph.D. programs are still running to make sure that good American kids are learning. . . that facts are made up, that there is no such thing as natural, unmediated, unbiased access to truth, that we are always prisoners of language, that we always speak from a particular standpoint, and so on, while dangerous extremists are using the very same argument of social construction to destroy hard-won evidence that could save our lives.

Has Latour in the post-truth age of "alternative facts" become a proponent of science, as the journalist Jop de Vrieze (2017) says? Not so. I was perhaps too charitable to credit him for this change of perspective (Sidky 2018: 42). But this is not a recantation. Latour goes on to say that the sublime elements of his ideas are still valuable and is unwilling to give up his constructivist perspective (Latour 2004: 227). In other words, despite what has happened, he meant well and that his ideas are still good. Sorry. This is too little too late because the damage has been done. Alberto Brandolini's law—which states that "the amount energy needed to refute bullshit is an order of magnitude bigger than to produce it"—applies here (Williamson 2016). Postmodern philosophy was indeed replete with bullshit and intellectual dishonesty. McIntyre (2015: 106) has rightly observed that such disingenuous remorse by an ideologue such as Latour whose life's work was devoted to disparaging truth and undermining science, which is our only means for detecting the truth, is "the feeble bargaining of a thoughtless bully who has gone too far and now wants us to believe that he never intended to hurt anyone."

There was no foresight on the part of any of the self-styled academic cultural critics about the broader impact of their ideas (McIntyre 2015: 107; Otto 2016: 189). The British philosopher and historian of ideas Isaiah Berlin (1969: 119) long ago alluded to the perils of such neglect on the part of those who make ideas their vocation:

> When ideas are neglected by those who ought to attend to them—that is to say, those who have been trained to think critically about ideas—they sometimes acquire an unchecked momentum and an irresistible power over multitudes of men that may grow too violent to be affected by rational criticism. Over a hundred years ago, the German poet Heine warned the French not to underestimate the power of ideas: philosophical concepts nurtured in the stillness of a professor's study could destroy a civilization.

Along the same lines the cognitive scientist and philosopher Daniel Dennett (2017) says:

> Maybe people will now begin to realise that philosophers aren't quite so innocuous after all. Sometimes, views can have terrifying consequences that might actually come true. I think what the postmodernists did was truly evil. They are responsible for the intellectual fad that made it respectable to be cynical about truth and facts (in Cadwalldar 2017).

Above all, the postmodern academic savants overlooked the great danger posed by their epistemic relativism. When the public believes that there are multiple voices and multiple truths and is unable to differentiate between what is truth and what is falsehood it is susceptible to the manipulation of ideologues with malignant anti-democratic agendas. History has shown how authoritarian and totalitarian regimes have thrived on the type of epistemic relativism that was being advocated by radicals in American institutions of higher learning and subsequently picked up by their right-wing beneficiaries operating today. Consider these chillingly postmodern and post-truth sounding statements:

> From the fact that all ideologies are of equal value, that all ideologies are mere fictions, [we] deduce that everybody is free to create for himself his own ideology and attempt to carry it out with all possible energy (Benito Mussolini, in Ross 1980: xvii).

> We stand at the end of the Age of Reason. A new era of the magical explanation of the world is rising. There is no truth, in the scientific sense. That which is called the crisis of science is nothing more than that the gentlemen are beginning to see on their own how they have gotten onto the wrong track with their objectivity (Adolf Hitler, in Slakey 1993).

Latour is not alone in his insipid, half-hearted, after the fact pretense that none of this was his doing. This was evident from the letters some of these true-believers wrote absolving themselves in response to my article "The War on Science, Anti-intellectualism, Supernaturalism, and "Alternative Ways of Knowing" in 21st Century United States" (2018). Such sham denials are indicative of the continued dishonesty shared by the science-denying postmodern savants.

Post-truth politics should alarm rational people because much of it comes from the playbook of fogyish fascist propagandists who were touting totalitarianism for the common good of "the people." We may not be there just yet, but we are on that road. As Snyder (2017: 71) correctly observes, "Post-truth is pre-fascism." It seems that Steve Tesich was spot-on eighteen years ago about the trajectory of American culture, observing that in a "very fundamental way we, as a free people, have freely decided that we want to live in some post-truth world" (Tesich 1992: 13). Such choices brought us to Trump's America. Indeed, as Steven Levitsky and Daniel Ziblatt observe in their book *How Democracies Die*, the election of Donald Trump, an individual known to have "dubious allegiances to democratic principles," occurred not simply because of public dissatisfaction but also by the choice of the Republican Party to allow "an extremist demagogue within its own ranks" to gain the nomination (Levitsky and Ziblatt 2018: 8). It remains to be seen just how far down that perilous road we will go before a semblance of reason and respect for truth and democratic principles will return, if they ever do.

Bibliography

Abel, Reuben 1976 *Man Is the Measure: A Cordial Invitation to the Central Problems of Philosophy*. New York: The Free Press.
Abraham, John, John Cook, John Fasullo, Peter Jacobs, Scott Mandia, and Dana Nuccitelli 2014 Review of the Consensus and Asymmetric Quality of Research on Human-Induced Climate Change. *Cosmopolis* 1: 3–18. https://mahb.stanford.edu/wp-content/uploads/2014/05/2014_Abraham-et-al.-Climate-consensus.pdf (Accessed March 11, 2019).
Abu-Lughod, Lila 1991 Writing Against Culture. In *Recapturing Anthropology*. Richard Fox (ed.). Santa Fe, NM: School of American Research Washington Press. Pp. 37–62.
Achinstein, Peter 2000 Proliferation: Is It a Good Thing? In *The Worst Enemy of Science: Essays in Memory of Paul Feyerabend*. John Preston, Gonzalo Munévar, and David Lamb (eds.). Oxford: Oxford University Press. Pp. 37–39.
Alcock, James 1985 Parapsychology As a 'Spiritual Science. In *A Skeptic's Handbook of Parapsychology*. Paul Kurtz (ed.). Buffalo, NY: Prometheus Books. Pp. 537–568.
Alloa, Emmanuel 2017 Post-Truth or: Why Nietzsche Is Not Responsible for Donald Trump. *The Philosophical Salon*. https://thephilosophicalsalon.com/post-truth-or-why-nietzsche-is-not-responsible-for-donald-trump/ (Accessed October 11, 2019).
Ambasciano, Leonardo 2018 *An Unnatural History of Religions: Academia, Post-Truth, and the Quest for Scientific Knowledge*. London: Bloomsbury.
Anderegg, William, James Prall, Jacob Harold, and Stephen Schneider 2010 Expert Credibility in Climate Change. *Proceeding of the National Academy of Sciences of the United States of America* 107(27): 12107–12109. https://doi.org/10.1073/pnas.1003187107 (Accessed December 15, 2019).
Andersen, Kurt 2017 *Fantasyland: How America Went Haywire*. New York: Random House.
Andreski, Stanislav 1972 *Social Science As Sorcery*. New York: St. Martin's Press.

Ardent, Hannah 1968 *Between Past and Future: Eight Exercises in Political Thought.* New York: Penguin.

—— 1951 *The Origins of Totalitarianism.* New York: Harcourt, Brace.

Arnold, Laurence 2020 QAnon, the Conspiracy Theory Creeping into U.S. Politics. *The Washington Post*, August 22, 2020. https://www.washingtonpost.com/business/qanon-the-conspiracy-theorycreeping-into-us-politics/2020/08/21/1a1d4940-e3dd-11ea-82d8-5e55d47e90ca_story.html (Accessed August 24, 2020).

Asimov, Isaac 1980 A Cult of Ignorance. *Newsweek* (January) 21: 19.

Audi, Robert 2011 *Epistemology: A Contemporary Introduction to the Theory of Knowledge.* New York: Routledge.

Ayala, Francisco, and Walter Fitch 1997 Genetics and the Origin of Species: An Introduction. *Proceeding of the National Academy of Sciences of the United States of America* 94(15): 7691–7697. https://www.pnas.org/content/pnas/94/15/7691.full.pdf (Accessed November 22, 2019).

Aylesworth, Gary 2015 Postmodernism. In *The Stanford Encyclopedia of Philosophy* (Spring 2015 Edition). Edward N. Zalta (ed.). https://plato.stanford.edu/archives/spr2015/entries/postmodernism (Accessed January 1, 2019).

Bacon, Francis 1902 *Novum Organum, or True Directions Concerning the Interpretation of Nature* [1620]. New York: P. F. Collier. https:// oll.libertyfund.org/ titles/ 1432 (Accessed September 1, 2018).

Baghramian, Maria 2010 A Brief History of Relativism. In *Relativism: A Contemporary Anthology.* Michael Krausz (ed.). New York: Columbia University Press. Pp. 31–50.

—— 2004 *Relativism: The Problems of Philosophy.* London: Routledge.

Baghramian, Maria, and Adam Carter 2019a Relativism. In *The Stanford Encyclopedia of Philosophy* (Winter 2019). Edward Zalta (ed.). https://plato.stanford.edu/archives/win2019/entries/relativism/ (Accessed August 15, 2019).

—— 2019b The Linguistic Relativity Hypothesis: Supplement to Relativism. In *The Stanford Encyclopedia of Philosophy* (Winter 2019). Edward Zalta (ed.). https://plato.stanford.edu/archives/win2019/entries/relativism/ (Accessed August 15, 2019).

Bailey, Frederick 1991 *The Prevalence of Deceit.* Ithaca, NY: Cornell University Press.

Bale, Jeffrey 2007 Political Paranoia vs. Political Realism: On Distinguishing Between Bogus Conspiracy Theories and Genuine Conspiratorial Politics. *Patterns of Prejudice* 41: 45–60. https://www.tandfonline.com/doi/full/10.1080/00313220601118751 (Accessed October 11, 2019).

Ball, James 2017 *Post-Truth: How Bullshit Conquered the World.* London: Biteback Publishing.

Bambach, Charles 2003 *Heidegger's Roots: Nietzsche, National Socialism, and the Greeks.* Ithaca, NY: Cornell University Press.

Barclay, Eliza 2020 The Conspiracy Theories About the Origins of the Coronavirus, Debunked. *Vox* (March 12). https://www.vox.com/2020/3/4/21156607/how-did-the-coronavirus-get-started-china wuhan-lab (Accessed March 15, 2020).

Barker, Gillian, and Philip Kitcher 2014 *Philosophy of Science: A New Introduction.* Oxford: Oxford University Press.

Barkun, Michael 2013 *A Culture of Conspiracy: Apocalyptic Visions in Contemporary America*. Los Angeles, CA: University of California Press.

Barnett, Paul, and James Kaufman 2018 Truth Shall Prevail. In *Pseudoscience: The Conspiracy Against Science*. Allison Kaufman and James Kaufman (eds.). Cambridge, MA: The MIT Press. Pp. 467–479.

Baudrillard, Jean 1995 *The Gulf War Did Not Take Place*. Bloomington: Indiana University Press.

Beals, Ralph 1978 Sonoran Fantasy or Coming of Age? *American Anthropologist* 80: 355–362.

Becker, Jasper 1996 *Hungry Ghosts: China's Secret Famine*. London: John Murray.

Beiner, Ronald 2018 *Dangerous Minds: Nietzsche, Heidegger, and the Return of the Far Right*. Philadelphia: University of Pennsylvania Press.

Bell, James 1994 *Reconstructing Prehistory: Scientific Method in Archaeology*. Philadelphia: Temple University Press.

Benestad, Rasmus, Dana Nuccitelli, Stephan Lewandowsky, Hans Olav Hygen, Katharine Hayhoe, Rob van Dorland, and John Cook 2016 Learning from Mistakes in Climate Research. *Theoretical and Applied Climatology* 126: 699–703. https://link.springer.com/article/10.1007/s00704-015-1597-5 (Accessed March 11, 2019).

Benson, Ophelia, and Jeremy Stangroom 2006 *Why Truth Matters*. London: Continuum International Publishing Group.

Bereiter, Carl 1994 Implications of Postmodernism for Science, or, Science As Progressive Discourse. *Educational Psychologist* 29: 1, 3–12. https://www.tandfonline.com/doi/abs/10.1207/s15326985ep2901_1 (Accessed March, 2019).

Berlin, Isaiah 1969 Two Concepts of Liberty. In *Four Essays on Liberty*. Oxford: Oxford University Press. Pp. 118–172.

Berman, Emily, and Jacob Carter 2018 Policy Analysis: Scientific Integrity in Federal Policymaking Under Past and Present Administrations. *Journal of Science Policy &Governance* 13(1). (September). http://www.sciencepolicyjournal.org/uploads/5/4/3/4/5434385/berman_emily__carter_jacob.pdf (Accessed December 19, 2019).

Bernard, Russell 1995 *Research Methods in Anthropology: Qualitive and Quantitative Approaches*. Walnut Creek, CA: AltaMira.

Bérubé, Michael 2011 The Science Wars Redux. *Democracy Journal* 19: 64–74 (Accessed September 1, 2019).

Best, Steven, and Douglas Kellner 1997 *The Postmodern Turn*. New York: Guilford Press.

Beyerstein, Barry 1995 *Distinguishing Science from Pseudoscience*. Victoria, Canada: Centre for Curriculum and Development.

Bielo, James 2015 *Anthropology of Religion: The Basics*. New York: Routledge.

Blaker, Kimberly (ed.) 2003a *The Fundamentals of Extremism: The Christian Right in America*. Michigan: New Boston Books.

——— 2003b Introduction: The Perils of Fundamentalism and the Imperilment of Democracy. In *The Fundamentals of Extremism: The Christian Right in America*. Kimberly Blaker (ed.). Michigan: New Boston Books. Pp. 7–24.

Blancke, Stefaan, and Johan de Smedt 2013 Evolutionary and Cognitive Foundations of Pseudoscience. In *Philosophy of Pseudoscience: Reconsidering the Demarcation Problem*. Massimo Pigliucci and Maarten Boudry (eds.). Chicago: University of Chicago Press. Pp. 361–380.

Blanco, Fernando, and Helena Matute 2108 The Illusion of Causality: A Cognitive Bias Underlying Pseudoscience. In *Pseudoscience: The Conspiracy Against Science*. Allison Kaufman and James Kaufman (eds.). Cambridge, MA: The MIT Press. Pp. 45–75.

Bloor, David 1981 The Strengths of the Strong Programme. *Philosophy of Social Sciences* 11: 199–213.

——— 1976 *Knowledge and Social Imagery*. London: Routledge and Kegan Paul.

Boas, Franz 1940 *Race, Language, and Culture*. New York: Macmillan.

Boghossian, Paul 2006 *Fear of Knowledge: Against Relativism and Constructivism*. Oxford: Oxford University Press.

Boseley, Sarah 2008 Mbeki AIDS Denial "Caused 300,000 Deaths." *Guardian* (November 26). https://www.theguardian.com/world/2008/nov/26/aids-south-africa.

——— 1996 What the Sokal Hoax Ought to Teach Us: The Pernicious Consequences and Internal Contradictions of "Postmodernist" Relativism. *Times Literary Supplement*, Commentary. December 13: 14–15. https://www.nyu.edu/gsas/dept/philo/faculty/boghossian/papers/bog_tls.html (Accessed July 19, 2019).

Boudry, Maarten, Stefaan Blancke, and Johan Braeckman 2010 How Not to Attack Intelligent Design Creationism: Philosophical Misconceptions About Methodological Naturalism. *Foundations of Science* 22: 921–949.

Bridges, Tristan 2017 There's an Intriguing Sociological Reason So Many Americans Are Ignoring Facts Lately. *Business Insider* (February 27). https://www.businessinsider.com/sociology-alternative-facts-2017-2 (Accessed July 19, 2019).

Bridgstock, Martin 2009 *Beyond Belief: Skepticism, Science and the Paranormal*. Cambridge: Cambridge University Press.

Brink, Susan 2020 When Public Figures Make Questionable Health Claims, Do People Listen? *NPR* (May 1). https://www.npr.org/sections/goatsandsoda/2020/05/01/847812806/when-public-figures-make-questionable-health-claims-do-people-listen (Accessed May 19, 2020).

Brook, Andrew, and Robert Stainton 2000 *Knowledge and Mind: A Philosophical Introduction*. Cambridge, MA: The MIT Press.

Brown, Donald 1991 *Human Universals*. New York: McGraw-Hill.

Brugger, Peter 2001 From Haunted Brain to Haunted Science: A Cognitive Neuroscience View of the Paranormal. In *Hauntings and Poltergeists: Multidisciplinary Perspectives*. James Houran and Rense Lange (eds.). Jefferson, NC: MacFarland. Pp. 195–213.

Buekens, Filip 2013 Agentive Thinking and Illusions of Understanding. In *Philosophy of Pseudoscience: Reconsidering the Demarcation Problem*. Massimo Pigliucci and Maarten Boudry (eds.). Chicago: University of Chicago Press. Pp. 439–458.

Cadwalladr, Carole 2017 Daniel Dennett: "I Begrudge Every Hour I Have to Spend Worrying about Politics." *Observer* (February 12). https://www.theguardian.com/science/2017/feb/12/daniel-dennett-politics-bacteria-bach-back-dawkins-trump-interview (Accessed November 7, 2019).

Calcutt, Andrew 2016 The Truth About Post-Truth Politics. *Newsweek* (November 21). https://www.newsweek.com/truth-post-truth-politics-donald-trump-liberals-to ny-blair-523198 (Accessed November 1, 2019).

Campbell, Colin 2002 The Cult, the Cultic Milieu and Secularization. In *The Cultic Milieu: Oppositional Subcultures in an Age of Globalization*. Jeffrey Kaplan and Heléne Lööw (eds.). Walnut Creek: AltaMira Press. Pp. 12–25.

Cannell, Fenella 2006 Introduction: Anthropology and Christianity. In *The Anthropology of Christianity*. Fenella Cannell (ed.). Durham, NC: Duke University Press. Pp. 1–50.

Capps, John 2019 The Pragmatic Theory of Truth. In *The Stanford Encyclopedia of Philosophy* (Summer Edition). Edward N. Zalta (ed.). https://plato.stanford.edu/arc hives/sum2019/entries/truth-pragmatic (Accessed March 1, 2019).

Card, Jeb 2018 *Spooky Archaeology: Myth and the Science of the Past*. Albuquerque, NM: University of New Mexico Press.

Carneiro, Robert 1995 Godzilla Meets New Age Anthropology: Facing the Postmodernist Challenge to a Science of Culture. *Europa* 3–21.

Carrier, Richard 2005 *Sense and Goodness Without God: A Defense of Metaphysical Naturalism*. USA: Author House.

Carter, Jacob, Gretchen Goldman, and Charise Johnson 2018 *Science Under Trump: Voices of Scientists Across 16 Federal Agencies*. Cambridge, MA: Union of Concerned Scientists. https://www.ucsusa.org/sites/default/files/images/2018/08/science-under-trump-report.pdf (Accessed August 16, 2019).

Carter, Jacob, Gretchen Goldman, Genna Reed, Peter Hansel, Michael Halpern, and Andrew Rosenberg 2017 *Sidelining Science Since Day One: How the Trump Administration Has Harmed Public Health and Safety in its First Six Months*. Cambridge, MA: Union of Concerned Scientists. https://www.ucsusa.org/resourc es/sidelining-science-day-one (Accessed August 16, 2019).

Cerroni-Long, E. L. 1999 Introduction: Anthropology at Century's End. In *Anthropological Theory in North America*. E. L. Cerroni-Long (ed.). Westport, CT: Bergin and Garvey. Pp. 1–18.

Chomsky, Noam 1994 *Keeping the Rabble in Line: Interviews with David Barsamian*. Monroe, MN: Common Courage Press.

Clarke, Arthur 2003 Credo. In *Science and Religion: Are They Compatible*. Paul Kurtz, Barry Karr, and Ranjit Sandhu (eds.). Amherst, NY: Prometheus Books. Pp. 181–187.

Clifford, James 1986 Introduction: Partial Truths. In *Writing Culture: The Poetics and Politics of Ethnography*. James Clifford and George Marcus (eds.). Berkeley, CA: University of California Press. Pp. 1–26.

Clifford, James, and George Marcus (eds.) 1986 *Writing Culture: The Poetics and Politics of Ethnography*. Berkeley, CA: University of California Press.

Conway, Philip 2017 Post-Truth, Complicity and International Politics. *E-International Relations*. https://www.e-ir.info/2017/03/29/post-truth-complicity-and-internation al-politics/PHILIP (Accessed March 18, 2019).

Cook, John, Stephan Lewandowsky, and Ullrich Ecker 2017 Neutralizing Misinformation through Inoculation: Exposing Misleading Argumentation Techniques Reduces Their Influence. *PLoS One* 12: e0175799. https://journals.plo s.org/plosone/article?id=10.1371/journal.pone.0175799 (Accessed July 8, 2018).

Coppins, McKay 2020 Trump's Dangerously Effective Coronavirus Propaganda. *The Atlantic* (March 11). https://www.theatlantic.com/politics/archive/2020/03/trump-c oronavirus-threat/607825/ (Accessed March 14, 2020).

Coyne, Jerry 2015 *Faith Versus Fact: Why Science and Religion Are Incompatible.* New York: Penguin Books.

Crapo, Richley 2003 *Anthropology of Religion: Unity and Diversity of Religions.* Boston: McGraw-Hill.

Creel, Richard 2001 *Thinking Philosophically: An Introduction to Critical Reflection and Rational Dialogue.* Malden, MA: Blackwell.

Crumley, Jack 1999 *An Introduction to Epistemology.* Mountain View, CA: Mayfield Publishing.

Curran, James, Des Freedman, and Natalie Fenton 2012a *Misunderstanding the Internet.* New York: Routledge. https://courses.helsinki.fi/sites/default/files/course material/4511752/CURRAN%20ET%20AL_Misunderstanding%20the%20intern et.pdf (Accessed July 1, 2019).

——— 2012b Reinterpreting the Internet. In *Misunderstanding the Internet.* James Curran, Des Freedman, and Natalie Fenton (eds.). New York: Routledge. Pp. 3–33.

D'Ancona, Matthew 2017 *Post-Truth: The War on Truth and How to Fight Back.* London: Ebury Press.

D'Andrade, Roy 1999 Culture Is Not Everything. In *Anthropological Theory in North America.* E. L. Cerroni-Long (ed.). Westport, CT: Bergin and Garvey. Pp. 85–103.

——— 1995 What Do You Think You Are Doing? *Anthropology Newsletter* 36(3): 399–408.

David, Marian 2016 The Correspondence Theory of Truth. In *The Stanford Encyclopedia of Philosophy* (Fall Edition). Edward N. Zalta (ed.). https://plato.s tanford.edu/archives/fall2016/entries/truth-correspondence (Accessed January 1, 2019).

Dawes, Robyn 2001 *Everyday Irrationality: How Pseudo-Scientists, Lunatics, and the Rest of Us Systematically Fail to Think Rationally.* New York: Routledge.

Dawkins, Richard 2006 *The God Delusion.* New York: Houghton Mifflin.

——— 1997 Obscurantism to the Rescue. *Quarterly Review of Biology* 72: 397–399.

De Man, Paul, Werner Hamacher, Neil Hertz, and Thomas Keenan 1988 *Wartime Journalism, 1939–1943.* Lincoln, NE: by the University of Nebraska Press.

De Mille, Richard 1990 *The Don Juan Papers: Further Castaneda Controversies.* Belmont, CA: Wadsworth.

——— 1976 *Castaneda's Journey: The Power of an Allegory.* Lincoln, NE: University.

De Vrieze, Jop 2017 Bruno Latour, a Veteran of the 'Science Wars,' Has a New Mission. *Science* 358(6360): 159. https://doi.org/10.1126/science.358.6360.159 (Accessed December, 2019).

Dean, Jodi 1998 *Aliens in America: Conspiracy Cultures from Outerspace to Cyberspace*. Ithaca, NY: Cornell University Press.

Dejong-Lambert, William 2012 *The Cold War Politics of Genetic Research: An Introduction to the Lysenko Affair*. London: Springer Science.

Del Vicario, Michela, Alessandro Bessi, Fabiana Zollo, Fabio Petroni, Antonio Scala, Guido Caldarelli, Harry Eugene Stanley, and Walter Quattrociocchi 2016 The Spreading of Misinformation Online. *Proceedings of the National Academy of Sciences of the United States of America* 113(3): 554–559. https://www.semanticscholar.org/paper/The-spreading-of-misinformation-online.-Vicario-Bessi/c44cd3b6864293e4449ce78191c54bf71313d544 (Accessed December 11, 2019).

Dembski, William 2003 Skepticism's Prospect for Unseating Intelligent Design. In *Science and Religion: Are They Compatible?* Paul Kurtz, Barry Karr, and Ranjit Sandhu (eds.). Amherst, NY: Prometheus Books. Pp. 89–97.

Dennett, Daniel 2006 *Breaking the Spell: Religion As a Natural Phenomenon*. New York: Penguin Books.

―――― 1995 *Darwin's Dangerous Idea: Evolution and the Meaning of Life*. New York: Simon and Schuster.

Derrida, Jacques 1976 *Of Grammatology*. Baltimore, MD: Johns Hopkins University Press.

―――― 1970 Structure, Sign and Play in the Discourse of the Human Sciences. In *The Languages of Criticism and the Sciences of Man: The Structuralist Controversy*. Richard Macksey and Eugenio Donato (eds.). Baltimore: Johns Hopkins Press. Pp. 247–272.

Derrida, Jacques, and Peggy Kamuf 1988 Like the Sound of the Sea Deep Within a Shell: Paul de Man's War. *Critical Inquiry* 14(3): 590–652.

Deuze, Mark, and Tamara Witschge 2018 Beyond Journalism: Theorizing the Transformation of Journalism. *Journalism* 19(2): 165–181. https://journals.sagepub.com/doi/10.1177/1464884916688550 (Accessed December 11, 2019).

Dew, James, and Mark Foreman 2014 *How Do We Know: An Introduction to Epistemology*. Downers Grove, IL: InterVarsity Press.

Dickson, E. J. 2020 Coronavirus Is Spreading—And So Are the Hoaxes and Conspiracy Theories Around It. *The Rolling Stone* (March 9). https://www.rollingstone.com/culture/culture-news/coronavirus-china-bat-patent-conspiracy-theory-942416/ (Accessed March 15, 2020).

Diethelm, Pascal, and Martin McKee 2009 Denialism: What Is It and How Should Scientists Respond? *European Journal of Public Health* 19: 2–4. https://academic.oup.com/eurpub/article/19/1/2/463780 (Accessed October 1, 2019).

Diggins, John 1992 *The Rise and Fall of the American Left*. New York: W.W. Norton.

Doran, Peter, and Maggie Zimmerman 2009 Examining the Scientific Consensus on Climate Change. *Eos* 90(3): 22–23. https://agupubs.onlinelibrary.wiley.com/doi/pdf/10.1029/2009eo030002 (Accessed October 22, 2019).

Douglas, Karen, Robbie Sutton, and Aleksandra Cichocka 2017 The Psychology of Conspiracy Theories. *Current Directions in Psychological Science* 26(6): 538–542. https://journals.sagepub.com/doi/pdf/10.1177/0963721417718261.

Dreyfuss, Emily 2017 Want to Make a Lie Sound True? Say It Again. And Again. And Again. *Wired* (February 11). https://www.wired.com/2017/02/dont-believe-lies-just-people-repeat (Accessed January 1, 2019).

Dugger, Celia 2008 Study Cites Toll of AIDS Policy in South Africa. *New York Times* (November 25). https://www.nytimes.com/2008/11/26/world/africa/26aids.html (Accessed January 7, 2019).

Dunning, David 2011 The Dunning–Kruger Effect: On Being Ignorant of One's Own Ignorance. *Advances in Experimental Social Psychology* 44: 247–296.

Edis, Taner 2008 *Science and Nonbelief*. Amherst, NY: Prometheus Books.

Edwards, Jeanette, Penny Harvey, and Peter Wade 2007 Introduction: Epistemologies in Practice. In *Anthropology and Science: Epistemologies in Practice*. Jeanette Edwards, Penny Harvey, and Peter Wade (eds.). New York: Berg Publishers. Pp. 1–18.

Egan, Lauren, and Mansee Khurana 2020 Trump Has Many Hunches About the Coronavirus. Here's What the Experts Say. *NBC News* (March 5). https://www.nbcnews.com/politics/donald-trump/just-my-hunch-trump-contradicts-health-experts-coronavirus-n1151006#anchor-TrumpsayswarmweathercouldkillthevirusExpertssaythatspremature (Accessed March 29, 2020).

Einstein, Albert 1936 Physics and Reality. *Daedalus* 132(4): 22–25. https://www.sciencedirect.com/science/article/pii/S0016003236910475 (Accessed October 1, 2019).

Einstein, Katherine, and David Glick 2015 Do I Think BLS Data Are BS? The Consequences of Conspiracy Theories. *Political Behavior* 37: 679–701.

Eliade, Mircea 1969 *The Quest*. Chicago, IL: University of Chicago Press.

——— 1963 *Patterns in Comparative Religion*. Cleveland: Meridian Books.

Evans-Pritchard, Edward 1965 *Theories of Primitive Religion*. Oxford: Clarendon Press.

——— 1960 Religion and the Anthropologists. *Blackfriars* 41(480): 104–118.

——— 1937 *Witchcraft, Oracles and Magic Among the Azande*. Oxford: Clarendon Press.

Fagan, Garrett, and Chris Hale 2001 The New Atlantis and the Dangers of Pseudo History. *Skeptic* 9(1): 78–87.

Faye, Emmanuel 2009 *Heidegger: The Introduction of Nazism into Philosophy*. New Haven, CT: Yale University.

Festinger, Leon, Henry Riecken, and Stanley Schachter 1956 *When Prophecy Fails*. Minneapolis: University of Minnesota Press.

Feyerabend, Paul 1995 *Killing Time: The Autobiography of Paul Feyerabend*. Chicago: University of Chicago Press.

——— 1993 *Against Method* (3rd Edition). London: Verso.

——— 1992 Atoms and Consciousness. *Common Knowledge* 1(1): 28–32.

——— 1981 *Realism, Rationalism and Scientific Method*. Cambridge: Cambridge University Press.

——— 1975 *Against Method*. London: New Left Books.

Feynman, Richard 1986 Appendix F—Personal Observations on the Reliability of the Shuttle. https://science.ksc.nasa.gov/shuttle/missions/51-l/docs/rogers-commission/Appendix-F.txt (Accessed March 10, 2019).

Field, Matt, and John Krzyzaniak 2020 Why Do Politicians Keep Breathing Life into the False Conspiracy Theory that the Coronavirus Is a Bioweapon? *Bulletin of the Atomic Scientists* (March 13). https://thebulletin.org/2020/03/why-do-politicians-keep-breathing-life-into-the-false-conspiracy-theory-that-the-coronavirus-is-a-bioweapon/ (Accessed March 15, 2020).

Fishman, Yonata 2009 Can Science Test Supernatural Worldviews? *Science and Education* 18: 813–837.

Fishman, Yonata, and Maarten Boudry 2013 Does Science Presuppose Naturalism (or Anything at All)? *Science and Education* 22: 921–949.

Forrest, Barbara 2002 The Newest Evolution of Creationism. *Natural History* 11(3): 80.

Forrest, Barbara, and Paul Gross 2004 *Creationism's Trojan Horse: The Wedge of Intelligent Design*. Oxford: Oxford University Press.

Forstenzer, Joshua 2018 Something Has Cracked: Post-Truth Politics and Richard Rorty's Postmodernist Bourgeois Liberalism. *Ash Center for Democratic Governance and Innovation, Harvard Kennedy School*. https://ash.harvard.edu/files/ash/files/post-truth-politics-rorty.pdf (Accessed October 11, 2019).

Foucault, Michel 1980 Truth and Power. In *Truth and Power: Selected Interviews and Other Writings 1972–1977*. Colin Gordon (ed.). New York: Pantheon. Pp. 109–133.

—— 1978 *The History of Sexuality*. New York: Pantheon Books.

Fountain, Philip, and Sin Wen Lau 2013 Anthropological Theologies: Engagements and Encounters. *The Australian Journal of Anthropology* 24: 227–234.

Fox, Robin 1997 State of the Art/Science in Anthropology. In *Flights from Science and Reason*. Paul Gross, Norman Levitt, and Martin Lewis (eds.). New York: Academia Press. Pp. 327–345.

—— 1992 Anthropology and the 'Teddy Bear' Picnic. *Society* 30(2): 47–55.

Frankenberry, Nancy, and Hans Penner 1999 Clifford Geertz's Long-Lasting Moods, Motivations, and Metaphysical Conceptions. *The Journal of Religion* 79(4): 617–640.

Frankfurt, Harry 2018 *On Truth*. New York: Alfred A. Knopf.

—— 2005 *On Bullshit*. Princeton, NJ: Princeton University Press.

Franklin, James 2009 *What Science Knows: And How It Knows It*. New York: Encounter Books.

—— 2002 Stove's Discovery of the Worst Argument in the World. *Philosophy* 77: 615–624.

—— 2000 Thomas Kuhn's Irrationalism. *New Criterion* 18(10): 29. https://search.ebscohost.com/login.aspx?direct=true&db=a9h&AN=3596800&site=ehost-live&scope=site (Accessed November 15, 2019).

French, Christopher 2001 *Paranormal Perception: A Critical Examination*. The Institute for Cultural Research. Monograph Series 42. Pp. 1–24.

French, Christopher, and Anna Stone 2014 *Anomalistic Psychology: Exploring Paranormal Belief and Experience*. New York: Palgrave Macmillan.

Futuyma, Douglas 1982 *Science on Trial: The Case for Evolution*. New York: Pantheon Books.

Gardner, Martin 1993 *The Whys of a Philosophical Scrivener*. New York: William Morrow and Company.

——— 1989 *Science: Good, Bad, and Bogus*. Buffalo, NY: Prometheus Books.

Gauch, Hugh 2009 Science, Worldviews, and Education. *Science and Education* 18: 667–695.

Geertz, Clifford 1988 *Work and Lives: The Anthropologist As Author*. Stanford, CA: Stanford University Press.

——— 1983 *Local Knowledge: Further Essays in Interpretive Anthropology*. New York: Basic Books.

——— 1980 Blurred Genres: The Reconfiguration of Social Thought. *The American Scholar* 49(2): 165–179.

——— 1973 Thick Description: Toward an Interpretive Theory of Culture. In *The Interpretation of Cultures: Selected Essays*. Glifford Geertz (ed.). New York: Basic Books. Pp. 3–30.

Gellner, Ernest 1992 *Postmodernism, Reason and Religion*. London: Routledge.

Gilovich, Thomas 1991 *How We Know What Isn't So: The Fallibility of Human Reason in Everyday Life*. New York: The Free Press.

Giuliani, Rudy 2018 Rudy Giuliani: "Truth Isn't Truth." *Meet The Press, NBC News*. https://www.youtube.com/watch?v=CljsZ7lgbtw (Accessed September 5, 2018).

Glaeser, Edward, Giacomo Ponzetto, and Jesse Shapiro 2005 Strategic Extremism: Why Republicans and Democrats Divide on Religious Values. *The Quarterly Journal of Economics* 120: 1283–1330. https://www.nber.org/papers/w10835 (Accessed October 1, 2019).

Glass-Coffin, Bonnie 2010 Anthropology, Shamanism, and Alternative Ways of Knowing-Being in the World: One Anthropologist's Journey of Discovery and Transformation. *Anthropology and Humanism* 35(2): 204–217.

Glass-Coffin, Bonnie, and Kiiskeentum 2012 The Future of a Discipline: Considering the Ontological/Methodological Future of the Anthropology of Consciousness, Part IV: Ontological Relativism or Ontological Relevance: An Essay in Honor of Michael Harner. *Anthropology of Consciousness* 23(2): 113–126.

Goertzel, Ted 2010 Conspiracy Theories in Science. *EMBO Reports* 11(7): 493–499. https://www.ncbi.nlm.nih.gov/pmc/articles/PMC2897118 (Accessed July 4, 2019).

——— 1994 Belief in Conspiracy Theories. *Political Psychology* 15: 731–742. https://www.jstor.org/stable/pdf/3791630.pdf (Accessed October 11, 2019).

Goldman, Alvin, and Matthew McGrath 2015 *A Contemporary Introduction to Epistemology*. Oxford: Oxford University Press.

Goldschmidt, Walter 1968 Forward to *The Teachings of Don Juan: A Yaqui Way of Knowledge*. Carlos Castaneda (ed.). Berkeley: University of California Press. Pp. xxi–xxii.

Golomb, Jacob 2002 How to De-Nazify Nietzsche's Philosophical Anthropology? In *Nietzsche, Godfather of Fascism?: On the Uses and Abuses of a Philosophy*. Jacob Golomb and Robert Wistrich (eds.). Princeton, NJ: Princeton University Press. Pp. 19–46.

Goode, Erich 2012 *The Paranormal: Who Believes, Why They Believe, and Why It Matter*. Amherst, NY: Prometheus Books.

Goodrick-Clarke, Nicholas 2005 *The Occult Roots of Nazism: Secret Aryan Cults and Their Influence on Nazi Ideology: The Ariosophists of Austria and Germany, 1890–1935*. New York: I.B. Tauris.

Gordin, Michael 2012 *The Pseudoscience Wars: Immanuel Velikovsky and the Birth of the Modern Fringe*. Chicago: University of Chicago Press.

Gorham, Geoffrey 2011 *The Philosophy of Science*. London: One World Books.

Goslinga, Gillian 2013 Spirited Encounters: Notes on the Politics and Poetics of Representing the Uncanny in Anthropology. *Anthropological Theory* 12(4): 386–406.

Gould, Stephen 2002 *The Structure of Evolutionary Theory*. Cambridge: Harvard University Press.

——— 2000 Deconstructing the "Science Wars" by Reconstructing an Old Mold. *Science* 287: 253–261.

——— 1999 *Rock of Ages: Science and Religion in the Fullness of Life*. New York: Ballantine Books.

Goulet, Jean-Guy 1994 Ways of Knowing: Towards a Narrative Ethnography of Experience among the Dene Tha. *Journal of Anthropological Research* 50(2): 113–139.

Goulet, Jean-Guy, and Bruce Miller 2007 Embodied Knowledge: Steps Toward a Radical Anthropology of Cross-Cultural Encounters. In *Extraordinary Anthropology: Transformations in the Field*. Jean-Guy Goulet and Bruce Miller (eds.). Lincoln: University of Nebraska Press. Pp. 1–14.

Goulet, Jean-Guy, and David Young 1994 Theoretical and Methodological Issues. In *Being Changed: Anthropology of Extraordinary Experience*. Jean-Guy Goulet and David Young (eds.). Orchard Park, NY: Broadview. Pp. 298–335.

Graham, Loren 2016 *Lysenko's Ghost: Epigenetics and Russia*. Cambridge, MA: Harvard University Press.

Greco, John, and Ernst Sosa (eds.) 1999 *The Blackwell Guide to Epistemology*. Malden, MA: Blackwell.

Grim, Ryan 2015 Senator Who Cited Snowball in Climate Change Debate Cites Scripture to Back Himself Up. *HuffPost* (March 6). https://www.huffpost.com/entry/jim-inhofe-genesis_n_6815270 (Accessed January 11, 2019).

Grindal, Bruce 1983 Into the Heart of Sisala Experience: Witnessing Death Divination. *Journal of Anthropological Research* 39(1): 60–80.

Gross, Paul, and Norman Levitt 1994 *Higher Superstition: The Academic Left and Its Quarrels with Science*. Baltimore, MD: The Johns Hopkins University Press.

Hacking, Ian 2010 Introduction to the Fourth Edition. In *Against Method* (4th Edition). Paul Feyerabend. London: Verso. Pp. vii–xvi.

Hales, Steven (ed.) 2002 *Analytical Philosophy: Classic Readings*. Belmont, CA: Wadsworth.

Hamacher, Werner, Neil Hertz, and Thomas Keenan 1989 *Responses: On Paul de Man's Wartime Journalism*. Lincoln, NE: University of Nebraska Press.

Hamilton, Lawrence 2011 Education, Politics and Opinions About Climate Change Evidence for Interaction Effects. *Climatic Change* 104: 231–242. https://link.springer.com/article/10.1007/s10584-010-9957-8 (Accessed July 11, 2019).

Hanlon, Aaron 2018 Postmodernism Didn't Cause Trump. It Explains Him. https://www.washingtonpost.com/outlook/postmodernism-didnt-cause-trump-it-explains-him/2018/08/30/0939f7c4-9b12-11e8-843b-36e177f3081c_story.html (Accessed July 11, 2019; Accessed April 19, 2019).

Hann, Chris 2007 The Anthropology of Christianity Per Se. *European Journal of Sociology* 48(3): 383–410.

Hanson, Norwood 1971 *What I Do Not Believe, and Other Essays*. Dordrecht, Holland: D. Reidel.

Harding, Sandra 1987 *The Science Question in Feminism*. Ithaca, NY: Cornell University Press.

Harding, Susan 1991 Representing Fundamentalism: The Problem of the Repugnant Cultural Other. *Social Research* 58(2): 373–393.

Harner, Michael 1999 Science, Spirits, and Core Shamanism. *Shamanism* (Spring/Summer) 12(1): 1–2.

Harris, Marvin 2001a *The Rise of Anthropological Theory: A History of Theories of Culture*. Walnut Creek, CA: AltaMira Press.

——— 2001b *Cultural Materialism: The Struggle for a Science of Culture*. Walnut Creek, CA: AltaMira.

——— 1999 *Theories of Culture in Postmodern Times*. Walnut Creek, CA: AltaMira.

——— 1995 Anthropology and Postmodernism. In *Science, Materialism, and the Study of Culture*. Martin Murphy and Maxine Margolis (eds.). Gainesville: University of Florida Press. Pp. 62–77.

Heath, Chip, and Dan Heath 2007 *Made to Stick: Why Some Ideas Take Hold and Others Come Unstuck*. London: Arrow Books.

Hedges, Chris 2006 *American Fascists: The Christian Right and the War on America*. New York: Free Press.

Heit, Helmut 2018 "There Are No Facts...": Nietzsche As Predecessor of Post-Truth? *Studia Philosophica Estonica* 11: 44–63. https://ojs.utlib.ee/index.php/spe/article/view/14404 (Accessed October 11, 2019).

Hellweg, Joseph, Joshua Englehardt, and Jesse Miller 2015 Raising the Dead: Altered States, Anthropology, and the Heart of Sisala Experience. *Anthropology and Humanism* 40(2): 206–224.

Hemple, Carl 1965 *Aspects of Scientific Explanation: And Other Essays in the Philosophy of Science*. New York: The Free Press.

Hénaff, Marcel 1998 *Claude Lévi-Strauss and the Making of Structural Anthropology*. Minneapolis: University of Minnesota Press.

Herzfeld, Michael 2017 Anthropological Realism in a Scientistic Age. *Anthropological Theory* 18 (1): 22.

——— 2001 *Anthropology: Theoretical Practice in Culture and Society*. Oxford: Blackwell.

Higgins, C. Francis 2006 Gorgias (483—375 B.C.E.). *Internet Encyclopedia of Philosophy*. https://www.iep.utm.edu/gorgias/#SH2a (Accessed January, 2018).

Higgins, Kathleen 2016 Post-Truth: A Guide for the Perplexed. *Nature* 540: 9. https://www.nature.com/news/post-truth-a-guide-for-the-perplexed-1.21054 (Accessed January, 2019).

Hines, Terence 2003 *Pseudoscience and the Paranormal*. Amherst, NY: Prometheus Books.

Hitler, Adolf 1939 *Mein Kampf*. London: Hurst and Blackett. http://gutenberg.net.au/ebooks02/0200601.txt (Accessed March 19, 2019).

Hoffmann, Banesh 1972 *Albert Einstein: Creator and Rebel*. New York: Viking.

Hofstadter, Richard 1963 *Anti-Intellectualism in American Life*. New York: Anchor Books.

Holt, Nicola, Christine Simmonds-Moore, David Luke, and Christopher French 2012 *Anomalistic Psychology*. Basingstoke: Palgrave Macmillan.

Holton, Gerald 1992 How to Think About the "Anti-Science" Phenomena. *Public Understanding of Science* 1: 103–128.

Horgan, John 1993 Profile: Paul Karl Feyerabend: The Worst Enemy of Science. *Scientific American* 268(5): 36–37. JSTOR. www.jstor.org/stable/24941475 (Accessed January, 2019).

Hospers, John 1988 *An Introduction to Philosophical Analysis*. Englewood Cliffs, NJ: Prentice Hall.

Howson, Colin, and Peter Urbach 2006 *Scientific Reasoning: The Bayesian Approach*. Peru, IL: Open Court.

Hoyningen, Paul 2000 Paul Feyerabend and Thomas Kuhn. In *The Worst Enemy of Science: Essays in Memory of Paul Feyerabend*. John Preston, Gonzalo Munévar, and David Lamb (eds.). Oxford: Oxford University Press. Pp. 102–114.

Huang, Yanzhong 2020 U.S.-Chinese Distrust Is Inviting Dangerous Coronavirus Conspiracy Theories and Undermining Efforts to Contain the Epidemic. *Foreign Affairs* (March/April). https://www.foreignaffairs.com/articles/united-states/2020-03-05/us-chinese-distrust-inviting-dangerous-coronavirus-conspiracy (Accessed March, 15).

Hufford, David 2010 Visionary Spiritual Experiences in an Enchanted World. *Anthropology and Humanism* 35(2): 142–158.

Hume, David 1902 [1748] *Enquiry Concerning Human Understanding*. Oxford: Clarendon Press. https://www.earlymoderntexts.com/assets/pdfs/hume1748.pdf (Accessed July 4, 2019).

Hunt, Julia 2017 Fake News' Named Collins Dictionary Word of the Year for 2017. *Independent* (November 2). http://www.independent.co.uk/news/uk/home-news/fake-news-word-of-the-year-2017-collins-dictionary-donald-trump-kellyanne-conway-antifa-corbynmania-a8032751.html (Accessed October 1, 2018).

Hunter, Jack 2018 *Engaging the Anomalous: Collected Essays on Anthropology, the Paranormal, Mediumship and Extraordinary Experience*. Hove, UK: White Crow Productions.

——— 2012 Anthropology and the Paranormal. In *Paranthropology: Anthropological Approaches to the Paranormal*. Jack Hunter (ed.). Bristol, UK: Paranthropology. Pp. 21–42.

Illing, Sean 2019 The Post-Truth Prophets: Postmodernism Predicted Our Post-Truth Hellscape: Everyone Still Hates It. *Vox* (November 16). https://www.vox.com/features/2019/11/11/18273141/postmodernism-donald-trump-lyotard-baudrillard (Accessed February 19, 2019).

Inhofe, James 2012 *The Greatest Hoax: How the Global Warming Conspiracy Threatens Your Future*. Washington, DC: WND Books.

Isaac, Jeffrey 2016 How Hannah Arendt's Classic Work on Totalitarianism Illuminates Today's America. *The Washington Post* (December 17). https://www.washingtonpost.com/news/monkey-cage/wp/2016/12/17/how-hannah-arendts-classic-work (Accessed October 22, 2019).

Isaak, Mark 2002 A Philosophical Premise of Naturalism? http:// www.talkdesign.org/faqs/naturalism.html (Accessed October 15, 2018).

Jackson, Michael 1989 *Path Toward a Clearing: Radical Empiricism and Ethnographic Inquiry*. Bloomington: Indian University Press.

Jacoby, Susan 2009 *The Age of American Unreason*. New York: Vintage Books.

Jacques, Peter 2012 A General Theory of Climate Denial. *Global Environmental Politics* 12: 9–17. https://www.mitpressjournals.org/doi/pdf/10.1162/GLEP_a_00105 (Accessed December 18, 2019).

Jacques, Peter, Riley Dunlap, and Mark Freeman 2008 The Organisation of Denial: Conservative Think Tanks and Environmental Scepticism. *Environmental Politics* 17: 349–385. https://www.tandfonline.com/doi/full/10.1080/09644010802055576 (Accessed December 18, 2019).

Jaffe, Alexandra 2017 Kellyanne Conway: WH Spokesman Gave "Alternative Facts" on Inauguration Crowd. *NBC News* (January 22). https://www.nbcnews.com/storyline/meet-the-press-70-years/wh-spokesman-gave-alternative-facts-inauguration-crowd-n710466 (Accessed October 11, 2019).

Jasny, Lorien, Joseph Waggle, and Dana Fisher 2015 An Empirical Examination of Echo Chambers in US Climate Policy Networks. *Nature Climate Change* 5: 782–786.

Johnson, Allen, and Orna Johnson 2001 Introduction to the Updated Edition. In *Cultural Materialism: The Struggle for a Science of Culture*. Marvin Harris (ed.). Walnut Creek, CA: AltaMira Press. Pp. vi–xiv.

Jolley, Daniel, and Karen Douglas 2013 The Social Consequences of Conspiracism: Exposure to Conspiracy Theories Decreases Intentions to Engage in Politics and to Reduce One's Carbon Footprint. *British Journal of Psychology* 105: 35–56.

Joravsky, David 1970 *Lysenko Affair*. Cambridge, MA: Harvard University Press.

Kafka, Peter 2016 An Astonishing Number of People Believe Pizzagate, the Facebook-fueled Clinton Sex Ring Conspiracy Story, Could Be True: Especially If They Are Trump Voters. *Vox* (December 9). https://www.recode.net/2016/12/9/13898328/pizzagate-poll-trump-voters-clinton-facebook-fake-news (Accessed December 18, 2019).

Kahn, Joel 2011 Understanding: Between Belief and Unbelief Acknowledgement of Difference May Be Turned into Respect. *The Australian Journal of Anthropology* 22: 76–88.

Kakutani, Michiko 2018 *The Death of Truth: Notes on Falsehoods in the Age of Trump*. New York: Tim Duggan Books.

Kalichman, Seth 2009 *Denying AIDS: Conspiracy Theories, Pseudoscience, and Human Tragedy*. New York: Springer.
Kaufman, Allison, and James Kaufman (eds.) 2018 *Pseudoscience: The Conspiracy Against Science*. Cambridge, MA: The MIT Press.
Kaufmann, Walter 1968 *Nietzsche: Philosopher, Psychologist, Antichrist*. New York Vintage Books.
Kay, Paul, and Willett Kempton 1984 What Is the Sapir-Whorf Hypothesis? *American Anthropologist* 86(1): 65–79.
Keane, Webb 2006 Epilogue: Anxious Transcendence. In *The Anthropology of Christianity*. Fenella Cannell (ed.). Durham, NC: Duke University Press. Pp. 308–323.
Keeley, Brian 1999 Of Conspiracy Theories. *The Journal of Philosophy* 96(3): 109–126.
Keener, Craig 2011 *Miracles: The Credibility of the New Testament Accounts* (Vols. 2). Grand Rapids, MI: Baker.
Kenny, Caroline 2018 Rudy Giuliani Says "Truth Isn't Truth." *CNN* (August 19). https://www.cnn.com/2018/08/19/politics/rudy-giuliani-truth-isnt truth/index.html (Accessed October 1, 2019).
Keyes, Ralph 2004 *The Post-Truth Era: Dishonesty and Deception in Contemporary Life*. New York: St. Martin's Press.
Klausner, William 1994 Going Native. *Anthropology Today* 10(3): 18–19.
Koertge, Noretta 1998 Postmodernism and the Problem of Scientific Literacy. In *A House Built on Sand: Exposing Postmodern Myths About Science*. Noretta Koertge (ed.). Oxford: Oxford University Press. Pp. 257–271.
Koss-Chioino, Joan 2010 Introduction: Do Spirits Exist. *Anthropology and Humanism* 35(2): 131–141.
Kossy, Donna 1994 *Kooks: A Guide to the Outer Limits of Human Belief*. Portland, OR: Feral House.
Kruger, Justin, and David Dunning 1999 Unskilled and Unaware of It: How Difficulties in Recognizing One's Own Incompetence Lead to Inflated Self-Assessments. *Journal of Personality and Social Psychology* 77(6): 1121–1134.
Kuhn, Thomas 1990 The Road Since Structure. In *PSA: Proceedings of the Biennial Meeting of the Philosophy of Science Association*. Pp. 3–13.
——— 1970 *The Structure of Scientific Revolutions*. Chicago: University of Chicago Press.
Kuklinski, James, Paul Quirk, Jennifer Jerit, David Schwieder, and Robert Rich 2000 Misinformation and the Currency of Democratic Citizenship. *The Journal of Politics* 62(3): 790–816.
Kurlander, Eric 2017 *Hitler's Monsters: A Supernatural History of the Third Reich*. New Haven, CT: Yale University Press.
Kutschera, Ulrich, and Karl Niklas 2004 The Modern Theory of Biological Evolution: An Expanded Synthesis. *Naturwissenschaften* 91: 255–276 (Accessed November 22, 2019).
Kuznar, Lawrence 2008 *Reclaiming a Scientific Anthropology*. Walnut Creek, CA: Altamira.

LaFrance, Adrienne 2020 The Prophecies of Q: American Conspiracy Theories are Entering a Dangerous New Phase. *The Atlantic* (June). https://www.theatlantic.com/magazine/archive/2020/06/qanon-nothing-can-stop-what-is-coming/610567/ (Accessed August 24, 2020).

Lang, Berel 2002 Misinterpretation As the Author's Responsibility (Nietzsche's Fascism, for Instance). In *Nietzsche, Godfather of Fascism?: On the Uses and Abuses of a Philosophy*. Jacob Golomb and Robert Wistrich (eds.). Princeton, NJ: Princeton University Press. Pp. 47–65.

Lash, Scott 1990 *Sociology of Postmodernism*. London: Routledge and Kegan Paul.

Latour, Bruno 2004 Why Has Critique Run Out of Steam? From Matters of Fact to Matters of Concern. *Critical Inquiry* 30: 225–248.

——— 1996 On the Partial Existence of Existing and Nonexisting Objects. In *Biographies of Scientific Objects*. Lorraine Daston (ed.). Chicago: Chicago University Press. Pp. 247–269.

——— 1988 A Relativistic Account of Einstein's Relativity. *Social Studies of Science* 18: 3–44.

——— 1985 *Science in Action: How to Follow Scientists and Engineers Through Society*. Cambridge: Harvard University Press.

——— 1983 Give Me a Laboratory and I Will Raise the World. In *Science Observed: Perspectives on the Social Study of Science*. Karin Knorr-Cetina and Michael Mulkay (eds.). New York: Sage Publications. Pp. 141–170.

Latour, Bruno, and Steve Woolgar 1986 *Laboratory Life: The Construction of Scientific Facts* (2nd Edition). Princeton, NJ: Princeton University Press.

——— 1979 *Laboratory Life: The Social Construction of Scientific Facts*. Beverly Hills, CA: Sage Publications.

Laudan, Larry 1990 *Science and Relativism: Some Key Controversies in the Philosophy of Science*. Chicago: University of Chicago Press.

——— 1983 The Demise of the Demarcation Problem. In *Physics, Philosophy and Psychoanalysis: Essays in Honor of Adolf Grünbaum*. Robert Cohen and Larry Laudan (eds.). Dordrecht, Holland: D. Reidel. Pp. 111–127.

Law, Stephen 2016 The X-Claim Argument Against Religious Belief. *Religious Studies* 54: 15–35.

Layton, Robert 1997 *An Introduction to Theory in Anthropology*. Cambridge: Cambridge University Press.

Leavitt, John 2006 Linguistic Relativities. In *Language, Culture, and Society*. Christine Jourdan and Kevin Tuite (eds.). Cambridge: Cambridge University Press. Pp. 47–81.

Lecourt, Dominique 1977 *Proletarian Science? The Case of Lysenko*. London: New Left Books.

Lehman, David 1991 *Signs of the Times: Deconstruction and Fall of Paul De Man*. New York: Poseidon Press.

Lett, James 1997a *Science, Reason, and Anthropology: The Principles of Rational Inquiry*. Lanham, MD: Rowman & Littlefield.

——— 1997b Science, Religion, and Anthropology. In *Anthropology of Religion: A Handbook*. Stephen Glazier (ed.). Westport, CT: Praeger. Pp. 103–120.

———— 1987 *The Human Enterprise: A Critical Introduction to Anthropological Theory*. Boulder, CO: Westview Press.
Levine, Alex 1999 T.S. Kuhn's "Non-Revolution": An Exchange. *The New York Review of Books* (February 18). https://www.nybooks.com/articles/1999/02/18/ts-kuhns-non-revolution-an-exchange (Accessed January 18, 2019).
Levitin, Daniel 2016 *Weaponized Lies: How to Think Critically in the Post-Truth Era*. New York: Dutton.
Levitsky, Steven, and Daniel Ziblatt 2018 *How Democracies Die*. New York: Broadway Books.
Levitz, Eric 2020 Does Trump Know Senate Republicans Can't Make the Coronavirus Go Away? *Intelligencer* (February 28). https://nymag.com/intelligencer/2020/02/trump-coronavirus-mick-mulvaney-lies.html (Accessed March 14, 2020).
Lewandowsky, Stephen, Gilles Gignac, and Klaus Oberauer 2013 The Role of Conspiracist Ideation and Worldviews in Predicting Rejection of Science. *PLoS One* 10(8): e75637. https://journals.plos.org/plosone/article?id=10.1371/journal.pone.0075637 (Accessed September 18, 2018).
Lewandowsky, Stephan, John Cook, and Elisabeth Lloyd 2016 The "Alice in Wonderland" Mechanics of the Rejection of (Climate) Science: Simulating Coherence by Conspiracism. *Synthese* 195: 175–196. https://link.springer.com/article/10.1007%2Fs11229-016-1198-6 (Accessed January 17, 2019).
Lewandowsky, Stephan, Klaus Oberauer, and Gilles Gignac 2013 NASA Faked the Moon Landing—Therefore, (Climate) Science Is a Hoax: An Anatomy of the Motivated Rejection of Science. *Psychological Science* 24(5): 622–633. https://journals.sagepub.com/doi/pdf/10.1177/0956797612457686 (Accessed September 18, 2018).
Lewandowsky, Stephan, Ullrich Ecker, and John Cook 2017 Beyond Misinformation: Understanding and Coping with the Post-truth Era. *Journal of Applied Research in Memory and Cognition* 6(4): 353–369. https://www.sciencedirect.com/science/article/pii/S2211368117300700 (Accessed January 1, 2019).
Lilienfeld, Scott 2018 Foreword: Navigating a Post-Truth World: Ten Enduring Lessons from the Study of Pseudoscience. In *Pseudoscience: The Conspiracy Against Science*. Allison Kaufman and James Kaufman (eds.). Cambridge, MA: The MIT Press. Pp. xi–xvii.
———— 2005 The 10 Commandments of Helping Students Distinguish Science from Pseudoscience. *Observer* 18: 39–40, 49–51. https:// www.psychologicalscience .org/ observer/ the- 10- commandments- of- helping- students- distinguish science from- pseudoscience- in- psychology (Accessed September 16, 2018).
Lingua Franca, Editors (eds.) 2000 *The Sokal Hoax: The Sham that Shook the Academy*. Lincoln, NE: University of Nebraska Press. Pp. 54–58.
Lockie, Stewart 2016 Post-Truth Politics and the Social Sciences. *Environmental Sociology* 3 (1): 1–5.
Loftus, Elizabeth 1993 The Reality of Repressed Memories. *American Psychologist* 48: 518–537.
Long, Joseph (ed.) 1977 *Extrasensory Ecology: Parapsychology and Anthropology*. Metuchen, NJ: Scarecrow Press.

Lotringer, Sylvere, and Jean Baudrillard 1986 Forgetting Baudrillard. *Social Text* 15: 140–144. https://www.jstor.org/stable/466498?seq=1#metadata_info_tab_contents.

Lucy, John 1997 Linguistic Relativity. *Annual Review of Anthropology* 26: 291–312. https://www.jstor.org/stable/2952524?seq=1#metadata_info_tab_contents291 (Accessed December 2, 2019).

Lukas, Scott 2013 Postmodernism. In *Theory in Social and Cultural Anthropology: An Encyclopedia*. R. Jon McGee and Richard L. Warms (eds.). Thousand Oakes, CA: Sage Publications. Pp. 639–645.

Lynch, Michael 2005 *True to Life: Why Truth Matters*. Cambridge: The MIT Press.

Lyotard, Jean-François 1984 *The Postmodern Condition: A Report on Knowledge*. Minneapolis: University of Minnesota Press.

Mack, John 1994 *Abduction: Human Encounters with Aliens*. New York: Charles Scribner's Sons.

Mahner, Martin 2013 Science and Pseudoscience: How to Demarcate After the (Alleged) Demise of the Demarcation Problem. In *Philosophy of Pseudoscience: Reconsidering the Demarcation Problem*. Massimo Pigliucci and Maarten Boudry (eds.). Chicago: University of Chicago Press. Pp. 29–43.

——— 2012 The Role of Metaphysical Naturalism in Science. *Science and Education* 21: 1437–1459.

Mair, Jonathan 2017 Post-Truth Anthropology. *Journal of the Royal Anthropological Institute* 33(3): 3–4. https://rai.onlinelibrary.wiley.com/doi/full/10.1111/1467-8322.12346 (Accessed August 1, 2019).

Marcus, George 1992 Introduction. In *Reading Cultural Anthropology*. George Marcus (ed.). Durham, NC: Duke University Press. Pp. vii–xiv.

——— 1986 Afterward: Ethnographic Writing and Anthropological Careers. In *Writing Culture: The Poetics and Politics of Ethnography*. James Clifford and George Marcus (eds.). Berkeley, CA: University of California Press. Pp. 165–193.

Marcus, George, and Michael Fischer 1986 *Anthropology As Culture Critique: An Experimental Moment in the Human Sciences*. Chicago: University of Chicago Press.

Marton, Yves 1994 The Experiential Approach to Anthropology and Castaneda's Ambiguous Legacy. In *Being Changed: The Anthropology of Extraordinary Experience*. David Young and Jean-Guy Goulet (eds.). Orchard Park, NY: Broadview. Pp. 273–297.

Masterman, Margaret 1970 The Nature of a Paradigm. In *Criticism and the Growth of Knowledge*. Imre Lakatos and Alan Musgrave (eds.). Cambridge: Cambridge University Press. Pp. 59–90.

Mathis-Lilley, Ben 2017 Trump-Endorsed Media Outlet Accuses NASA of Operating Child Slave Colony on Mars. *Slate* (June 30). https://slate.com/news-and-politics/2017/06/alex-jones-trump-endorsed-infowars-site-exposes-nasa-s-martian-slave-colony.html (Accessed September 18, 2018).

McCright, Aaron, and Riley Dunlap 2011a Cool Dudes: The Denial of Climate Change Among Conservative White Males in the United States. *Global Environmental Change* 21: 1163–1172.

—— 2011b The Politicization of Climate Change and Polarization in the American Public's Views of Global Warming, 2001–2010. *The Sociological Quarterly* 52: 155–194.

—— 2010 Anti-Reflexivity: The American Conservative Movement's Success in Undermining Climate Science and Policy. *Theory, Culture & Society* 27: 100–133. https://journals.sagepub.com/doi/abs/10.1177/0263276409356001 (Accessed January 12, 2020).

—— 2003 Defeating Kyoto: The Conservative Movement's Impact on U.S. Climate Change Policy. *Social Problems* 50: 348–373. https://stephenschneider.stanford.edu/Publications/PDF_Papers/McCrightDunlap2003.pdf (Accessed January 12, 2020).

McCutcheon, Russell 2001 *Critics Not Caretakers: Redescribing the Public Study of Religion*. Albany, NY: State University of New York Press.

McIntyre, Lee 2019 *The Scientific Attitude*. Cambridge, MA: The MIT Press.

—— 2018 *Post-Truth*. Cambridge, MA: The MIT Press.

—— 2015 *Respecting Truth: Willful Ignorance in the Internet Age*. New York: Routledge.

McKee, Martin, and Pascal Diethelm 2010 Christmas 2010: Reading Between the Lines: How the Growth of Denialism Undermines Public Health. *British Medical Journal* 341: 1309–1311.

Meacham, Christopher 2016 Understanding Conditionalization. *Canadian Journal of Philosophy* 45(5–6): 767–797.

Mead, Margaret 1977 An Anthropological Approach to Different Types of Communication and the Importance of Differences in Human Temperaments. In *Extrasensory Ecology: Parapsychology and Anthropology*. Joseph Long (ed.). Metuchen, NJ: Scarecrow Press. Pp. 47–50.

Medvedev, Zhores 1969 *Rise and Fall of T.D. Lysenko*. New York: Columbia University Press.

Merrin, William 1994 Uncritical Criticism? Norris, Baudrillard and the Gulf War. *Economy and Society* 23(4): 433–458. https://doi.org/10.1080/03085149400000019 (Accessed January 12, 2020).

Menand, Louis 2014 The De Man Case: Does a Critic's Past Explain His Criticism? *The New Yorker* (March 24). https://www.newyorker.com/magazine/2014/03/24/the-de-man-case (Accessed January 11, 2018).

Merton, Thomas 1979 *The Sociology of Science*. Chicago: Chicago University Press.

Milbank, John 1990 *Theology and Social Theory: Beyond Secular Reason*. Oxford: Blackwell.

Mooney, Chris 2011 Once and For All: Climate Denial Is Not Postmodern. *DeSmog Blog.com* (February). https://www.desmogblog.com/once-and-all-climate-denial-not-postmodern (Accessed November 1, 2019).

Mooney, Chris, and Sheril Kirshenbaum 2009 *Unscientific America: How Scientific Illiteracy Threatens our Future*. New York: Basic Books.

Moore, Jerry 2019 *Visions of Culture: An Introduction to Anthropological Theory*. Lanham, MD: Rowman and Littlefield.

Muirhead, Russell, and Nancy Rosenblum 2019 *A Lot of People Are Saying: The New Conspiracism and the Assault on Democracy*. Princeton, NJ: Princeton University Press.

Murdock, George 1980 *Theories of Illness: A World Survey*. New York: Columbia University Press.

Murguía, Salvador 2019a Introduction. In *Trumping Truth: Essays on the Destructive Power of "Alternative Facts."* Salvador Murguía (ed.). Jefferson, NC: MacFarland and Company Publishing Company, Inc., Publishers. Pp. 3–11.

――― (ed.) 2019b *Trumping Truth: Essays on the Destructive Power of "Alternative Facts."* Jefferson, NC: MacFarland and Company Publishing Company, Inc., Publishers.

Murphy, Martin, and Maxine Margolis 1995 An Introduction to Cultural Materialism. In *Science, Materialism, and the Study of Culture*. Martin Murphy and Maxine Margolis (eds.). Gainesville: University Press of Florida. Pp. 1–4.

Musgrave, Alan 1993 *Common Sense, Science and Scepticism: A Historical Introduction to the Theory of Knowledge*. Cambridge: Cambridge University Press.

Nagel, Jennifer 2014 *Knowledge: A Very Short Introduction*. Oxford: Oxford University Press.

Nagle, Angela 2017 *Kill All Normies: Online Culture Wars From 4Chan and Tumblr to Trump and the Alt-Right*. Alresford, UK: Zero Books.

National Academy of Science (NAS) 1998 *Teaching About Evolution and the Nature of Science*. Washington, DC: National Academy Press.

Negroponte, Nicholas 1996 *Being Digital*. London: Hodder and Stoughton.

Nehamas, Alexander 2002 Nietzsche and "Hitler." In *Nietzsche, Godfather of Fascism?: On the Uses and Abuses of a Philosophy*. Jacob Golomb and Robert Wistrich (eds.). Princeton, NJ: Princeton University Press. Pp. 90–105.

Newman, Hannah 2005 Blavatsky, Helena P. (1831–1891) In *Antisemitism: A Historical Encyclopedia of Prejudice and Persecution*. Richard Levy (ed.). Santa Barbara: ABC-CLIO. Pp. 72–73.

Nichols, Tom 2017 *The Death of Expertise: The Campaign Against Established Knowledge and Why it Matters*. Oxford: Oxford University Press.

Nietzsche, Friedrich 2003 *Writings from the Late Notebooks*. Cambridge: Cambridge University.

――― 1990 *Twilight of the Idols/The Anti-Christ*. London: Penguin.

Norris, Christopher 2002 *Deconstruction: Theory and Practice*. New York: Routledge.

――― 1997 *Against Relativism: Philosophy of Science, Deconstruction and Critical Theory*. Oxford: Blackwell.

――― 1992 *Uncritical Theory: Postmodernism, Intellectuals and the Gulf War*. London: Lawrence & Wishart.

Nyhan, Brendan, Ethan Porter, Jason Reifler, and Thomas Wood 2019 Taking Fact-Checks Literally But Not Seriously? The Effects of Journalistic Fact-Checking on Factual Beliefs and Candidate Favorability (January 7, 2019). *Political Behavior*. https://ssrn.com/abstract=2995128 (Accessed March 4, 2019).

Nyhan, Brendan, and Jason Reifler 2019 The Roles of Information Deficits and Identity Threat in the Prevalence of Misperceptions. *Journal of Elections, Public Opinion and Parties* 29 (2). https://www.tandfonline.com/doi/abs/10.1080/174572 89.2018.1465061 (Accessed January 1, 2019).

———— 2010 When Corrections Fail: The Persistence of Political Misperceptions. *Political Behavior* 32: 303–330. https://doi.org/10.1007/s11109-010-9112-2 (Accessed March 4, 2019).

O'Connor, Cailin, and James Weatherall 2019 *The Misinformation Age: How False Beliefs Spread*. New Haven, CT: Yale University Press.

Okasha, Samir 2016 *Philosophy of Science: A Very Short Introduction*. Oxford: Oxford University Press.

O'Meara, Tim 1995 Comment on "Objectivity and Militancy: A Debate" by Roy D'Andrade and Nancy Scheper-Hughes. *Current Anthropology* 36 (3): 427–428.

O'Reilly, Sean 2019 Of Crowd Sizes and Casualties: The Ominous Similarities Between Trump-era America and Wartime Japan in the Abuse of Alternative Facts. In *Trumping Truth: Essays on the Destructive Power of "Alternative Facts."* Salvador Murguía (ed.). Jefferson, NC: MacFarland and Company Publishing Company, Inc., Publishers. Pp. 139–149.

Oppy, Graham 2018 *Naturalism and Religion: A Contemporary Philosophical Investigation*. New York: Routledge.

Oreskes, Naomi, and Erik Conway 2011 *Merchants of Doubt: How a Handful of Scientists Obscured the Truth on Issues from Tobacco Smoke to Global Warming*. New York: Bloomsbury Press.

Ortner, Sherry 2006 *Anthropology and Social Theory*. Durham, NC: Duke University Press.

Ott, Brian 2017 The Age of Twitter: Donald J. Trump and the Politics of Debasement. *Critical Studies in Media Communication* 34: 59–68. https://www.tandfonline.com /doi/full/10.1080/15295036.2016.1266686 (Accessed November 28, 2019).

Otto, Shaw 2016 *The War on Science: Who Is Waging It, Why It Matters, What Can We Do About It*. Minneapolis: Milkweed.

———— 2011 *Fool Me Twice: Fighting the Assault on Science in America*. New York: Rodale Books.

Paine, Thomas 1880 *The Age of Reason: An Investigation of True and Fabulous Theology*. London: Freethought Publishing Company (Part I [1794], Part II [1795], Part III [1807]). https:// openlibrary.org/ works/ OL60357W/ The_ Age_ of_ Reason (Accessed January 11, 2018).

Painter, James, Erviti, María, Richard Fletcher, Candice Howarth, Silje Kristiansen, Bienvenido León, Alan Ouakrat, Adrienne Russell, and Mike Schäfer 2016 *Something Old, Something New: Digital Media and the Coverage of Climate Change*. Oxford: Reuters Institute for the Study of Journalism. https://science policy.colorado.edu/students/stpr4100/painter_2016.pdf (Accessed September 1, 2019).

Pandian, Jacob 2003 The Dangerous Quest for Cooperation Between Science and Religion. In *Science and Religion: Are They Compatible?* Paul Kurtz, Barry Karr, and Ranjit Sandhu (eds.). Amherst, NY: Prometheus Books. Pp. 161–169.

Pandian, Kevin 2002 Waiting for the Watchmaker. *Science* 295(5564): 2373–2374.

Papazoglou, Alexis 2016 The Post-Truth Era of Trump Is Just What Nietzsche Predicted. *The Conversation* (December 14). https://theconversation.com/the-post-truth-era-of-trump-is-just-what-nietzsche-predicted-69093 (Accessed January 6, 2019).

Pariser, Eli 2011 *The Filter Bubble: What the Internet Is Hiding From You.* New York: Penguin Press.

Pennock, Robert 2010 The Postmodern Sin of Intelligent Design Creationism. *Science and Education* 19: 757–778.

——— 1999 *Tower of Babel: The Evidence Against the New Creationism.* Cambridge, MA: The MIT Press.

Pennycook, Gordon, James Cheyne, Nathaniel Barr, Derek Koehler, and Jonathan Fugelsang 2015 On the Reception and Detection of Pseudo-Profound Bullshit. *Judgment and Decision Making* 10(6): 549–563.

Perrin, Andrew 2017 Stop Blaming Postmodernism for Post-Truth Politics. *Chronicle of Higher Education* (August 4). https://www.chronicle.com/article/Stop-Blaming-Postmodernism-for/240845 (Accessed January 10, 2019).

Persinger, Michael, and Katherine Makarec 1987 Temporal Lobe Epileptic Signs and Correlative Behaviors Displayed by Normal Populations. *Journal of General Psychology* 114: 179–195.

Pfohl, Stephen 1997 Reviewed Work: *The Gulf War Did Not Take Place* by Jean Baudrillard. *Contemporary Sociology* 26 (2): 138–141. www.jstor.org/stable/2076743 (Accessed January 29, 2020).

Phillip, Abby, and Mike DeBonis 2017 Without Evidence, Trump Tells Lawmakers 3 Million to 5 Million Illegal Ballots Cost Him the Popular Vote. *WashingtonPost.com* (23 January). https://www.washingtonpost.com/news/post-politics/wp/2017/01/23/at-white-house-trump-tells-congressional-leaders-3-5-million-illegal-ballots-cost-him-the-popular-vote (Accessed July 1, 2019).

Philipse, Herman 2014 *God in the Age of Science? A Critique of Religious Reason.* Oxford: Oxford University Press.

Pierce, Charles 2009 *Idiot America: How Stupidity Became a Virtue in the Land of the Free.* New York: Anchor Books.

Pigliucci, Massimo 2013 The Demarcation Problem: A (Belated) Reply to Laudon. In *Philosophy of Pseudoscience: Reconsidering the Demarcation Problem.* Massimo Pigliucci and Maarten Boudry (eds.). Chicago: University of Chicago Press. Pp. 9–28.

Pigliucci, Massimo, and Maarten Boudry 2013a Introduction. In *Philosophy of Pseudoscience: Reconsidering the Demarcation Problem.* Massimo Pigliucci and Maarten Boudry (eds.). Chicago: University of Chicago Press. Pp. 1–5.

——— (eds.) 2013b *Philosophy of Pseudoscience: Reconsidering the Demarcation Problem.* Chicago: University of Chicago Press.

Piltz, Rick 2010 Sen. Inhofe Inquisition: Seeking Ways to Criminalize and Prosecute 17 Leading Climate Scientists. *Climate Science & Policy Watch* (February 24). http://www.climatesciencewatch.org/2010/02/24/sen-inhofe-inquisition-seeking-ways-to-criminalize-and-prosecute-17-leading-climate-scientists/ (Accessed December 11, 2019).

Pinker, Steven 2018 *Enlightenment Now: The Case for Reason, Science, Humanism, and Progress.* New York: Viking.
────── 2007 *The Stuff of Thought.* New York: Penguin Book.
Pipes, Daniel 1996 Review of The Gulf War Did Not Take Place by Jean Baudrillard. *Middle East Quarterly* 3(1). https://www.meforum.org/1098/the-gulf-war-did-not-take-place (Accessed December 11, 2019).
Plantinga, Alvin 2009 Games Scientists Play. In *The Believing Primate: Scientific, Philosophical, and Theological Reflections on the Origins of Religion.* Jeffrey Schloss and Michael Murray (eds.). New York: Oxford University Press. Pp. 139–167.
Pollitt, Katha 2007 Pomolotov Cocktail. In *Subject to Debate* (Kindle Edition). New York: Random House Publishing Group.
Popper, Karl 1972 *Objective Knowledge: An Evolutionary Approach.* Oxford: Oxford University Press.
Preston, John 2000 Science As Supermarket: "Postmodern" Themes in Paul Feyerabend's Later Philosophy of Science. In *The Worst Enemy of Science: Essays in Memory of Paul Feyerabend.* John Preston, Gonzalo Munévar, and David Lamb (eds.). Oxford: Oxford University Press. Pp. 80–102.
Preston, John, Gonzalo Munévar, and David Lamb (eds.) 2000 *The Worst Enemy of Science: Essays in Memory of Paul Feyerabend.* Oxford: Oxford University Press.
Price, Robert 2010 Jesus: Myth and Method. In *The Christian Delusion: Why Faith Fails.* John Loftus (ed.). Amherst, NY: Prometheus Books. Pp. 273–290.
Quercia, Jacopo della 2019 The Alternative Electorate: Mapping Trumped-Up Claims of Voter Fraud in the 2016 Election. In *Trumping Truth: Essays on the Destructive Power of "Alternative Facts."* Salvador Murguía (ed.). Jefferson, NC: MacFarland and Company Publishers. Pp. 171–177.
Raab, Marius, Nikolas Auer, Stefan Ortlieb, and Claus-Christian Carbon 2013 The Sarrazin Effect: The Presence of Absurd Statements in Conspiracy Theories Makes Canonical Information Less Plausible. *Frontiers in Psychology* 4(453): 1–8. https://www.ncbi.nlm.nih.gov/pmc/articles/PMC3714455/pdf/fpsyg-04-00453.pdf (Accessed July 11, 2019).
Rabin-Havt, Ari 2016 *Lies Incorporated: The World of Post-Truth Politics.* New York: Anchor Books.
Rabinow, Paul 1968 Representations Are Social Facts: Modernity and Postmodernity in Anthropology. In *Writing Culture: The Poetics and Politics of Ethnography.* James Clifford and George Marcus (eds.). Berkeley, CA: University of California Press. Pp. 234–261.
Radin, Paul 1939 The Mind of Primitive Man. *The New Republic* 98: 300–303.
Regal, Brian 2009 *Pseudoscience: A Critical Encyclopedia.* Santa Barbara, CA: ABC-CLIO.
Rennie, John 2002 15 Answers to Creationist Nonsense. *Scientific American* (July): 78–85.
Reyna, S. P. 1994 Literary Anthropology and the Case Against Science. *Man* (New Series) 29(3): 555–581.

Robbins, Bruce, and Andrew Ross 2000 Response: Mystery Science Theater. In *The Sokal Hoax: The Sham that Shook the Academy*. Lingua Franca (ed.). Lincoln, NE: University of Nebraska Press. Pp. 54–58.

Robbins, Joel 2006 Anthropology and Theology: An Awkward Relationship? *Anthropological Quarterly* 79(2): 285–294.

Rodriguez, Barrera, Sergei Guriev, Emeric Henry, and Ekaterina Zhuravskaya 2019 Facts, Alternative Facts, and Fact Checking in Times of Post-Truth Politics. *Journal of Public Economics* (Forthcoming). https://ssrn.com/abstract=3004631 (Accessed December 15, 2019).

Rorty, Richard 1998 *Truth and Progress: Philosophical Papers* (Vol. 3). Cambridge: Cambridge University Press.

——— 1992 A More Banal Politics. *Harper's Magazine* (May). Pp. 16–21.

Rosdolsky, Roman 1977 *The Making of Marx's Capital*. London: Pluto Press.

Ross, Eric 1980 Introduction. In *Beyond the Myth of Culture: Essays in Cultural Materialism*. Eric Ross (ed.). New York: Academic Press. Pp. xv–xvi.

Roughgarden, Joan 2006a *Evolution and Christian Faith: Reflections of an Evolutionary Biologist*. Washington, DC: Island Press.

——— 2006b Beyond Belief: Science, Reason, Religion & Survival Symposium, Session 3 (November 5–7). https://www.youtube.com/watch?v=kbkOJr8klhA (Accessed December 17, 2018).

Roy, Rustum 2005 Scientism and Technology As Religions. *Zygon* 40(4): 835–844.

Ruse, Michael 2018 Democracy and the Problem of Pseudoscience. In *Anti-Science and the Assault on Democracy*. Michael Thompson and Gregory Smulewicz-Zucker (eds.). Amherst, NY: Prometheus Books. Pp. 241–270.

Russell, Bertrand 1961 *History of Western Philosophy*. London: Allen and Unwin.

Ryan, Alan 1992 Princeton Diary. *London Review of Books* 14(6): 21.

Sagan, Carl 2001 The Burden of Skepticism. In *Magic, Witchcraft, and Religion: An Anthropological Study of the Supernatural*. Arthur Lehman and James Myers (eds.). Mountain View, CA: Mayfield. Pp. 389–394.

——— 1995 *The Demon-Haunted World: Science As a Candle in the Dark*. New York: Random House.

——— 1993 *Broca's Brain: Reflections on the Romance of Science*. New York: Ballantine Books.

——— 1980 Encyclopaedia Galactica. *Cosmos* (episode 12. 01:24 minutes, first aired December 14, 1980 on PBS). https:// www.youtube.com/watch?v=Bxdsh6RjnQI (Accessed March 5, 2018).

Sahlins, Marshall 1999 What Is Anthropological Enlightenment? *Annual Review of Anthropology* 18: i–xxiii.

Salzman, Philip 2001 *Understanding Culture: An Introduction to Anthropological Theory*. Prospect Heights, IL: Waveland.

Samir, Okasha 2016 *Philosophy of Science: A Very Short Introduction*. Oxford: Oxford University Press.

Sangren, Steven 1988 Rhetoric and the Authority of Ethnography: Postmodernism and the Social Reproduction of Texts. *Current Anthropology* 29(3): 405–435.

Sapir, Edward 1929 The Status of Linguistics As a Science. *Language* 5: 207–214.

Sapire, David 1989 Comment on Ethnography Without Tears by Paul Roth. *Current Anthropology* 30(5): 564–565.

Scheper-Hughes, Nancy 1995 The Primacy of the Ethical: Propositions for a Militant Anthropology. *Current Anthropology* 36: 409–420.

Schick, Theodor, and Lewis Vaughn 2014 *How to Think About Weird Things: Critical Thinking for a New Age.* New York: McGraw-Hill.

Scott, Eugenie 2008 Science and Religion, Methodology and Humanism. https://ncse.com/religion/science-religion-methodology-humanism (Accessed January 11, 2018).

——— 2001 My Favorite Pseudoscience. In *Skeptical Odysseys: Personal Accounts by the World's Leading Paranormal Inquirers.* Paul Kurtz (ed.). Amherst, NY: Prometheus Books. Pp. 245–256.

——— 1999 The "Science and Religion Movement:" An Opportunity for Improved Public Understanding of Science? *Skeptical Inquirer* 23: 29–31.

Scriven, Michael 1966 *Primary Philosophy.* New York: McGraw-Hill.

Searle, John 1998 *Mind, Language and Society.* New York: Basic Books.

Segal, Robert 1983 In Defense of Reductionism. *Journal of the American Academy of Religion* 51(1): 97–124.

——— 1980 The Social Sciences and the Truth of Religious Belief. *Journal of the American Academy of Religion* 48(3): 403–413.

Service, Elman 1985 *A Century of Controversy: Ethnological Issues from 1860 to 1960.* Orlando: Academic Press.

Shackel, Nicholas 2013 Pseudoscience and Idiosyncratic Theories of Rational Belief. In *Philosophy of Pseudoscience: Reconsidering the Demarcation Problem.* Massimo Pigliucci and Maarten Boudry (eds.). Chicago: University of Chicago Press. Pp. 397–443.

Sharlet, Jeff 2010 *C Street: The Fundamentalist Threat to American Democracy.* New York: Little Brown.

Shermer, Michael 2011 *The Believing Brain.* New York: St. Martin's Press.

——— 2002a *The Skeptic Encyclopedia of Pseudoscience* (Vols. 2). Santa Barbara, CA: ABC-CLIO.

——— 2002b *Why People Believe Weird Things: Pseudoscience, Superstition, and Other Confusions of Our Time.* New York: St. Martin's Griffin.

Shotwell, David 2003 From the Anthropic Principle to the Supernatural. In *Science and Religion: Are They Compatible?* Paul Kurtz, Barry Karr, and Ranjit Sandhu (eds.). Amherst, NY: Prometheus Books. Pp. 47–49.

Shweder, Richard 1991 *Thinking Through Cultures: Expeditions in Cultural Psychology.* Cambridge: Harvard University Press.

Sidky, H. 2020 *Religion, Supernaturalism, the Paranormal, and Pseudoscience: An Anthropological Critique.* New York: Anthem Press.

——— 2018 The War on Science, Anti-Intellectualism, and "Alternative Ways of Knowing" in 21st-Century America. *Skeptical Inquirer* 42: 38–43.

——— 2015 *Religion: An Anthropological Perspective.* New York: Peter Lang.

——— 2008 *Haunted by the Archaic Shaman: Himalayan Jhakris and the Discourse on Shamanism.* Lanham, MD: Lexington Books.

——— 2007a War, Changing Patterns of Warfare, State Collapse, and Transnational Violence in Afghanistan: 1978–2001. *Modern Asian Studies* 41(4): 849–888.

——— 2007b Cultural Materialism, Scientific Anthropology, Epistemology, and "Narrative Ethnographies of the Particular." In *Studying Societies and Cultures: Marvin Harris's Cultural Materialism and its Legacy*. Lawrence Kuznar and Stephen Sanderson (eds.). Boulder, CO: Paradigm Publishers. Pp. 66–77.

——— 2004 *Perspectives on Culture: A Critical Introduction to Theory in Cultural Anthropology*. Upper Saddle River, NJ: Prentice Hall.

——— 1997 *Witchcraft, Lycanthropy, Drugs and Disease: An Anthropological Study of the European Witch-Hunts*. New York: Peter Lang.

Silverman, David 1975 *Reading Castaneda: A Prologue to the Social Sciences*. London: Routledge and Kegan Paul.

Slakey, Francis 1993 When the Lights of Reason Go Out. *New Scientist* (September 11). https://www.newscientist.com/ article/ mg13918905- 000- forum- when- the lights-of- reason- go- out- francis-slakey- ponders- the- faces- of- fantasy- and- new- age- scientists (Accessed January 23, 2018).

Slezak, Peter 2012 Review of *Science and Spirituality: Making Room for Faith in the Age of Science*, by Michael Ruse. *Science and Education* 21: 403–413.

——— 1994a Sociology of Scientific Knowledge and Scientific Education: Part I. *Science & Education* 3(3): 265–294.

——— 1994b Sociology of Scientific Knowledge and Science Education, Part 2: Laboratory Life Under the Microscope. *Science & Education* 3(4): 329–355.

Smith, James 2015 Science As Cultural Performance: Leveling the Playing Field in the Theology and Science Conversation. In *Scientism: The New Orthodoxy*. Richard Williams and Daniel Robinson (eds.). New York: Bloomsbury. Pp. 177–191.

Smith, Jonathan 2010 *Pseudoscience and Extraordinary Claims of the Paranormal*. West Sussex, UK: Wiley-Blackwell.

Smulewicz-Zucker, Greogry 2018 The Myth of the Expert As Elite: Postmodern Theory, Right-Wing Populism, and the Assault on Truth. In *Anti-Science and The Assault on Democracy*. Michael Thompson and Gregory Smulewicz-Zucker (eds.). Amherst, NY: Prometheus Books. Pp. 203–222.

Snyder, Timothy 2017 *On Tyranny: Twenty Lessons from the Twentieth Century*. New York: Tim Duggan Books.

Sober, Elliott 2006 The Design Argument. In *Debating Design: From Darwin to DNA*. William Dembski and Michael Ruse (eds.). Cambridge: Cambridge University Press. Pp. 98–129.

Sobieraj, Sarah, and Jeffrey Berry 2011 From Incivility to Outrage: Political Discourse in Blogs, Talk Radio, and Cable News. *Political Communication* 28: 19–41. https://www.tandfonline.com/doi/full/10.1080/10584609.2010.542360 (Accessed December 11, 2019).

Sokal, Alan 2008 *Beyond the Hoax: Science, Philosophy and Culture*. Oxford: Oxford University Press.

——— 1997 Professor Latour's Philosophical Mystifications. *Le Monde* (January 31). https://physics.nyu.edu/faculty/sokal/le_monde_english.html (Accessed December 1, 2019).

—— 1996a Transgressing the Boundaries: Towards a Transformative Hermeneutics of Quantum Gravity. *Social Text* 46/47: 217–252. https://physics.nyu.edu/faculty/sokal/transgress_v2/transgress_v2_singlefile.html (Accessed November 11, 2018).

—— 1996b Revelation: A Physicist Experiments with Cultural Studies. *Lingua Franca* (May/June): 62–64. https://physics.nyu.edu/faculty/sokal/lingua_franca_v4/lingua_franca_v4.html (Accessed November 17, 2018).

Sokal, Alan, and Jean Bricmont 1998 *Fashionable Nonsense: Postmodern Intellectuals' Abuse of Science*. New York: Picador.

Soyfer, Valery 1994 *Lysenko and the Tragedy of Soviet Science*. New Brunswick, NJ: Rutgers University Press.

Spaulding, Albert 1988 Distinguished Lecture: Archaeology and Anthropology. *American Anthropologist* 90(2): 263–271.

Specter, Michael 2009 *Denialism: How Irrational Thinking Hinders Scientific Progress, Harms the Planet, and Threatens Our Lives*. New York: Penguin.

Sperber, Dan 2010 The Guru Effect. *Review of Philosophy and Psychology* 1(4): 583–592.

Spiro, Melford 1982 Collective Representations and Mental Representations in Religious Symbol Systems. In *On Symbols in Anthropology: Essays in Honor of Harry Hoijer* (Vol. 2). James Fernandez, Melford Spiro, and Melton Singer (eds.). Los Angeles: University of California Press. Pp. 45–72.

Stracqualursi, Veronica 2020 Trump Promotes a Doctor Who Has Claimed Alien DNA Was Used in Medical Treatments. *CNN Politics*, July 29, 2020. https://www.cnn.com/2020/07/29/politics/stella-immanuel-trump-doctor/index.html (Accessed July 30, 2020).

Staley, Kent 2014 *Introduction to the Philosophy of Science*. Cambridge: Cambridge University Press.

Stanley, Jason 2018 *How Fascism Works: The Politics of Us and Them*. New York: Random House.

Staski, Edward, and Jonathon Marks 1992 *Evolutionary Anthropology: An Introduction to Physical Anthropology and Archaeology*. New York: Holt, Rinehart, and Winston.

Stellino, Paolo 2017 Nietzsche and the Responsibility of Intellectuals. In *Friedrich Nietzsche: Legacy and Prospects*. Yulia Sineokaya and Ekaterina Poljakova (eds.). Moscow: LRC. Pp. 467–477.

Stenger, Victor 2012 *God and the Folly of Faith: The Incompatibility of Science and Religion*. Amherst, NY: Prometheus Books.

—— 2007 *God: The Failed Hypothesis: How Science Shows That God Does Not Exist*. Amherst, NY: Prometheus Books.

—— 2003 *Has Science Found God? The Latest Results in the Search for Purpose in the Universe*. Amherst, NY: Prometheus Books.

—— 1990 *Physics and Psychics: The Search for a World Beyond the Senses*. Buffalo, NY: Prometheus Books.

Stephanopoulos, George 2020 Transcript for "So yes, I do blame the Chinese" for Coronavirus Pandemic: Peter Navarro (ABC News, May 17, 2020). https://abcnews.go.com/ThisWeek/video/blame-chinese-coronavirus-pandemic-peter-navarro-70729064 (Accessed July 1, 2020).

Stocking, S. Holly, and Lisa Holstein 2009 Manufacturing Doubt: Journalists' Roles and the Construction of Ignorance in a Scientific Controversy. *Public Understanding of Science* 18: 23–42. https://journals.sagepub.com/doi/10.1177/0963662507079373 (Accessed December 11, 2019).

Stoller, Paul, and Cheryl Olkes 1989 *In Sorcery's Shadow: A Memoir of Apprenticeship Among the Songhay of Niger*. Chicago: University of Chicago Press.

Stove, David 2008 *Scientific Irrationalism: Origins of a Postmodern Cult*. London: Transaction Publishers.

——— 1995 Judge's Report on the Competition to Find the Worst Argument in the World. In *Cricket Versus Republicanism and Other Essays by David Stove*. Sydney: Quakers Hill Press. Pp. 66–67.

——— 1991 *The Plato Cult and Other Philosophical Follies*. Oxford: Basil Blackwell.

Strehle, Samuel 2014 A Poetic Anthropology of War: Jean Baudrillard and the 1991 Gulf War. *International Journal of Baudrillard Studies* 11(2). https://baudrillardstudies.ubishops.ca/a-poetic-anthropology-of-war-jean-baudrillard-and-the-1991-gulf-war/.

Strong, S. I. 2017 Alternative Facts and the Post-Truth Society: Meeting the Challenge. *University of Pennsylvania Law Review Online* 165(1): 137–146. https://scholarship.law.upenn.edu/penn_law_review_online/vol165/iss1/14 (Accessed November 2, 2019).

Sunstein, Cass, and Adrian Vermeule 2009 Conspiracy Theories: Causes and Cures. *Journal of Political Philosophy* 17: 202–227.

Swain, Harriet 2017 Richard Evans Interview: The Film Denial "Shows There Is Such a Thing As Truth." *The Guardian* (February 14). https://www.theguardian.com/education/2017/feb/14/richard-evans-interview-holocaust-denial-film (Accessed January 3, 2019).

Sznajder, Mario 2002 Nietzsche, Mussolini, and Italian Fascism. In *Nietzsche, Godfather of Fascism?: On the Uses and Abuses of a Philosophy*. Jacob Golomb and Robert Wistrich (eds.). Princeton, NJ: Princeton University Press. Pp. 235–262.

Thompson, Damian 2008 *Counter Knowledge: How We Surrendered to Conspiracy Theories, Quack Medicine, Bogus Science and Fake History*. New York: W.W. Norton and Company.

Thompson, Michael, and Gregory Smulewircz-Zuker (eds.) 2018a *Anti-Science and the Assault on Democracy*. New York: Prometheus Books.

——— 2018b Introduction. In *Anti-Science and the Assault on Democracy*. Michael Thompson and Gregory Smulewircz-Zuker (eds.). Amherst, NY: Prometheus Books. Pp. 8–14.

Thorsrud, Harald 2014 *Ancient Scepticism*. London: Routledge.

Tiles, Mary, and Jim Tiles 1993 *An Introduction to Historical Epistemology: The Authority of Knowledge*. Oxford: Blackwell.

Trivers, Robert 2011 *The Folly of Fools: The Logic of Deceit and Self-Deception in Human Life*. Philadelphia, PA: Perseus Books.

Truzzi, Marcello 1978 On the Extraordinary: An Attempt at Clarification. *Zetetic Scholar* 1(1): 11–19.

Turner, Edith 2010 Discussion: Ethnography As a Transformative Experience. *Anthropology and Humanism* 35(2): 218–226.

—— 1998 *Experiencing Ritual: A New Interpretation of African Healing.* Philadelphia: University of Pennsylvania Press.

—— 1994 A Visible Spirit Form in Zambia. In *Being Changed: The Anthropology of Extraordinary Experience*. David Young and Jean-Guy Goulet (eds.). Orchard Park, NY: Broadview. Pp. 71–95.

Tyler, Stephen 1987 *The Unspeakable*. Madison, WI: University of Wisconsin Press.

—— 1986 Post-Modern Anthropology. In *Discourse and the Social Life of Meaning*. Phyllis Chock and June Wyman (eds.). Washington, DC: Smithsonian Institution Press. Pp. 23–49.

Wallace, Ruth, and Alison Wolf 1991 *Contemporary Sociological Theory: Continuing the Classical Tradition*. Ottawa: University of Ottawa Press.

Wang, Amy 2016 "Post-Truth" Named 2016 Word of the Year by Oxford Dictionaries. *Washington Post* (November 16). https://www.washingtonpost.com/news/the-fix/wp/2016/11/16/post-truth-named-2016-word-of-the-year-by-oxford-dictionaries/?utm_term=.12aaa7361b38 (Accessed December 11, 2019).

Warner, Judith 2011 Fact Free Science. *New York Times Magazine* (February 25). https://www.nytimes.com/2011/02/27/magazine/27FOB-WWLN-t.html (Accessed October 1, 2019).

Wasson, Gordon 1958 The Divine Mushroom: Primitive Religion and Hallucinatory Agents. *Proceedings of the American Philosophical Society* 102(3): 221–223.

—— 1957 Seeking the Magic Mushroom. *Life Magazine* (May) 13: 100–102, 109–120.

Webster, Anthony, and Leighton Peterson 2011 Introduction: American Indian Languages in Unexpected Places. *American Journal of Indian Culture and Research Journal* 35(2): 1–18.

Wehner, Peter 2016 The Theology of Donald Trump. *New York Times* (July 5). https://www.nytimes.com/2016/07/05/opinion/campaign-stops/the-theology-of-donald-trump.html (Accessed October 1, 2019).

Weinberg, Steven 1998 The Revolution that Didn't Happen. *New York Review of Books* (October 8). https://www.physics.utah.edu/~detar/phys4910/readings/fundamentals/weinberg.html (Accessed July 4, 2019).

—— 1996 Sokal's Hoax. *New York Review of Books* (August). https://www.nybooks.com/articles/1996/08/08/sokals-hoax.http://www.1st-deg-innov.com/pdf/Weinberg-Sokal's%20Hoax.pdf (Accessed January 1, 2017).

White, Leslie 1987a Evolutionism in Cultural Anthropology: A Rejoinder. In *Leslie A. White: Ethnological Essays*. Beth Dillingham and Robert Carniero (eds.). Albuquerque, NM: University of New Mexico Press. Pp. 85–96.

—— 1987b Kroeber's *Configuration of Culture Growth* (1946). In *Leslie A. White: Ethnological Essays*. Beth Dillingham and Robert Carniero (eds.). Albuquerque, NM: University of New Mexico Press. Pp. 199–214.

—— 1949 *The Science of Culture: A Study of Man and Civilization*. New York: Grove Press.

Whorf, Benjamin 1944 The Relation of Habitual Thought and Behavior to Language. *A Review of General Semantics* 1(4): 197–215. https://www.jstor.org/stable/pdf/42581315.pdf?refreqid=excelsior%3Ac5293f070babf455fc603cf50eb569e9 (Accessed August 15, 2019).

Wiebe, Donald 1984a Beyond the Sceptic and the Devotee: Reductionism in the Scientific Study of Religion. *Journal of the American Academy of Religion* 52(1): 157–165.

—— 1984b The Failure of Nerve in the Academic Study of Religion. *Studies in Religion* 13(4): 401–422.

Wilkes, Barbara 2007 Reveal or Conceal? In *Extraordinary Anthropology: Transformations in the Field*. Jean-Guy Goulet and Bruce Miller (eds.). Lincoln: University of Nebraska Press. Pp. 53–84.

Williams, Michael 2001 *Problems of Knowledge: A Critical Introduction to Epistemology*. Oxford: Oxford University Press.

Williamson, Phil 2016 Take the Time and Effort to Correct Misinformation. *Nature News* (December 6). https://www.nature.com/news/take-the-time-and-effort-to-correct-misinformation-1.21106 (Accessed March 11, 2017).

Windschuttle, Keith 1998 Forward to *Scientific Irrationalism: Origins of a Postmodern Cult*. David Stove (ed.). London: Transaction Publishers. Pp. 1–18.

Wolff, Phillip, and Kevin Holmes 2011 Linguistic Relativity. *Cognitive Science* 2(3): 253–265. https://onlinelibrary.wiley.com/doi/10.1002/wcs.104 (Accessed December 18, 2019).

Wolin, Richard 2004 *The Seduction of Unreason: The Intellectual Romance with Fascism from Nietzsche to Postmodernism*. Princeton: Princeton University Press.

Wood, Michael, Karen Douglas, and Robbie Sutton 2012 Dead and Alive: Beliefs in Contradictory Conspiracy Theories. *Social Psychological and Personality Science* 3(6): 767–773. https://journals.sagepub.com/doi/pdf/10.1177/1948550611434786 (Accessed July 4, 2019).

Young, James 2018 The Coherence Theory of Truth. *The Stanford Encyclopedia of Philosophy* (Fall Edition). Edward N. Zalta (ed.). https://plato.stanford.edu/archives/fall2018/entries/truth-coherence (Accessed January 1, 2019).

Zimring, James 2019 *What Science Is and How It Really Works*. Cambridge: Cambridge University Press.

Zirkle, Conway 1946 The Early History of the Idea of the Inheritance of Acquired Characters and of Pangenesis. *Transactions of the American Philosophical Society* 35(2): 91–151. https://www.jstor.org/stable/pdf/1005592.pdf (Accessed November 11, 2019).

Zusne, Leonard, and Warren Jones 1989 *Anomalistic Psychology: A Study of Magical Thinking*. Hillsdale, NJ: Lawrence Erlbaum Associates.

Index

Abduction: Human Encounters with Aliens (1994) by John Mack, 63
Abel, Reuben (American philosopher): on the influence of belief on hypothesis, 42; on the pragmatic justification of knowledge of the external world, 71; on radical epistemological skepticism, 31
academic Left in America, 23; adoption of postmodern ideas by, 31, 36; contribution of skepticism of science to post-truth, 19; disingenuous assault of upon science, 74, 79; flirtation of with postmodernism proving compatible with right-wing populism, 166, 167, 168; political failure of leading to the adoption of postmodern ideas, 20, 32; political irrelevance of in the present, 77; why contempt of science became a preoccupation of, 20
Achinstein, Paul (professor of philosophy): critique of Feyerabend's epistemic anarchism, 65
Against Method: Outline of an Anarchic Theory of Knowledge (1975) by Paul Feyerabend, 64
agency-detection cognitive module and perception of ghosts and spirits, 114

Age of American Unreason (2008) by Susan Jacoby, 8
Alcock, James (Canadian professor of psychology and skeptic): on the cognitive mechanisms for paranormal experiences, 149
Aliens in America (1998) by Jodi Dean, 117
alternative facts, 5, 133, 136, 178; based on the premise that there are two sides to the story, 12; dangers of to deliberative democracy, 5; features of, 5; a legacy of academic postmodernism, 19; in paranormal anthropology, 153; prevalence of in post-truth U.S., 107; in theistic anthropology, 161; use of by science deniers in the post-truth era, 12
Ambasciano, Leonardo (historian of religion), 9; on the fideistic partiality of academic studies of religion, 160
American Association for the Advancement of Science (AAAS): reliance of on Gould's NOMA, 93
Andersen, Kurt (commentator on American culture), 7; on America as a fantasyland, 106; critique of Castaneda's paranormalism, 142; on the role of academics in the fostering

post-truth, 116, 118, 142, 172; on spread of postmodern ideas outside the academy and into the public mind, 165
Andreski, Stanislave (Polish-British sociologist): on the pretentious and vague verbosity in the social sciences, 46, 78
Anthropology and Science: Epistemologies in Practice (2007) edited by Edwards, Harvey, and Wade, 125
Anthropology as Cultural Critique (1986) by George Marcus and Michael Fisher, 129
anti-intellectualism, 6; fostered in the United States by the tobacco and fossil fuel industries and academic institutions, 10; as an overt feature of postmodern philosophy, 30, 33, 81, 123, 126, 129, 133; reasons for the rise of, 10; role of American academics in the spread of, 19, 140; in the United States, 8, 43, 47, 125
An Unnatural History of Religions (2018) by Leonardo Ambasciano, 160
apophenia (perception of connections and meaningful patterns in random information), 114
Arendt, Hanna (political philosopher), 3; relevance of work to post-truth America, 4; on truth, 4
Ariosophy (German white supremacy doctrine), 115
Asimov, Isaac (scientist and author): on anti-intellectualism in U.S. politics and cultural life, 6
Azande witchcraft beliefs, 86

backfire effect (cognitive bias), 8, 16, 37, 114
Bacon, Francis (English philosopher and developer of the scientific method), 42
Bale, Jeffrey (expert on right-wing extremism and cults): on the widespread belief in paranormal phenomena, 172
Ball, James (investigative journalist): on the negative effects of the Internet, 170
Bannon, Steve (right-wing populist and Trump propogandist), 166
Barndolini, Alberto: bullshit asymmetry principle of, 8, 178
Barnett, Paul (educational psychologist): on fighting for truth as a battle against masses of true-believers armed with ignorance and misinformation, 106; on the self-correcting nature of science, 91
Baudrillard, Jean-François (postmodern philosopher), 20, 35, 168; definition of postmodernism by, 36; on the nonexistence of the Gulf War, 44, 45; on nonexistence of truth, 55, 146
Bayesian confirmation theory, 102
Bayesian statistics, 101
Beiner, Ronald (Canadian professor of political science), 21; on the correlations between Nietzsche's ideas, postmodernism, and post-truth, 22; on the postmodernists' imprudent and uncritical adoption of Nietzsche's ethically problematic ideas, 23, 35
Benson, Ophelia (American philosopher), 53; on the absurdity of Sandra Harding's feminist critique of science, 54, 55; on the self-evident existence of an external reality, 70
Bereiter, Carl (education researcher): on the impact of postmodernism on science education, 163
Berlin, Isaiah (British philosopher and historian of ideas): on the intellectual responsibility of philosophers regarding the impact of their ideas, 178
Bernard, Russell (American cultural anthropologist): on the success of science, 90

Berry, Jeffrey (political scientist): on the incivility of post-truth political discourse, 171

Bérubé, Michael (postmodern thinker), 177; after-the-fact recognition by of the errors of science studies, 177; on the influence of Thomas Kuhn on the postmodern view of science, 63

Beyond the Hoax: Science, Philosophy and Culture (2008) by Alan Sokal, 50

Bielo, James (theistic anthropologist), 156

Blavatsky, Helena (Russian occultist, con artist, and co-founder of the Theosophical Society): impact of the idea of root races of on the Nazi racialist theories, 115

Bloor, David (British sociologist): Edinburgh School Strong Programme of, 63

Boas, Franz (founding figure of American anthropology): failed atheoretical approach of, 133

Boghossian, Paul (American philosopher), 37; on evidentiary justification of truth, 86; on independence of thought and reality, 83; on postmodernists' conflation of representation and things represented, 74; on the problematic nature of the notion of incomprehensibility of paradigms, 62; on the self-defeating aspect of postmodernism as an approach to social justice, 123; on the Sokal hoax, 51, 85

Boudry, Maarten (Belgian philosopher and skeptic): on the dangers of pseudoscience, 107; on lack of scientific confirmation for paranormal phenomena, 150

Brexit (withdrawal of the United Kingdom from the European Union in 2016), 1

Bricmont, Jean (Belgian theoretical physicist and philosopher of science), 50; on the incomprehensibility and vacuous nature of postmodern discourse about science, 51; on the scientific method, 72

Bridges, Tristan (sociologist): on the backfire effect, 16

burden of proof: and pseudoscientific theories, 111; and the scientific assessment of propositions, 102, 112

Bush, George W. use of post-truth lexicon by, 16

Campbell, Collin (sociologist), 6

Card, Jeb (American archaeologist), 145

Carneiro, Robert (American anthropologist): on obscurity of postmodern discourse, 36, 37

Castaneda, Carlos (Peruvian-American cultural anthropologist and paranormalist): assertions about the existence of an alternate reality, 142; revealed as a plagiarist and con artist, 116, 136; work of as inspiration for paranormal anthropologists, 145; work of containing standard ingredients of postmodern dogma, 136; work of lauded by postmodernists, New Age gurus, wizards, and pseudoscientists, 136

Challenger disaster (January 28, 1986), 84

Christopher Norris (British philosopher and literary critic), 28, 45, 87; on the ethical problems of postmodernism, 34; on Thomas Kuhn's idea of knowledge relative to linguist framework, 58

Clarke, Arthur C. (skeptic, humanist, and author): on the hijacking of morality by religion, 158; on the proliferation of pseudoscience around the world, 118

Clifford, James (American postmodern anthropologist), 129, 130, 131

climate science politicization of, 14
climate science denial, 14; endorsement of by conservative think tanks, 14, 173, 176; linkage of with beliefs in other conspiracy theories, 173
Coker, Rory (American physicist): on pseudoscience, 115
confirmation bias (cognitive bias), 37, 171
confirmation bias (cognitive predisposition), 113
conspiracy theories, 2; differences between contemporary versions and classic varieties, 176; difficulties in refutation of, 175; diffusion of from the cultic milieu to cultural mainstream, 172; entrenchment of in the public mind, 15; and the human fascination with the supernatural and the mysterious, 173; on the Internet, 6, 170; links of with broad-based rejection of science, 173; in post-truth United States, 5, 6; psychological underpinnings of, 173, 174; relating to AIDS in Africa, 107; as simplistic answers to complex issues, 174; touted by Donald Trump, 82; use of as rhetorical devices to generate social and psychological effects, 175; warranted verses unwarranted varieties of, 173
Conway, Eric (historian of science), 10, 11, 12, 13, 15, 169
Conway, Kellyanne (Trump propogandist and sycophant), 166
Cotton, Tom (Republican senator, ARK): conspiracy theories of, 174
COVID-19 pandemic, 5, 55, 82
COVID-19 posited conspiracy theories regarding, 173, 174
Coyne, Jerry (American biologist): on the absence of evidence for the paranormal, 150
Crapo, Richley (American anthropologist): methodological agnosticism of in the study of religion, 144
cultic milieu (the cultural margin or space where fringe beliefs and heterodox views exist and interact), 6, 172
cultural anthropology: advocacy of anti-intellectualism by proponents of, 125, 129; beliefs in the ontological reality of paranormal phenomena by many members of, 143; conversion of many members of to endorsers and proselytizers of nonsensical and incoherent postmodernist philosophical precepts, 125; deceptive portrayal of by postmodernists as a field dominated by scientific paradigms, 130; encouragement of paranormalism and pseudoscientific beliefs by proponents of, 141; as an entirely humanistic, interpretive, and meaning-oriented enterprise, 133; interpretive orientation of, 126; paucity of scientific perspectives in, 125, 133; postmodern version of as writing ethnographies, 132; preoccupation of postmodern variety of with teasing apart texts, 26; reception of postmodern ideas in, 136
cultural relativism: difference of from epistemic relativism, 127; meaning of in anthropology, 143, 147
Cuomo, Chris (American journalist), 168
Curran, James (professor of communication): on the ill effects of the Internet, 169

Darwin, Charles (English naturalist and biologist known for his theory of evolution), 108
Darwin on Trial (1991) by Phillip Johnson, 122

Das Kapital (1867) by Karl Marx, 110
Dawes, Robyn (American psychologist): on the epistemic meaninglessness of self-contradictory claims, 86
Dean, Jodi (postmodernist political scientist), 117; as defender of alien abductees and proponents of other irrational beliefs, 117
deconstructionism, 20, 25, 28
De Man, Paul (postmodern philosopher): fascist orientation of, 29, 78
Dembski, William (philosopher of Intelligent Design Creationism): use of the logical fallacy of popular consensus by to support his pseudoscientific claims, 120
Dennett, Daniel (American cognitive scientist and philosopher): on the academic smokescreen that impedes the scientific study of religion, 160; on intellectual irresponsibility of postmodern philosophers, 178
Denying AIDS: Conspiracy Theories, Pseudoscience, and Human Tragedy (2009) by Seth Kalichman, 107
Derrida, Jacques (postmodern philosopher), 20, 21, 35, 126, 164, 168; bogus defense of Paul de Man by, 29, 78; construal of language by, 28; and deconstructionism, 25, 28; delegitimization of science by, 29; disdain of for the rationalist tradition of the Enlightenment, 35; on language and truth, 25; scientific illiteracy of, 52
de Vrieze, Jop (journalist), 178
Dialectics of Nature (1876) by Friedrich Engels: influence of on Lysenkosim, 108
Diggins, John (American professor of history): on the adoption of postmodern theory by the academic Left, 23
Discovery Institute (religionist think tank that advocates the pseudoscientific concept of Intelligent Design), 122
Dunning-Kruger Effect (cognitive bias), 37, 76, 139

echo chambers (custom-designed online information environments based on user algorithms), 171
Einstein, Albert (German-born theoretical physicist and creator of the theory of relativity), 62; on the comprehensibility of the world and universe, 83; on science as the most precious possession of humankind, 85
Eliade, Mircea (Romanian historian of religion): construal of religion as an autonomous self-generating phenomenon that has sociopolitical effects, but itself has no causes, 159; construal of religious phenomena as intrinsically different from all other aspects of experience, 159; deferential treatment of religion by, 155
Engels, Friedrich (German socialist, philosopher, and collaborator of Karl Marx), 108
epistemic relativism, 69; in American postmodern anthropology, 127; appeal to authority and rhetoric by proponents of, 75; contribution of to post-truth, 164, 167, 169, 178; David Stove's critique of, 77; and the idea of multiple realities/truths, 75, 79, 83, 86, 106; massive advocacy of by postmodernists in social sciences and humanities departments, 117; and the present-day proliferation of irrationalism and pseudoscience, 105, 118, 152; reasons for rejection of, 71, 73; treated by postmodern anthropologists as the road to emancipation, 132; use of by creationists to advance their

supersititons, 122; in the work of Richard Rorty, 166
epistemic skepticism among postmodern writers, 57, 82, 85, 88, 147
epistemology, 81, 132; meaning of, 81
evangelical Christianity: efforts of to replace science with the Bible, 94; intrusion of in American cultural anthropology, 91, 96
Evans-Pritchard, Edward (British social anthropologist): conversion of to Catholicism by and theistic anthropologists, 156; methodological agnosticism of in the study of religion, 143
extraordinary anthropology. *See* paranormal anthropology
Extrasensory Ecology: Parapsychology and Anthropology (1977) by Joseph Long, 143

fake news, 2, 5, 19, 44, 168, 170
false equivalence between science and nonsense created by media granting matching credence to both sides of issues, 12, 14
Fantasyland: How America Went Haywire (2017) by Kurt Andersen, 7, 116
Fashionable Nonsense: Postmodern Intellectuals' Abuse of Science (1998) by Alan Sokal and Jean Bricmont, 50
Feyerabend, Paul (Austrian-born American philosopher), 64; an admirer of Carlos Castaneda, 116; advocacy of for creationism to be taught in schools, 65; anarchic approach of to knowledge, 65, 66; collaboration of with Thoma Kuhn, 64; principle of proliferation of approaches of, 65; treatment of science by as having epistemic parity with other belief systems, 64, 65

Feynman, Richard (American theoretical physicist): on the Challenger disaster, 84
Fischer, Michael (postmodern anthropologist), 130, 146; admirations of for Castaneda's work, 146
Fisher, Ronald (British statistician), 102
Fishman, Yonata (neuroscientist): on the ability of science to investigate supernatural claims, 100; on lack of scientific confirmation for paranormal phenomena, 100, 150
Forstenzer, Joshua (philosopher): on the contribution of Rorty's ideas to post-truth politics, 166
Foucault, Michel (postmodern philosopher), 20, 21, 35, 164, 168; disdain of for the rationalist tradition of the Enlightenment, 35; dismissal of scientific knowledge by, 146; influence of Nietzschean doctrine on thinking of, 22; on the relation of truth and power, 24, 25
Fountain, Philip (religionist scholar), 154
Fox, Robin (Anglo-American evolutionary anthropologist): on fanaticism of postmodern anti-science writers, 34
Frankfurt, Harry (American philosopher), 7, 70; on bullshit, 73; on impact of postmodern epistemic relativism on public discourse, 74
Franklin, Benjamin, 9
Franklin, James (Australian philosopher and mathematician), 30; on the obscure nature of postmodern rhetoric, 36
French, Christopher (anomalous psychologist): on pseudoscience, 106
fundamentalist religion: threat of to democracy and civil society, 91
Futuyma, Douglas (American evolutionary biologist): on the

hallmarks of science, 89; on Lysenko's fiasco, 110

Gardner, Martin (mathematician and philosopher of science): on the existence of a mind-independent reality, 71
Gates, Bill (American business magnate, software developer, and philanthropist): conspiracy theories about as the mastermind behind the COVID-19 pandemic, 173
Geertz, Clifford (American cultural anthropologist), 138, 146, 159; culture as text idea of, 127, 131; influence of work of on postmodern anthropology, 126, 127
Gellner, Ernest (British-Czech philosopher and social anthropologist): on the dilemmas faced by postmodern anthropologists, 134
Gilovich, Thomas (American psychologist): on the dangers of flawed thinking and irrationalism, 115
Giuliani, Rudy (Trump's lawyer and sycophant), 168; truth denialism of, 168
Glass-Coffin, Bonnie (paranormal anthropologist), 146; belief of in the ontological reality of ghosts and spirits, 149
Gonzo journalism news reporting without claims of objectivity and on the premise that both sides of an issue are equally valid, 15
Gopnik, Adam (author), 7
Gordin, Michael (historian), 36; on Lysenkosim, 108; on the problematic nature of the term pseudoscience, 111
Gorgias (Greek sophist rhetorician circa 483—375 BCE), 26, 31; usefulness of ideas of to postmodernists, 26

Gorham, Geoffrey (philosopher of science): on the empirical world as the ultimate arbiter in science, 88; on science as a unique attribute of humankind, 82
Gould, Stephen J. (American evolutionary biologist and historian of science): compatibility of NOMA idea of with post-truth, 95; erroneous construal of religion by, 94; NOMA concept of overlooking the fundamental incompatibility of science and religion, 94; possible influence of postmodern ideas on conceptualization of religion and science by, 95; religionists' rejection of NOMA concept of, 96, 154; on the science wars, 39, 40; on the separate domains of science and religion, or non-overlapping magisteria (NOMA), 93
Goulet, Jean-Guy (paranormal anthropologist), 150; influence of work of on theistic anthropology, 157
Greatest Hoax: How the Global Warming Conspiracy Threatens Your Future (2012) by James Inhofe (R-Oklahoma), 8
Grindal, Bruce (American cultural anthropologist and paranormalist), 146, 152; paranormal experience of during fieldwork, 146
Gross, Paul (American biologist and author): on the postmodernists' assumption that paying attention to words would give the analyst world-changing powers, 32
group-think (cognitive bias), 37, 46, 113, 139
Gulf War (1990–1991): the nonexistence of according to Baudrillard, 44; and post-truth, 1
Gulf War Did Not Take Place (1995) by Jean-François Baudrillard, 44, 45

Hanson, Norwood (American philosopher of science): on the God hypothesis, 102

Harding, Sandra (philosopher of feminist theory and postmodern icon); absurdity of anti-science claims of, 55, 74; rape metaphors of and science, 54

Harding, Susan (American cultural/anthropologist/religionist), 154, 155

Harner, Michael (American cultural anthropologist and self-professed shaman), 146

Harris, Marvin (American scientific cultural anthropologist): on the uniqueness of science compared to other ways of knowing, 89

Hegel, Georg Wilhelm Friedrich (German idealist philosopher), 30

Heidegger, Martin (German philosopher): icon of the postmodernists and a Nazi, 22

Higgins, C. Francis (philosopher), 26

hindsight bias (cognitive predisposition), 113

Hines, Terence (professor of neurology): on pseudoscience, 106

Hitler, Adolf: big lies of, 7; impact of Nietzsche's philosophy on Nazi ideology of, 21, 114; postmodern/post-truth notions of, 179; on the power of grand falsehoods, 8; rise to power by during an intellectual climate of paranormalism and anti-science, 115

House Built on Sand: Exposing Postmodern Myths about Science (1998) by Noretta Koertge, 163

How Democracies Die (2018) by Steven Levitsky and Daniel Ziblatt, 4, 179

How Fascism Works (2018) by Jason Stanely, 12, 177

Hume, David (Scottish Enlightenment philosopher), 54, 118; on miracles, 102, 158; on priestly power and pious fraud, 119; on the propensity of humans for the extraordinary and the marvelous, 173

Idiot America (2009) by Charles Pierce, 2, 120

ignotum per ignotius (logical fallacy), 120

Immanuel, Stella (con artist and paranormalist), 106; Trump's endorsement of absurd ideas of, 106

incommensurability: of competing paradigms, 60, 62, 64, 66, 69; of cultures, 62, 127

information silos (online news, opinion and discussion communities of people with the same point of view), 172

Inhofe, James (R-Oklahoma, climate change denier), 8; use of Bible by to refute climate change science, 110; use of group prayers by to halt rising sea levels, 55

In Sorcery's Shadow: A Memoir of Apprenticeship among the Songhay of Niger (1989) by Paul Stoller, 147

Intelligent Design Creationism, 67, 97, 119, 121, 122, 156; absence of positive theory in, 119; efforts of proponents to justify their superstitions through public relations, 120; entire agenda of to demonize science and forward archaic superstitions in it place, 119; a religionist pseudoscience, 119

Internet: contribution of to the proliferation of conspiracy theories, 172; creation by of an unchecked cyber space for the spread of lies, racism, and fascist extremism, 170

Interpretation of Culture (1973) by Clifford Geertz, 127

intrinsic methodological naturalism, 96; as an erroneous characterization of science, 97, 100

Iran-Contra affair, 1, 173
Iraq war (2003): deceptions regarding as a foretaste of post-truth, 17
Isaac, Jeffrey (historian), 4
Islamic State in Iraq and Syria (ISIS [Levant], the jihadist proto-state that emerged in the wake of the Iraq war), 16

Jacoby, Susan (American author), 8
Jefferson, Thomas, 9
Johnson, Phillip (architect of the Intelligent Design movement): acknowledgment by of use of postmodernist ideas to promote creationism, 122
John Wheeler (American theoretical physicist): on parapsychology as a pathological pseudoscience, 143

Kahn, Joel (religionist scholar), 154
Kakutani, Michiko (American literary critic): on the appropriation of dumbed-down corollaries of postmodernism by the Right, 168
Kaufman, James (American psychologist): on fighting for truth as a battle against masses of true-believers armed with ignorance and misinformation, 106; on the self-correcting nature of science, 91
Keener, Craig (Christian apologist), 98; belief of in the reality of resurrection of the dead past and present, 153
Kirshenbaum, Sheril (science writer), 97; erroneous characterization of science entailing intrinsic methodological naturalism, 98
Kitzmiller v. Dover Area School District (2005): legal case regarding the teaching of Intelligent Design in schools, 97
Klausner, William (cultural anthropologist): on the limitations of attaining the insider's point of view, 159
Kossy, Donna (sociologist): on conspiracy theories, 174
Kuhn, Thomas (American philosopher of science), 57, 67, 146; collaboration of with Paul Feyerabend, 64; confusion by of scientific knowledge and persons conveying that knowledge, 74; construal of science amenable to pseudoscience, paranormalism, and spiritual worldviews, 105, 117; construal of science used by creationists, 122; impact of work of on science studies and Bloor's Strong Programme, 63; on the incommensurability of new and old paradigms, 59, 61; irrationalist construal of scientific revolutions by, 58; questionable claims of about the growth of scientific knowledge, 63; work of as a radical form of anti-realism regarding science, 60; work of used as a concise argument that science is biased by U.S. industry seeking to dodge environmental safty, 63; work of used by paranormalists to challenge science, 63; work of used by postmodernists to delegitimize science, 58

Laboratory Life: The Social Construction of Scientific Facts (1979) by Bruno Latour and Steve Woolgar, 40, 41
Lacan, Jacques (postmodern philosopher), 20
Lamarck, Jean-Baptise (French naturalist): idea of evolution through inheritance of acquired characteristics, 108
Langbehn, Julius (German philosopher): anti-science ideals of lauded by the Nazis, 114

Latour, Bruno (postmodernist and self-styled anthropologist of science), 40, 76, 131; effort of to exonerate himself for right-wing appropriation of postmodern anti-science ideas, 177, 179; inane anthropological approach of to the study of science, 41; indifference of to the cogency of his assertions, 45; influence of the ideas of Kuhn upon, 63; on the impossibility of acquisition of objective scientific data, 43; on the mummy of Pharaoh Ramses II and diagnosis of tuberculosis, 44; response of to the Sokal hoax, 52; scientific illiteracy of, 41, 53

Lau, Sin Wen (religionist scholar), 154

Laudan, Larry (American philosopher of science and epistemologist), 30; on incommensurability of paradigms, 59; on postmodernists' deceptive use of conclusions from philosophy of science, 47; prediction of post-truth by, 47; on pseudoscience and the demarcation problem, 111; surprise of over widespread academic acceptance of epistemic relativism, 37; on theory-ladenness argument, 59

Law, Stephen (English philosopher): construal of pseudoscientific/religious beliefs as shaped by systematically unreliable cognitive predispositions, 113

Lett, James (American scientific anthropologist), 160; critique of paranormalism in American cultural anthropology, 143; on faith and revelation as problematic paths to knowledge, 99; on the falseness of religious beliefs, 144, 161; on intellectual dishonesty of postmodernist academics, 71; on the need to scientifically address the evidentiary basis of religious claims, 96

Lévi-Strauss's, Claude (French structural anthropologist): wholesale adoption of structuralism of by American cultural anthropologists, 126

Levitin, Daniel (American-Canadian cognitive psychologist): on the creation of false equivalency by a media conditioned to submissively present both sides of scientific issues without weighing merit of the evidence, 14

Levitsky, Steven (Harvard political scientist), 4; on the Republican Party's role in enabling Donald Trump's candidacy, 179

Levitt, Norman (American mathematician): on the postmodernists' assumption that paying attention to words would give the analyst world-changing powers, 32

Lewandowsky, Stephen (psychologist): on post-truth as an alternative epistemology, 8; on the correlation between endorsement of conspiracy theories and climate science denial, 176; on the correlation of science rejection and reliance on the Internet for information, 169; on the distrust of experts in the post-truth world, 172; on the hallmarks of post-truth, 2

Lilienfeld, Scott (professor of psychology): on the difference between science and pseudoscience, 111

Limbaugh, Rush (rightwing American ideologue): conspiracy theories of, 174

Lingua Franca (American magazine about intellectual and literary life in academia), 50

linguistic relativity. *See* Sapir-Whorf Hypothesis

Local Knowledge (1983) by Clifford Geertz, 127
Lockie, Stewart (Australian environmental scientist), 2
Long, Joseph (paranormal anthropologist): belief of in the ontological reality of ghosts, poltergeists, psychic surgery, etc., 143
Lots of People Are Saying: The New Conspiracism and the Assault on Democracy (2019) by Russell Muirhead and Nancy Rosenblum, 176
Lynch, Michael (professor of philosophy): on the obscurity of postmodern rhetoric, 36
Lyotard, Jean-François (postmodern philosopher), 20, 116
Lysenko, Trofim Denisovich (Director of Genetics in the Soviet Union), 108, 114; agricultural disaster caused by bogus genetic science of, 109; agricultural disaster in China due to his pseudoscience, 110; genetic theory of similar to Lamarkian inheritance of acquired characteristics, 108; rejection of Darwinian biology by, 109; terrible consequences of his imposing political authority upon science, 109; treatment the science of genetics in the West as an ideology supporting class inequalities, 108

Mack, John (American psychiatrist): construal of science as a theology, 63; use of Kuhn's ideas by to support his claim regarding the reality of alien abductions, 117
Mahner, Martin (German biologist and philosopher of science): on the flaws of omni-explanatory propositions, 119
Mair, Jonathan (anthropologist), 170

Mao Zedong (chairman of the Communist Party of China): eight rules of for agriculture based on Lysenko's pseudoscience, 109; famines during Great Leap Forward of, 110
Marcus, George (American postmodern cultural anthropologist), 130, 133, 146; admiration of for Castaneda's work, 136, 146
Marx, Karl (German political theorist), 24, 110
Mbeki, Thabo (South African politician and the second president of South Africa): rejection of antiretroviral drugs against AIDS in favor of lemon juice and garlic, 107
McCutcheon, Russell (Canadian religious scholar): on the reasons for the deferential approach to religion by religious scholars, 160
McIntyre, Lee (philosopher and historian of science): on the contribution of science-denial to post-truth, 10; on the distinguishing characteristics of science, 89; on the roots of post-truth, 14; on science as the best way to respect truth, 84; on science as the opposite of ideology, 89; on truth, 84; on the use of postmodern theories by conservative critics of science, 122, 168; on the weaknesses of postmodernist criticisms of science, 31
Mead, Margaret (American cultural anthropologist and paranormalist): as espouser of supernatural bunkum in lectures and writings, 143; instrumental role of in obtaining membership for the pseudoscientific Parapsychological Association into the American Association for the Advancement of Science, 143
Mein Kampf (1939) by Adolf Hitler, 8, 29

memory conformity (cognitive bias), 113
Menand, Louis (American literary critic): on the efforts of postmodernists to defend Paul de Man's Nazism, 29; on the inherent problems of deconstruction, 30
Mendel, Gregor (pioneer in the field of modern genetics): ideas of suppressed in the Soviet Union, 108
Merchants of Doubt (2011) by Naomi Oreskes and Erik Conway, 15
Merton, Thomas (American sociologist): the sociological study of science by, 39
Metaphysics (350 BCE) by Aristotle, 82
methodological agnosticism, 144; as a barrier to the scientific study of religion, 144; employment of by anthropologists studying religion, 143; rejection of by theistic anthropologists, 154
Milbank, John (English Anglican theologian), 158
Miracles: The Credibility of the New Testament Accounts (2011) by Craig Keener, 153
Mooney, Chris (journalist and science writer), 97; denial of ideological influence of Left wing academics on right-wing populists, 164; erroneous characterization of science entailing intrinsic methodological naturalism, 98
Murguía, Salvador (sociologist): on alternative facts, 5
Mussolini, Benito (Italian Fascist leader), 21; postmodern/post-truth notions of, 179

Nagle, Angela (author), 169
NASA, 6; bogus claims regarding conspiratorial activities of, 9, 173; and the Challenger disaster, 84

National Academy of Sciences (NAS): public stance of on the scope of science, 94; reliance of on Gould's NOMA, 93
National Socialists. *See* Nazis
Navarro, Peter (Trump official and propogandist): COVID-19 conspiracy theory of, 174
Nazis, 21, 22, 114, 115; opposition of to Enlightenment ideals and the rational scientific worldview, 114; pseudosciences developed by as alternatives to real science, 115; racial theories of based on pseudoscience, 115
New Age beliefs/mysticism as the non-academic counterpart of postmodernism, 35, 52, 56, 136, 142, 155
Nichols, Tom (international affairs specialist), 2; on post-truth discourse, 167
Nietzsche, Friedrich (German philosopher): as an apostle of anti-science movements, including present day right-wing populism, 1; appeal of to fascists, racists, relativist, and post-truth white power activists, 22; endorsement of the extermination of inferior races by, 21; ethically problematic nature of work of, 22, 23; idea of *übermensch* or super-race or supermen, 21; on language as a prison house of thought, 26; and Nazism, 21, 22; and postmodernism, 1, 22, 35, 168; post-truth ideas of, 22; reception of ideas of by postmodernists, 22; similarity of perspectivism of to post-truth, 1
Noll, Mark (evagelical Christian apologist): fallacious understanding of science as a faith-based belief system, 98
non-overlapping magisteria (NOMA): opening space by for other ways of

knowing and alternative knowledge, 93, 94. *See also* Gould, Stephen J. (American evolutionary biologist and historian of science)

Okasha, Samir (professor of philosophy of science): on conditionalization in science, 101; on science and intellectual curiosity, 82; on science and unobservable reality, 92

O'Meara, Tim (American anthropologist): on the evils of postmodernists' epistemic relativism, 139

On Bullshit (2005) by Harry Frankfurt, 73

Oppy, Graham (Australian philosopher): on the abundance of solidly corroborated evidence on the unreality of paranormal/psi phenomena to rule out likelihood of a future science recognizing such things, 101; on the problematic nature of attaining the insider's point of view, 159

Oreskes, Naomi (historian of science), 10, 11, 12, 13, 15, 169

Origins of Totalitarianism (1951) by Hanna Arendt, 3

Ott, Brian (professor of communication studies): on nature of discourse encouraged by Twitter, 171

Otto, Shawn (American writer and science advocate), 105: on the impact of postmodern anti-science thinking outside university campuses, 163; on the impact of postmodernism on post-truth, 165; on postmodernist's rejection of scientific evidence and their dependence on authority, 34; on the profound misunderstanding of science by postmodern thinkers, 74; on the societal impact of academic science delegitimation, 19

Paine, Thomas, 9; on the unreliability of anecdotal accounts of religious revelations, 151

Pandian, Jacob (American cultural anthropologist): on the incompatibility of science and religion, 94

Pandora's Hope: Essays on the Reality of Science Studies (1999) by Bruno Latour, 41

Pangermanismus (19th-century pan-nationalist political/racialist idea to unify all the German-speaking people), 115

paranormal anthropology, 141; as an alternative way of knowing and counter-knowledge, 153; compatibility of with post-truth, 153; exclusive reliance on subjective impressions, anecdotal accounts, and hearsay, 151; extraordinary claims of offered by proponents without extraordinary evidence, 151; as foundation of theistic anthropology, 153; politicization of ontological relativism in, 150; postmodernist elements in, 145; a priori acceptance of the reality of ghosts and spirits by proponents of, 149, 151; rejection of conventional evidentiary and methodological criteria in, 152; rejection of cultural relativism by advocates of, 147; scientific illiteracy of its exponents, 150; as understanding of religion with endorsement, 148; works of Castaneda as inspiration for, 145

paranthropology. *See* paranormal anthropology

pareidolia (a tendency to see faces in random patterns), 114

Pennock, Robert (philosopher of science): on the fascination of humans with the mysterious, paranormal, and unknown, 173; on

the role of postmodern theory in the development of Intelligent Design, 121, 122
Pennycook, Gordon (American cognitive psychologist): on pseudo-profound bullshit, 73
Perrin, Andrew (sociologist): denial by of the impact of postmodern theory on post-truth, 164
Philipse, Herman (Dutch professor of philosophy): on the need to scientifically address the evidentiary basis of religious claims, 96
Philosophiæ Naturalis Principia Mathematica (1687) by Isaac Newton, 54
Pierce, Charles (author and social commentator), 2; on American idiocy, 106; on creationism, 120
Pigliucci, Massimo (professor of philosophy): on the dangers of pseudoscience, 107
Pinker, Steven (Canadian-American cognitive psychologist and linguist), 26; characterization of postmodernism by as self-refuting relativism, 35; on Nietzsche as architect of 20th century anti-science movements as well as post-truth, 23; on the relation between language and perception, 27
Pipes, Daniel (American historian and Middle East expert): on Baudrillard's assertions regarding the Gulf War, 45
Pizzagate conspiracy, 9. *See also* QAnon conspiracy
Plantinga, Alvin (American theologian and Christian apologist): defects of anti-science assertions of, 91, 92, 95, 96; use of postmodern anti-science ideas in support of his religionist assertions, 99
Plato (Athenian philosopher), 30
Popper, Karl (Austrian-born British philosopher), 72, 102

populism (right-wing), 118; adoption of postmodernist arguments for its authoritarian agenda, 43, 79, 122, 123, 167, 168; association of with post-truth politics, 4; devotion to Trump by advocates of, 167; a feature of Trump's post-truth America, 17, 47; Nietzsche as an apostle of, 1; as a threat to democracy, 9
postmodern anthropology, 125; characterized by profusion of moralistic platitudes, sanctimonious posturing, and intellectual dishonesty, 127; an enterprise devoid of any canons of verifiability, replicability, and the possibility of objective knowledge, 129; radical epistemic relativism as foundation of, 127; role of in spread of anti-intellectualism, irrational modes of thinking and science illiteracy, 126
Postmodern Condition: A Report on Knowledge (1979) by Jean-François Lyotard, 36
postmodernism, 31, 37, 49, 71, 156; attributes of, 20; as the creation of a coterie of fringe French philosophers, 20; defects within ensuring ultimate failure of, 77; as a form of epistemic relativism, 55; as an ideology disguised as scholarship, 34, 76; impact of on American cultural anthropology, 62, 126; indelible influence of on mainstream intellectual life and popular culture in the U.S., 164, 165; intellectual dishonesty of proponents of, 52; obscurity of as reason for its popularity, 36; and post-truth, 166; post-truth and anti-democratic populism as legacy of, 79; post-truth as dumbed down version of in contemporary U.S. politics, 168; pseudoscience

and New Age mysticism as non-academic counterparts of, 56, 142; role of in scientific illiteracy in the U.S., 163; role of in the proliferation of irrational beliefs in the U.S., 163; self-refuting nature of tenets of, 122; similarities of with Nazi ideology, 114; usefulness of for right-wing populists, 166; use of ideas of by creationists as a defense of their superstitions, 121, 122; various meaning of the term, 36

postmodern philosophy: role of in the fostering post-truth, 167, 168; role of in the fostering scientific illiteracy, 123

post-truth: and the 2016 U.S. Presidential elections, 1; as an alternative epistemology, 8, 9, 105, 106, 164; attributes of, 1, 2; as dumbed-down postmodern dogma, 168; falsehoods of similar to Hitler's big lies, 8; use of term by Ralph Keyes in 2004, 1

Post-Truth Era: Dishonesty and Deception in Contemporary Life (2004) by Ralph Keyes, 1

post-truth media: an enterprise based on fair and balanced reporting minus any appraisals of the evidentiary credence of the claims, 12; role of in creating post-truth, 13

post-truth politicians bogus claims of, 7

post-truth politics, 2, 3, 73; association of with right-wing populism, racism, and xenophobia, 4; extreme incivility of, 171; fascist attributes of, 4; involvement of postmodernism in development of, 164; as politics of debasement, 5

Post Truth: The New War on Truth and How to Fight Back (2017) by Matthew D'Ancona, 9

Price, Robert (American philosopher and New Testament scholar): on dignifying credulity as a method, 141

provisional methodological naturalism as an accurate characterization of science, 100

pseudoscience: attributes of, 112; beliefs in bolstered by postmodern theories, 105; definition of, 105, 106; and the demarcation problem, 111; differences of from science, 111, 112; harmful nature of, 114; Nazi regime bolstered by, 114

Pseudoscience and the Paranormal (2003) by Terence Hines, 106

Pseudoscience Wars (2012) by Michael Gordin, 111

pseudoscientific beliefs: as an expression of archaic irrational pre-scientific modes of thought, 113; varieties of in post-truth U.S., 106

Pyrrho of Elis (Greek skeptic philosopher circa fourth century BCE), 55

QAnon conspiracy, 9; association of with right-wing militants, 175; touted by Donald Trump, 175

Raab, Marius (psychologist): on the difficulty of falsifying conspiracy theories, 175

Rabin-Havt, Ari (political analyst): on corporate-funded science delegitimation as the largest mass deception in history, 14; on the existence of an organized industry of falsehoods, 11

relativism, 62, 66. *See also* epistemic relativism; fundamental incoherence of, 77; long history of in Western thought, 55; postmodern cultural anthropology as a form of, 127; work of French postmodern writers as a repackaging of, 55

Rennie, John (science writer): on nonsensical and deceptive creationist claims, 119

Republican politicians attacks of on science, 163
Responses: On Paul de Man's Wartime Journalism (1989) by Hamacher et al., 29
Robbins, Bruce (co-editor of the postmodern journal Social Text): dishonesty of in responding to the Sokal Hoax, 52
Robbins, Joel (theistic anthropologist), 158
Rorty, Richard (American postmodern/ pragmatic philosopher), 87; contributions of to post-truth, 166; the usefulness of work of to Intelligent Design ideologues, 122
Ross, Andrew (co-editor of the postmodern journal Social Text): intellectual dishonesty of in responding to the Sokal hoax, 52
Roughgarden, Joan (Christian biologist): treatment of biblical supersitions as having equal parity with the findings of science, 66
Ruse, Michael (British-born Canadian philosopher of science): on pseudoscience, 106
Russell, Bertrand (British philosopher and mathematician): on the concept of truth, 84, 85
Ryan, Alan (British political scientist): on the incoherence of postmodern assertions about truth, 35

Sagan, Carl (American astronomer, astrophysicist, and author), 17; axiom of that extraordinary claims require extraordinary evidence, 102; on the dangers of fraudulent claims about scientific knowledge, 82; evolutionary reason offered by for rejection of epistemic relativism, 73; on the role of skepticism in scientific thought, 89; on the self-correcting nature of science, 90; on the societal dangers of abandoning critical thinking, 105, 116, 171
Sangren, Steven (cultural anthropologist), 138; on postmodernists' conflation of textual authority and societal power, 33, 138
Sapir, Edward (American linguistic anthropologist): on the relation between language, thought, and perception, 26
Sapir-Whorf Hypothesis, 26, 27
Saussure, Ferdinand de (Swiss linguist), 31; on the self-referential nature of language, 26
Schick, Theodor (American philosopher): on the attributes of pseudoscience, 112; on the flaw of Thomas Kuhn's incommensurability of paradigms, 62; on fundamental incoherence of relativism, 77; on the importance of science and rationality in democratic societies, 116
science: aims of, 87, 88; and the assessment of nonfalsifiable claims, 101; assements of supernatural claims in, 150; clash of with religion as the clash of rationalism and irrationalism or rationality and superstition, 99; consilience or a unified view of the world and a convergence of conclusions in, 83; the differences in between context of discovery and justification, 88; distinction from pseudoscience, 113; distinguishing features of, 89; meaning of objectivity in, 90; as a method of discovering the truth, not a particular body of truth, 98; objective of to pursue the truth on the basis of evidence and to eradicate false beliefs from the public sphere, 97, 98, 100; and provisional methodological naturalism, 100; self-correcting nature of, 91; stance of regarding

the unsubstantiated nature of paranormal/supernatural phenomena based on *a posteriori* conclusions from scientific evidence, 100; truth claims in judged against empirical facts or objective reality, 88; validation of propositions in, 88, 89
science de-legitimation, 10; definition of, 10; and the emergence of the post-truth epistemology, 164; as the self-appointed task of postmodern academics, 58
science-denial, 10, 15, 16, 19, 93, 95; blueprint of provided by the tobacco, fossil fuel, and agrochemical industries, 10; definition of, 10; and post-truth, 10; in post-truth U.S., 91
Science in Action: How to Follow Scientists and Engineers Through Society (1985) by Bruno Latour, 41
Science on Trial (1982) by Douglas Futuyma, 110
science studies: after-the-fact recognition by some proponents of its imprudence as an intellectual enterprise, 177; confusion in works generated by of authority of science and persons conveying scientific knowledge, 74; derision of science by contributing to post-truth, 19; a disingenuous enterprise devoted to demystifying science and rationality, 39, 40, 41, 42; gross misunderstanding of anthropological methods by proponents of, 41; the gross misunderstanding of science by advocates of, 41; inauguration of by Bruno Latour, 40; rationale of drawn from the works of Kuhn and Feyerabend, 67; use of Kuhn's *Structure of Scientific Revolutions* as a canonical text in, 58
science wars, 39, 40; special issue of the postmodern journal *Social Text* devoted to, 49

scientific method, 42, 49, 86, 90; attributes of, 72
Scott, Eugenie (former director of the National Center for Science Education): detrimental adoption by of Gould's NOMA concept, 94
Scriven, Michael (British-born Australian philosopher): on the nonexistence of paranormal entities and mythical creatures, 102
Searle, John (American philosopher): on the existence of reality and truth as a default position in human thought, 70, 71
Seduction of Unreason (2004) by Richard Wolin, 19
Segal, Robert (religious studies scholar), 148
Sextus Empiricus (ancient Greek philosopher and skeptic, circa second or third centuries BCE), 55
Shotwell, David (American mathematician): on the impossibility of translating creationism into a scientific research program, 119
simulacrum, 44
skepticism: of Gorgias, 31; problems of when misapplied, 90; in science, 66, 89, 90
Slezak, Peter (Australian philosopher): on Bruno Latour's indifference to the cogency of his assertions, 45; on Bruno Latour's science studies, 40, 42; on the corruption of standards of thought and honest inquiry by postmodernists, 47; on Feyerabend's alleging epistemic parity between science and religion, 65; on the impenetrability of postmodern discourse, 36; on the strength of science as a way of knowing, 103
Smulewircz-Zuker, Gregory (political scientist): on the impact of postmodernism outside academia,

165; on post-truth as vulgar postmodernism, 168
Snyder, Timothy (American philosopher and historian): on dangers of dismissing facts, 167; on fascism and post-truth, 179
Sobieraj, Sarah (sociologist): on the incivility of post-truth political discourse, 171
Social Text (postmodern journal), 51, 52, 53; and the Sokal hoax, 49
Sociology of Postmodernism (1990) by Scott Lash, 164
Sokal, Alan (professor of physics), 50; condemnation of the academic Left by for its anti-science stance, 79; hoax of in *Social Text* revealing the nonsensical nature of postmodern rhetoric on science, 49, 50, 51; reaction of postmodernists to hoax of, 51, 52, 53; on the scientific method, 72; treatment of pseudoscience and magical thinking as counterparts of postmodernism, 56
Sokal Hoax, 49, 51, 53; *New York Times* article on, October 22, 1996, 85; response to by academics, 50
Sokal Hoax: The Sham that Shook the Academy (2000): compiled by the editors of Lingua Franca, 50
Sperber, Dan (French social and cognitive scientist): on group-think, 46; on the infatuation of believers with French postmodern gurus, 37
Spicer, Sean (Trump's White House Press Secretary and spin doctor), 166
Spooky Archaeology: Myth and the Science of the Past (2018) by Jeb Card, 141
Stalin, Joseph (premier of the Soviet Union), 109; and Lysenko's pseudoscience, 108; outlawing by of Mendelian genetics in the Soviet Union, 108

Stangroom, Jeremy (British philosopher), 53; on the absurdity of Sandra Harding's feminist critique of science, 54, 55; on the difference between rhetoric and argument based on sound evidence, 75; on the self-evident existence of an external reality, 70
Stanley, Jason (philosopher): on conspiracy theories and fascism, 177
Stenger, Victor (American physicist and philosopher): on the nonexistence of paranormal phenomena, 149; on the unreliability of anecdotal evidence, 112
Stoller, Paul (American cultural anthropologist): paranormal experience of during fieldwork, 147
Stone, Anna (anomalous psychologist): on pseudoscience, 106
Stove, David (Australian philosopher), 26; on the depths of the absurdity of Feyerabend's work, 65; description of postmodernist epistemic relativism as the worst argument in the world, 31; on epistemic relativism, 69; on the impact of Kuhn's ideas on the humanities, 62; on the intellectual irresponsibility and dishonesty of postmodern ideologues, 45; on Kuhn's strategy of espousing irrational views of science, 61; on the massive success of Western science, 72; on the self-refuting nature of epistemic relativism, 77
Strathern, Marilyn (British anthropologist and postmodernist): rejection by of the observer and observed dichotomy, 128
Strong, S. I (professor of law): on alternative facts and their dangers to deliberative democracy, 5
Structure of Scientific Revolutions (1970 [1962]) by Thomas Kuhn, 57, 61

Stuff of Thought (2007) by Steven Pinker, 26

Teachings of Don Juan: A Yaqui Way of Knowledge (1968) by Carlos Castaneda, 136
Tesich, Steve (playwright): the first use of term post-truth by in 1992 in reference to Watergate scandle and the Iran-Contra Affair, 1; on post-truth, 179
theistic anthropology, 141, 153; as an effort to transform anthropology into an enterprise for giving witness to the risen Lord, 157, 161; as enterprise based on alternative ways of knowing, alternative facts, and private subjective insights, 161; epistemic assumptions of, 154; faulty premises of, 158; a field dominated by evangelical Christians, 161; reliance on the approach of paranormalists, such as Edith Turner and Jean-Guy Goulet, 157; subscription of advocates of to Christian exceptionalism or the conviction that they alone possess the one true faith, 158; use of postmodern anti-science assertions in, 153
Theology and Social Theory: Beyond Secular Reason (1990) by John Milbank, 158
theory-ladenness argument, 59, 92
theory of mind the generation of paranormal experiences by, 114
Theosophy. *See* Blavatsky, Helena (Russian occultist, con artist, and co-founder of the Theosophical Society)
Thompson, Damian (sociologist of religion), 6; on counter-knowledge or pseudoscience, 106; on role of postmodern philosophy in forstering alternative facts and post-truth, 116

Trump, Donald, 3, 47, 83, 166, 168, 179; attacks on science by, 9; bogus remedies recommended by for COVID-19, 75, 106; bogus story of about 3 million illegal votes in the 2016 Presidential election, 7; dismissal of global warming by as a hoax, 15, 55; distrust and denigration of experts by, 170; endorsement of Stella Immanuel's bogus ideas by, 106; and fake news, 2; false statements by, 7; misrepresentation of the COVID-19 pandemic by, 5, 55, 82, 106; populist devotees of, 167; post-truth America of, 17
truth: assault on by American academics, 19; Bertrand Russell on, 84; Carl Sagan on, 82; devaluation of in post-truth U.S., 4; Hannah Arendt on., 4; Lee McIntyre on, 84; new understanding of in post-truth U.S., 2, 3, 6, 13; Nietzsche on, 22; postmodernists' understanding of, 20, 24, 25, 30; undermining of by purported fair and balanced reporting without consideration of evidentiary credence, 12; understanding of in science, 85, 87, 88, 89, 90, 98
truth by coherence, 85, 127
truth by consensus, 85, 86
truth by correspondence, 85; the centrality of to science, 87
truth by pragmatism, 85, 87
Turner, Edith (English-American paranormal anthropologist); belief of in the reality of spirits, 148; influence of work of on theistic anthropology, 157; purported paranormal experience of during fieldwork, 157
Twitter, 172; conducive to farce and fanaticism, 171
Tyler. Stephen (American postmodern cultural anthropologist), 134, 135

underdetermination of scientific theories argument, 47, 58
Untermenschen the term used by Nazis for purported inferior races, 115

Vaughn, Lewis (American philosopher): on the attributes of pseudoscience, 112; on the flaw of Thomas Kuhn's incommensurability of paradigms assertions, 62; on the fundamental incoherence of relativism, 77; on the importance of science and rationality in democratic societies, 116
völkisch (people's groups dedicated to pseudoscience active in Germany during World War I and after), 114
von Liebenfels, Lanz (Austrian political and racial theorist and occultist): ideas of embraced by the Nazis, 115
von List, Guido (Austrian occultist): ideas of embraced by the Nazis, 115

Walker, Anthony (British social anthropologist): on Edward Evans-Pritchard's conversion to Catholicism, 156
Wallace, Ruth (sociologist), 32
War on Science (2016) by Shawn Otto, 12
Wartime Journalism (1988) by De Man et al., 29
Watergate scandal, 173
Wedge (strategy by creationists to justify their pseudoscientific perspective by popular vote), 120
Weinberg, Steven (theoretical physicist): on the dangers of irrational views of science and dismissal of the leveling effects of evidence, 53; on the rarity of Kuhnian types of revolutions in the history of science, 63; on the Sokal hoax and the nonsensical aphorisms found in postmodern texts on science, 52, 53

Whorf, Benjamin (American linguist): on the relationship between language, thought, and perception, 26
Wiebe, Donald (philosopher of religion): on the unwillingness of scholars to subject religion to ontological study as a failure of nerve, 160
Williamson, Phil (climate engineer): on the Internet, 169
Windschuttle, Keith (Australian historian): on the agricultural disaster resulting from the Chinese application of Lysenko's bogus science, 109; on the impact of Kuhn on science studies, 58, 62
witchcraft beliefs in early Modern Europe, 86
Wittgenstein, Ludwig (Austrian-British philosopher): on language as a prison house of thought, 26
Wolf, Alison (sociologist), 32
Wolin, Richard (American intellectual historian), 19; on the embrace of Nietzsche's ethically problematic ideas by postmodern academics, 22; on the impact of postmodern ideas on American academics, 21; on postmodernists' transformation of radicalism into an entirely conceptual and ethereal enterprise, 32
Woolgar, Steve (British sociologist and colleague of Bruno Latour), 40
Writing Culture (1986) edited by James Clifford, 130
Wuhan Institute of Virology, 173

Young, David (paranormal anthropologist), 150

Ziblatt, Daniel (Harvard political scientist), 4; on Republican Party's role in enabling Donald Trump's candidacy, 179

About the Author

H. Sidky is professor of anthropology at Miami University (Ohio), United States, specializing in the anthropology of religion, entheogens, ecological anthropology, anthropological theory/history of anthropological thought, and the paranormal and pseudoscience. He is the author of numerous books and scholarly articles.

www.ingramcontent.com/pod-product-compliance
Lightning Source LLC
Chambersburg PA
CBHW050903300426
44111CB00010B/1359